Expanding Curriculum Theory

Dis/positions and Lines of Flight

Studies in Curriculum Theory
William F. Pinar, Series Editor

Expanding Curriculum Theory

Dis/positions and Lines of Flight

Edited by

William M. Reynolds
Georgia Southern University

Julie A. Webber
Illinois State University

LAWRENCE ERLBAUM ASSOCIATES, PUBLISHERS
2004 Mahwah, New Jersey   London

Copyright © 2004 by Lawrence Erlbaum Associates, Inc.
All rights reserved. No part of this book may be reproduced in any form, by photostat, microform, retrieval system, or any other means, without prior written permission of the publisher.

Lawrence Erlbaum Associates, Inc., Publishers
10 Industrial Avenue
Mahwah, New Jersey 07430

Cover design by Kathryn Houghtaling Lacey

Library of Congress Cataloging-in-Publication Data

Expanding curriculum theory : dis/positions and lines of flight / edited by William M. Reynolds, Julie A. Webber.
    p. cm. — (Studies in curriculum theory)
    Includes bibliographical references and index.
ISBN 0-8058-4664-6 (cloth : alk. paper)
ISBN 0-8058-4665-4 (pbk. : alk. paper)
    1. Curriculum planning. 2. Education—Curriculua.
    3. Curriculum change. I. Reynolds, William M., 1953–
    II. Webber, Julie A., 1972-   III. Series.

LB2806. 15.E96 2004
375'.001—dc22   2003056120
                                                    CIP

Books published by Lawrence Erlbaum Associates are printed on acid-free paper, and their bindings are chosen for strength and durability.

Printed in the United States of America
10 9 8 7 6 5 4 3 2 1

This book is dedicated to
William F. Pinar

Contents

Preface

This edited collection of essays on curriculum studies appears during a historical period of change. It is a time of Empire (Hardt & Negri, 2000).[1] We have moved through what Foucault (Rabinow, 1984) described as disciplinary societies in which people passed through various disciplinary institutions such as schools and factories that regulated habits, customs, and discourses to what Deleuze (1995) elaborated as control societies. These control societies operate with power in a more complex and pervasive manner:

> Power is now exercised through machines that directly organize the brains (in communication systems, information networks, etc.) and bodies (in welfare systems, monitored activities, etc.) toward a state of autonomous alienation from the sense of life and the desire for creativity. The society of control might thus be characterized by an intensification and generalization of normalizing apparatuses of disciplinarity that internally animate our common and daily practices, but in contrast to discipline, this control extends well outside the structured sites of social institutions through flexible and fluctuating networks. (Hardt & Negri, 2000, p. 23)

This movement toward Empire has consequences in academic fields. The movement toward disciplinarity, a narrowing of focus in particular disciplines (specifically curriculum studies, as in the Introduction to this volume), is contingent with the movement toward Empire. As Lyotard (1992) suggested, during this period there is a call in many disciplines to shut down experimentation and creativity. Unity is valued and difference is not. This is the historical moment in which this book is poised. This book attempts in a tactical way to address the sense of alienation from scholarship and creativity that exists. Thus, a book that encourages and demonstrates creativity, multidisciplinarity, and lines of flight is a momentary space within Empire to express difference and hope.

---

[1]As described in their text empire is a concept that is "characterized fundamentally by a lack of boundaries: Empire's rule has no limits. First and foremost, then, the concept of Empire posits a regime that effectively encompasses the spatial totality, or really a regime that rules over the entire 'civilized' world. No territorial boundaries limit its reign" (Hardt & Negri, 2000, p. XIV).

As the field of curriculum studies also experiences, to a limited extent, this call to return to unity and origins, it is significant that the spirit that animated the original reconceptualization of the field is still alive in the writers in this volume. The writing that is contained within the chapters draws from various disciplines and knowledges. Although there is this call in the field to return to the essence of curriculum (if the field ever had one), the writers in this volume do not limit themselves to strict disciplinary constraints. The texts in this book are connected by the authors' shared concern for viewing curriculum from alternative perspectives that are not method driven, but instead are derived from the insights of a dis/position that seeks to disentangle curriculum from its traditional dependence on formalities. The authors have attempted to dwell in alternative methodologies such as textual analysis, discourse theory, hermeneutics, and poststructuralism while triangulating them with the important perspectives of race, class, gender, and sexual orientation. The chapters blur disciplinary boundaries and interweave curriculum theory with cultural studies, political theory, psychoanalysis, dance, technology, and other fields. All of this is done within an overall poststructural framework. This is part of the book's uniqueness and its contribution to the field of curriculum studies. It is also a line of flight that expands curriculum theory. Additionally, the scholar, teacher, and student will notice that we have included prior to each chapter a section entitled "Thinking Beyond." These sections are designed to assist in understanding the various chapters, as well as in comparing, contrasting, and connecting the chapters to each other. The questions are intended to produce a more pedagogically friendly book.

We trust that within the current historical climate, this text will cause you to reflect on the curriculum studies field and its significance to education in our times, and that the book is a contribution to the conversation that is the curriculum studies field.

ACKNOWLEDGMENTS

We wish to thank William Pinar, to whom the book is dedicated. His continued support and faith in this project as well as in the editors themselves is deeply treasured. We also express our highest admiration and appreciation to Naomi Silverman, senior editor at Lawrence Erlbaum Associates. Naomi always seems to know what we are trying to do and consistently adds great ideas. Her support of this project and the curriculum studies field in general is of lasting value. We both wish to thank the reviewers, whose insightful comments and critiques made this book much better, particularly Greg Dimitriadis and Susan Edgerton.

Bill wishes to acknowledge the support of his colleagues and friends Mary Aswell Doll, Ming Fang He, Marla Morris, and John Weaver. Many times these colleagues have expressed support and given me ideas that contribute greatly to my thinking, not to mention much laughter. Julie Webber has also been a wonderful co-editor. Her ideas have made a lasting contribution to this volume. Bill would also like to thank the contributors for their patience through this process. He acknowledges his many doctoral students for listening to him and helping him think through these ideas.

Julie wishes to thank friends and colleagues for their very gracious support as she worked on the manuscript and presented versions of many ideas for them over the telephone. First, she thanks Bill Pinar and Bill Reynolds for their constant support in the curriculum field. Next, she is grateful to Diane Rubenstein for her continued mentoring and friendship on all things French. Finally, she wishes to thank her supportive colleagues from Politics and Government who mulled over many of her drafts: Jyl Josephson, Janie Leatherman, and Ali Riaz. Thanks to Manfred Steger for discussing Empire and reviewing Empire. Finally, thanks to Deems Morrione for friendship, intellectual companionship, and support. Without all these open-minded and interdisciplinary folks, including the special tolerance of the individual contributors, this book might not have been possible.

REFERENCES

Deleuze, G. (1995). *Negotiations 1972–1990*. New York: Columbia University Press.
Hardt, M., & Negri, A. (2000). *Empire*. Cambridge, MA: Harvard University Press.
Lyotard, J.-F. (1992). *The postmodern explained*. (D. Barry, B. Mather, J. Perfanis, V. Spate, & M. Thomas, Trans.) Minneapolis: University of Minnesota Press.
Rabinow, P. (Ed.). (1984). *The Foucault reader*. New York: Pantheon.

Chapter 1

Introduction:
Curriculum Dis/positions

William M. Reynolds
Georgia Southern University

Julie A. Webber
Illinois State University

> As forms of this newer kind of practice continue to erupt in multiple ways, in multiple locations, for multiple reasons, inside and outside the grids of defined research categories, the sphere of scholarly inquiry has become an extraordinary animated site for a diverse and experimental analytic production by a number of thinkers not hesitant to situate inquiry in a vast epistemological space. (Jipson & Paley, 1997, p. 3)

> From Plato and a tradition which lasted throughout the classical age, Knowledge is a hunt. To know is to put to death.... To know is to kill, to rely on death.... The reason of the strongest is reason by itself. Western Man is a wolf of science. (Serres, 1983, p. 198)

What counts as curriculum research? What procedures are considered legitimate for the production of knowledge? What forms shape the making of explanations? What constitutes proof? These questions swirl inside and outside the field of curriculum studies (see Jipson & Paley, 1997). Considerable attention is centered on the debate in curriculum among competing theoretical points of view. It has been tempestuous at times and vitriolic at others. Paradigm after paradigm, debate after debate, the firm foundations of educational research remain intact and settle again. And we researchers wonder why nothing has changed for the schools or ourselves, in our role as practitioners. Engaging in that remorseless form of debate is most definitely not the aim of this volume. Instead, we aim to bring to the forefront in this series of chapters work by scholars who are interested in looking at educational problems from a different vantage point. In this historical milieu of postmodernity, the troubling of all structures is the problem to be addressed. Can those very structures be deterritorialized to allow for the creation of new lines of flight in curriculum research to emerge? Deleuze commented on lines of flight:

The constant threat to revolutionary apparatuses comes from taking a puritanical view of interests, so that the only people who ever gain anything are a small section of the oppressed class, and this section of them just produces one more thoroughly oppressive caste and hierarchy. The higher one goes up a hierarchy, even a pseudo revolutionary one, the less scope there is for expression of desire (but, you always find it, however distorted, at the basic level of organization). We set against this fascism of power active, positive lines of flight, because these lines open up desire, desire's machines and the organization of a social field of desire: it's not a matter of escaping "personally from oneself, but allowing something to escape, like bursting a pipe or a boil." Opening up flows beneath social codes that seek to channel and block them. (Deleuze, 1995, p. 19)

We wish to distinguish this volume from current models of research and offer the possibility of refusing them, questioning them, and directing practitioners toward this idea of adopting lines of flight or multiplicities. This volume suggests that the adoption of these lines of flight will dis/position curriculum research. It advocates multiplicity. By refusing to create a new research hierarchy and allowing these lines of flight, we can avoid the pitfalls of debate. We address contingent dis/positions, not absolute positions or universal standpoints. By creating new venues for the epistemological, ontological, and axiological questions of our time, we are able to see education from multiple perspectives. Less professional and more creative, this research is enriched and old paradigms ruptured; this is a positive thing. It is not a question of analyzing the universal and eternal; in curriculum studies, we believe, it is a question of discovering the conditions under which something new might be produced. This discovery of or working toward the new is at the heart of multiplicities and lines of flight. Again, we are not interested in getting engaged in the same old tired exhausting debates that have perpetuated in the curriculum studies field (e.g., that curriculum studies is too nebulous, that the reconceptualization has led us away from the true nature of curriculum). Deleuze said that those types of debates are the bane of philosophy and we would suggest curriculum studies.

Students in curriculum studies can benefit from this multiplicity—lines of flight scholarship. Serres described the manner in which the multiple is indispensable: "The multiple as such, unhewn and little unified, is not an epistemological monster, but on the contrary the ordinary lot of situations, including that of ordinary scholar, regular knowledge, everyday work, in short, our common object" (Serres, 1999, p. 5). Rather than the contentious debates that we have witnessed in different fields in education—including, but not limited to, foundations and curriculum studies—we agree with Serres in his notion of multiple perspectives to address various issues.

Curriculum theory moves when in multiplicities and lines of flight, not in dualisms or either/ors. Curriculum theory IS *not* this or that—defining it *leads to* this or that. Curriculum theory considered as the number of ideologies or methodologies *does* not define multiplicity, because we can always add a 10th, a 17th, or a 201st:

> We do not escape dualism in this way, since the elements of any set whatever can be related to a succession of choices, which are themselves binary. It is not the elements or sets which define the multiplicity. What defines it is the **AND**, as something, which has its place between the elements or between the sets. **AND, AND, AND,**—stammering. And even if there are only two terms, there is an **AND** between the two, which is neither the one nor the other, nor the one which becomes the other, but which constitutes the multiplicity. (Deleuze & Parnet, 1977, p. 34)

This **AND**-stammering, these lines of flight, this multiplicity is construed by some in the field as disarray (Foshay, in Marshall, Sears, & Schubert, 2000), a contamination of genuine curriculum improvement and getting nowhere (Rubin, in Marshall et al., 2000), and a feeling of edginess (Marshall in Marshall et al., 2000). *Disarray* is an interesting choice of words. It can be defined as a lack of order or sequence. Maybe that is the strength of this multiplicity thinking in curriculum studies—it disrupts, troubles order. Lyotard, in *The Postmodern Explained* (1992), discussed the fact that we are in a moment of "relaxation." He listed a number of movements that are thought to need order. There is the urging to give up experimentation in the arts and everywhere. He noted that he had "read in a French weekly that people were unhappy with *A Thousand Plateaus* [Deleuze & Guattari, 1987] because, especially in a book of philosophy, they expect to be rewarded with a bit of sense" (p. 2). Lyotard stated that in all these controversies over experimentation or lines of flight or multiplicities, there is a "call to order, a desire for unity, identity, security, popularity (in the sense of *offentlichkeit*, finding a public)" (p. 4). There is the call even in curriculum theory to close down those lines of flight, that nomadic movement of multiplicity in the type of all-encompassing manner that Lyotard discussed. It frequently manifests itself in a discussion of what curriculum IS or should BE.

This multiplicity, this stammering does not settle in the comfortable IS of definitions. Expanding curriculum theory can be unsettling, **AND** energizing. This multiplicity thinking helps to clarify the notion of a line of flight. It hinges on Deleuze's argument for the priority of the conjunction *and* over the verb *to be*, multiplicity over either, or thinking:

> One must go further: one must make the encounter with relations penetrate and corrupt everything, undermine being, make it topple over. Substitute the **AND** for **IS**. A *and* B. The **AND** is not even a specific relation or conjunction, it is that which subtends all relations, the path of all relations, which makes relations shoot outside their terms and outside the of their terms, and outside everything which

could be determined as Being, One, or Whole. The **AND** as extra-being, inter-being. Relations might still establish themselves between their terms, or between two sets, from one to the other, but the **AND** gives relations another direction, and puts to flight terms and sets, the former and the latter on the line of flight which it actively creates. Thinking with **AND**, instead of thinking **IS**, instead of thinking for **IS**: empiricism has never had another secret. (Deleuze & Parnet, 1977, p. 57)

Curriculum theory should be about developing new lines of flight—lines of flight (becomings) that allow, however, contingently, briefly, or momentarily, for us to soar vertically like a bird or slither horizontally, silently like a snake weaving our way amid the constant reconfigurations, cooptations, and movements of the ruins. It is part of Deleuze's philosophy of multiplicities.

This became a major point in Deleuze and Guattari's political philosophy. It is the "in-between," the AND—becoming; new ways of thinking always proceed from the "in-between." This is where lines of flight take shape. The possibilities for creative curriculum thought for one lie in those multiplicities, which emerge in the "in-between." This shows not what curriculum thought should BE but how AND can be productive for it.

AND is neither one thing or the other, it is always in-between, between two things; it's the borderline, there's always a border, a line of flight or flow, only we don't see it, because it the least perceptible of all things. And yet it's along this line of flight that things come to pass, becomings evolve, revolutions take shape. The strong people aren't the ones on one side or the other, power lies on the border. (Deleuze & Parnet, 1977, p. 64)

This can reframe our thinking about the manner in which we can discuss the nature of curriculum studies poststructurally. The "struggle" is to keep on finding lines that disrupt and overturn, and tactically weave through the globalized corporate order. "An AND, AND, AND, which each time marks a new threshold, a new direction of the zigzagging line, a new course for the border" (Deleuze 1995, p. 45; see also Reynolds, 2003).

There are three issues/questions this volume raises: How is research determined politically and discursively (i.e., what counts as research)? How can research be deterritorialized or dis/positioned? What are some new possibilities, lines of flight for educational research in postmodernity?

WHAT IS CURRICULUM STUDIES RESEARCH?

[Postmodern curriculum is] a fascinating, imaginative realm (born of the echo of God's laughter) wherein no one owns the truth and everyone has the right to be understood. (Doll, 1993, p. 15)

Terry Eagleton, in *Literary Theory* (1983), asked the question "What is literature?" His answer was that literature is historically contingent and politically determined. Literature is what the dominant class determines literature to be. It is discourse that perpetuates and maintains social privilege. Through this discourse of power, knowledge, and imagination, the dominant class creates the literature that maintains the fantasy of order and social intelligibility. In order to be of this class you need to be immersed in its knowledge/power nexus and to believe yourself to be of this class—you need to engage its imagination through literature and fantasy. The subsequent development of a literary "canon," as in Western culture, is an attempt to maintain this persuasive power, and it operates to exclude and marginalize what is not in alignment with the codes and symbols implicit in it (Bloom, 1988; Gates, 1993; Hirsch, 1988). The struggle over the "canon" in literature is the struggle over the symbolic order, over how the story of what is "normal" will be told. Who controls and manipulates symbolic capital? Who determines the signs, symbols, and codes through which our identities are formulated? We would suggest that the struggle over curriculum research has many of the same intricacies and consequences. The determination of what constitutes legitimate curriculum research is a question of power operating to exclude and marginalize those voices raised in creative and imaginative struggle to think alternatively. This struggle over this research and the attitude toward it joins voice with a "growing number of educational thinkers, research workers and cultural theorists who have established a powerful, differently-constituted set of imperatives for reconstructing the coordinates of analytic practice in the post-positive movement" (Jipson & Paley, 1997, p. 5; see also Aronowitz & Giroux, 1991; Deleuze, 1995; Deleuze & Guatarri, 1987; Doll, 2000; Greene, 1994; Lather, 1991; Morris, Doll, & Pinar, 1999; Webber, 2003; Pinar, Reynolds, Slattery, & Taubman, 1995; Reynolds).

This is the point: The troubling of established practices or positions in some curriculum research will provoke the consternation we mentioned earlier. This kind of disruption *is* political because, although it seems like an "inconvenience" to those who are interested in maintaining the status quo of developing curriculum, to those who wish to disrupt it, it is to open up a "line of flight" in power and meaning for the use of those who are marginalized and excluded. We see these upheavals as political, in that such (research) practices about the status of pedagogic, representational, and research authority pulse with the power of individual imagination, they seem to force their way through the present densities of analytic production in efforts to articulate "why and how that-which-is" might no longer be "that-which-is" (Foucault, 1980). The sense of "that-which-is" becomes a sense of "what-can-be," always ready to just break loose (Jipson & Paley, 1997):

In the existing regime of frenzied "disciplinarization," such a breach in the regularity of the system constitutes the critical moment of disequilibrium and dis/illumination.... It is in these moments of "breach" and "disequilibrium," "dis/illumination" and what-can-be that the imaginative then may function as

a powerful political force: the power of making and breaking, concealing and
revealing, learning and burning. (Jipson & Paley, 1997, p. 8)

The reaction to this type or dis/positioning is predictable. It is reminiscent
of the initial and continuing reactions to the reconceptualization of curriculum
since the mid-1970s. Having lived through and survived those criticisms, Bill
can address the reactions to lines of flight research from a historical perspective. As a student of a totally different, if "slacker" generation, Julie views these
debates as unproductive means used by senior university scholars to block the
entrance of new scholars into the field. These criticisms are politically generated, exclusionary, and demeaning, and are at worse dismissive. The politically
generated criticism can be addressed briefly. The major problem with these
debates is that they are, unfortunately, modeled and ordered according to the
"established" and embedded understanding of critique that we find so problematic. As the reader can see in this volume, the kind of critique found here is
not overt or obvious. It is not a "challenge" to a debate, nor is it a challenge to
another author or thinker—that transparent, self-knowing author (and
reader) is dead (Barthes, 1986; Foucault, in Rabinow, 1984).

The first criticism of alternative modes of research is that they are not
research. This is the political tool of dismissal. Bill can recall vividly the
charge that curriculum theorists involved in the reconceptualization were
not real curriculum scholars, but instead "educational critics" in that they
wrote educational editorial, not sound curriculum research. Writing
sound curriculum research at the time—and even now, in some cases—apparently was producing endless derivations of Tylerian curriculum development. Curriculum theorists producing reconceptualizing scholarship
were relegated to the margins.

Times have changed. Curriculum scholarship is now an inclusive conversation. This conversation was called for in *Understanding Curriculum*
(1995); and Bill reemphasized it in 1999, at the Professors of Curriculum
meeting in Montreal (Reynolds, 2003). Finally, as Pinar et al. noted, "We
are not suggesting, of course, that the field requires more order that its
diversification is a problem. On the contrary, we call for collaboration,
conversation and disciplinary autonomy to increase the complexity of
the field" (Pinar et al., 1995, p. 867).

We are suggesting for research in curriculum what Henry Louis Gates Jr.
called for while writing about African American Studies: "We are scholars.
For our field to grow we need to encourage a true proliferation of ideologies
and methodologies, rather than to seek uniformity or conformity" (Gates,
1993, p. 126). Thus, instead of shutting down new modes of inquiry, we
should avoid becoming armchair researchers who wait for the curriculum
practitioners to confirm our hypotheses.

The other criticism is that this type of curriculum research lacks rigor and
scholarship. Rigor depends on who is defining it and how it is defined. Freire
defined rigor in a manner consistent with the rigor evidenced in dis/posi-

tioned research. Discussing critical pedagogy with Ira Shor, Freire expressed the desire of research:

> I am sure, Ira[,] that we have to fight with love, with passion, in order to demonstrate that what we are proposing is absolutely rigorous. We have, in doing so, to demonstrate that rigor is not synonymous with authoritarianism, that "rigor" does not mean "rigidity." Rigor lives with freedom, needs freedom. I cannot understand how it is possible to be rigorous without being creative. For me it is very difficult to be creative without having freedom. Without being free, I can only repeat what is being told me.
>
> Rigor is a desire to know, a search for an answer, a critical method of learning. Maybe rigor is also a communication, which challenges the other to take part, includes the other in an active search. (Shor & Freire, 1987, pp. 78, 84)

Research, then, is politically and ideologically determined. Alternative types of line of flight research that are currently being pursued in education are facing a struggle over the political borders of those determinations.

Research can also be discussed discursively. Discourse, according to Foucault, is a practice through which it forms the objects of which it speaks. It consists of words spoken or written that group themselves according to certain rules established within discourse, and certain conditions, that make their existence possible. For Foucault, discourse was an anonymous field in that its origin or locus of formation resides in neither a sovereign nor a collective consciousness. It exists at the level of "it is said." It indicates certain circumscribed positions from which, he wrote: "One may speak that which is already caught up in the play of 'exteriority'" (Foucault, 1972, p. 122). Because discourses can cut across normally accepted unities such as the academic disciplines or books, one can speak, for instance, of a psychological discourse, a medical discourse, or a curriculum research discourse, or one can speak of a discourse on madness or sexuality. Discourse not only forms the objects of which it speaks, it also disperses the subject of sovereign consciousness into various subject positions and it inserts researchers into paradigms and models. The assumed unity of the Self or the "I" of consciousness becomes a position attached to and retrospectively formed by the discourse surrounding it (Pinar et. al., 1995, p. 463). The purpose of discourse analysis is not to determine what the discourse means, but to investigate how it works, what conditions make it possible (its exteriority), how it interacts with nondiscursive practices, and how it is connected to power and knowledge:

> It is in discourse that power and knowledge are joined together. And for this very reason, we must conceive discourse as a series of discontinuous segments whose tactical function is neither uniform nor stable. To be more precise, we must not imagine a world of discourse divided between accepted discourse and excluded discourse ... but as a multiplicity of discursive ele-

ments that can come into play in various strategies…. Discourse can be both as instrument and an effect of power, but also a hindrance, a stumbling block, a point of resistance and a starting point for opposing strategies. (Foucault, 1980, pp. 100–101)

The discourses in which we speak about curriculum research and the manner in which it is questioned and discussed give it an aura of common sense or normalcy. This normalcy (or perhaps the nostalgia for certainty) gives these discourses a troubling power to shape thought and to hinder other questions. Research discourses and their very place in the realm of commonsense is what should be questioned so that the effects, values, ideologies, or trajectories can be brought into focus. In another way, we can say that these questions imply a norm of judgment: A very shifting and unstable meaning and essence are better and more important than a discussion of "how things work" or "where they come from." That is, within the normal procedures of our discipline (curriculum/pedagogy research) and the knowledge-producing system they make up, these commonsensical questions are more important than are functional questions. This discourse is a form of cognitive control and yet it is not exclusively repressive.

A curriculum perspective that "chooses" not to answer the commonsense questions appears to be naïve, obfuscating, needlessly difficult, or simply wrong, confused, or fuzzy. An analysis of discourse allows us to describe that the self-evident and commonsensical are what have the privilege of unnoticed power, and this power produces instruments of control. This does not mean, as Marx and Freud would have it, that it is control by repression or exclusion; instead, it is a control of positive production. That is a kind of power that generates certain kinds of questions, placed within systems that legitimize support and answer those questions: a kind of power that, in the process, includes within its systems all those it produces as agents capable of acting within them (Bove, 1992). These are questions that altogether justify certain interpretations and block our apprehension of others.

From Foucault's (1972) point of view, all intellectuals, all teachers, all students, and all researchers within any discipline are to some extent incorporated within these systems of control based on a mode of knowledge and truth production that defines much of our social world. There is, in other words, no place to stand outside of it, no Jamesian "ego of apperception," as our modelers would have us believe (James, 1997). Thus, the intriguing question is how do the various research discourses function? How does the discourse get produced and regulated? What are the effects of such discourse? Hence, a description of the surface linkages among power, knowledge, institutions, intellectuals, the control of populations, and the modern state as these intersect in the function of systems of thought in research can produce some fascinating results.

The focus of questions could swirl around the characterization of curriculum research as a technique of management. The point is that disciplinary, reform, or managerial techniques were and have been developed into a technology of cognitive control and positive production. These "new" techniques (discourses) do not inflict violence on the body. Instead of inflicting pain, the new techniques instill controlling habits and value-sustaining self-images—the intent was/is the increase of universalizable, efficient subjugation and control. These techniques proliferate/operate in all institutions involving the management of large numbers of people: the convent, the school, the barracks, and the corporation/university. It is also true for standardized research formulas in education. This becomes what Foucault delineated as a political technology of the body. The aim of this technology is not mere control, as in the effective impositions of restrictions and prohibitions, but rather pervasive management gained through enabling as well as restrictive conceptions, definitions, and descriptions that generate and support behavior-governing norms. This is a type and degree of complicity of those managed in a way not imagined before, because it demands not only obedience to laws and commandments, but also the deep internalization of a carefully orchestrated, value-laden understanding of the self. As researchers in education internalize these discourses, their subject position as educational researchers is formed. The discourses of acceptable educational research as they are internalized become less necessary as individuals begin to monitor themselves, so that the standardized and codified educational dispositions advocated in the discourse disperse the sovereign consciousness into a particular subject position and we become who we say we are, because we have internalized whom the discourses say we are and we produce the research discourses that say who we are. It is a form of power that makes individuals subjects:

> There are two meanings to the word subject: subject to someone else by control and dependence, and tied to his own identity by a conscience or self-knowledge. Both meanings suggest a form of power which subjects and makes subjects to ... nowadays, the struggle against the forms of subjugation against the submission of subjectivity—is becoming more and more important, even though the struggles against forms of domination and exploitation have not disappeared. Quite the contrary. (Foucault, 1982/1983, pp. 212–213)

Research in curriculum and education is intertwined within discursive constructions, which, as stated previously, determine those research questions that are legitimated and those that are relegated to dismissive formulations of the naïve, the obfuscating, the needlessly difficult, or simply wrong, and confused. How power operates through discursive formations in educational research and research in general is a topic that could generate much productive practice.

DIS/POSITIONING RESEARCH

> Control is not only the ghost in the clock of curriculum—to use the predominant modernist, mechanistic, metaphor—it is the ghost, which actually runs

the clock. It is time to put this ghost to rest, let it retire peacefully to the land of no return and to liberate curriculum to live a life of its own. (Doll, 2002)

In this section, the curriculum studies field is used as an example of the type of thinking that can dis/position in general. This line of flight research is connected by its shared concern for viewing educational phenomena from alternative perspectives that are not method driven, but instead derived from the insights of a disposition that seeks to disentangle research from its traditional dependence on formalities. Ever since reconceptualization, formal curriculum theorizing as well as educational research have dominated the field as scholars have attempted to gain acceptance for alternative methodologies such as textual analysis, discourse theory, hermeneutics, cultural studies, psychoanalysis, and poststructuralism while triangulating them with the important perspectives of race, class, gender, and sexual orientation. Although the enormity of this reconceiving process has produced innovative and challenging work, the place from which the author speaks has been, for the most part, ignored to the benefit of professionalism as an ideology in the academy. That is, although the research topics and methods that have recast curriculum orientations have made the field a much stronger contender within the larger field of education, they have not yet touched on the crucial role that method defending plays in unwittingly supporting a privileged position, that of theorist.

The positions that can teach us the most about curriculum are those that are in a dissed position vis-à-vis the formalisms of the field. Research in curriculum studies has tried to reinvent those positions in order to view the field from that dis/position because of the methodological imperative that drives most theorizing. We can see in some research this view that the choice of method is secondary to subjective positioning. Thus, instead of taking a formal position in curriculum theory and then choosing to understand a topic through its lens, researchers have chosen a subjective dis/position and let the concerns heard, seen, felt, and witnessed—at that place—dictate the methodological focus of the theorizing. The place from which theory is constructed is not always already framed by formal discourse, and our inability to see this disposition perhaps stems from our professional need to defend a measuring device, often to the detriment of our subject. To eradicate this human error (which, ironically, stems from our antihuman methodological tendencies; Althusser, 1971), we can choose to emphasize nomadic thinking. The movement of the thought in question is flexible and nomadic, transversal and nonhierarchical; this thought is able to move between the formations of the state, the unconscious, or language, and not just exclusively within one formation.

Like the navigator who in one trajectory uses the metro, the bus, and the foot in combination thereby integrating a network of bodily and mechanic locomotion into one 'assemblage' a rhizomatic or nomadic thought would forge linkages or connections between different systems of knowledge formation. (Kaufman & Heller, 1998, p. 5)

Research in this nomadic/line of flight manner would share an undisclosed disillusionment with viewing education from the perspective of curriculum criticizing or from formal training. Research could be derived from theorists whose experiences in their nonprofessional lives have dictated their focus of study. In a sense, they would be nomads, both professionally and theoretically, preferring to "do curriculum" on an alternate playing field. The Deleuzian nomad would view curriculum theorizing and research from this perspective, viewing its role in theory construction as one that comes from uninhabited (and perhaps uninhabitable) spaces and speaks about the unspeakable. Irreverent, mobile, and at times offensive, the nomad finds knowledge and feeling in unframed, ambiguous, and common places. Unlike the scholar of the week, the Deleuzian nomad does not occupy the place of the subject in order to speak knowledge to power, but only visits temporarily, deriving the insights necessary to enrich understanding. Speaking the dislocated position, the theorist admits that there is no new frontier to conquer, but only those left out of the curriculum/research loop by the profession. There is one last point to elaborate in this area of dis/positioning. Researchers in this nomadic, dis/positioned line of flight cannot abrogate the political responsibility of their work. Simply admitting that research, curriculum studies, and the rest are the result of political and ideological struggles, constructed through discourse and potentially nomadic, limits the very essence and function of the research. There needs to be investment in the political agency that can be engendered by this work. Recently, Bill attended a conference on Popular Culture. He thought that there he would find this type of research, the multidisciplinary nomadic type. And, to a certain extent, he did, but what was missing and what we should be ever vigilant about is that the research should always be connected to the larger sociopolitical situations of our times and the children—that educational/curriculum studies research isn't simply a means of social amelioration and as an end for professional advancement. And yet we are cautious that involving one's self in practice without a critical perspective only reinforces the status quo.

THE CHAPTERS

The chapters in this text reflect the conceptualizations we have discussed. Although they cover divergent areas, they do share this line of flight notion, this nomadic orientation to curriculum scholarship. It is a nomadic curriculum scholarship of difference:

The new, with its power of beginning, and beginning again, remains forever new, just as the established was always established from the outset, even if a certain

amount of empirical time was necessary for this to be recognized. What becomes established with the new is precisely not the new. For the new—in other
words, difference—calls forth forces in thought which are not the forces of recognition, today or tomorrow, but the powers of a completely other model, from
an unrecognized and unrecognizable *terra incognita*. (Deleuze, 1995, p. 136)

In *Understanding Curriculum* (1995), we (Pinar, Reynolds, Slattery, &
Taubman) provided a map of the curriculum field. In *Curriculum: Toward
New Identities* (1998), Pinar's collection emphasizes one area of the progress
of curriculum studies centering on identity. Perhaps this collection demonstrates that curriculum studies can center on difference. A healthy multiplicity is evident with these chapters. We hope that in this collection the
chapters will demonstrate the variety and extent to which research in curriculum studies is healthy, fluid, and nomadic.

In chapter 2, a discussion of corporations and the brand-named corporate order, Bill Reynolds moves curriculum thinking toward cultural curriculum studies with a Deleuzian twist. Ever mindful that we are all working
within the corporate order and that we can never stand outside it, Reynolds
advocates that by studying our immersion in the order it is possible to develop contingent, momentary spaces that allow for thinking otherwise. He
encourages us to think in the AND instead of the IS. This multiplicity thinking is the basis for curriculum dis/positions. Avoiding the rubric of the us
against them binary mentality, a Deleuzian "in-between" is emphasized.
Reynolds states, "The 'struggle' is to keep on finding lines that disrupt and
overturn the brand-name corporate order. An AND, AND, AND, which
each time marks a new threshold, a new direction of the zigzagging line, a
new course for the border" (Deleuze, 1995, p. 45). Never resting, always being in the AND. This AND thinking is the line of flight for Reynolds, who
recognizes all lines of flight, all curriculum dis/positions are temporary.
Each new line is closed down and new ones must continually be proposed.
This chapter sets the stage for those that follow.

Don Livingston's chapter, "Wondering About a Future Generation:
Identity Disposition Disposal, Recycling and Creation in the 21st Century"
(chap. 3) transports the reader directly into the line of flight reasoning we
have outlined in this introduction. Taking as his point of departure the debate in curriculum studies that problematizes the notion of the "individual"
as the end goal of educational reproduction, Livingston queries the effect of
new technologies on subjective experience in the 21st century. Postulating
that instead of forming individuals, new media force people to experience
themselves as "dividuals," Livingston continues the theoretical work necessary to understand Deleuze and Guattari's "part object." As people come to
experience themselves as dividuals, they lose the body and materiality as
the interpretive center for meaning making while at the same time giving
that interpretive power over to the technologies they use as mediums for
communication and experience.

Livingston cautions the reader against any utopian fantasies they might form about the effects of these technologies by recalling the interpretive strengths of Foucault's analysis of power. As Livingston writes, "Because dividuals openly expose their identities, social institutions that monitor such activities will have little trouble controlling dividuated behaviors. Because of this outward orientation, the regimes of truth will find it much easier to control fragmented dividuals." Unable to call on former institutions that rely on the body for the material experience of intersubjective communication, dividuals will become dependent a benevolent technocratic elite for their opinions, beliefs, and attitudes toward social life. But it is not a question of returning to the body or abandoning it completely for Livingston; instead, he calls on the reader to rethink this paradox and encourage researchers to transform experience in light of social justice and curriculum, rather than view technology as a tool that produces an either/or disposition.

In chapter 4, Karen Ferneding examines educational reform rhetoric in "The Discourse of Inevitability and the Forging of an Emergent Social Vision: Technology Diffusion and the Dialectic of Educational Reform Discourse" in order to apprehend the "discourse of inevitability" that dominates conversations concerning technology and education. In this chapter, Ferneding's ability to catch the "as if" moment in policy reform discussions and write persuasively about it situates her chapter squarely within the tradition of technology critique. The chapter makes this clear at the beginning, when she argues, "The diffusion of electronic technologies, the control of teacher's work, and the reconfiguring of public education to further a globalized market economy are inevitable. This situation effectively closes down the spaces for alternative perspectives, voices, and interpretations regarding the naming of the nature of public education's general condition and the imagining of its future."

What Ferneding's chapter ultimately does for the reader is demonstrate that although a critique of the content of education policy has been traditionally viewed as a valid point of departure for understanding its ultimate intent and ideological positioning, today it is perhaps more important to pin down the sensibility behind the message through an examination of its rhetoric. Finally, Ferneding's chapter argues that the language of this reform discourse insinuates that what the public wants from technology is to be delivered from the work implied in maintaining social relationships and cultivating a public discourse that has traditionally been viewed as the mission of the school in a democratic society. This "mythinformation" is pervasive and utopian in our public discourse because it concerns the schools.

Julie A. Webber, in chapter 5—which combines political science, psychoanalysis, and curriculum theory—discusses what she refers to as a countermovement in response to school violence or school shootings. That reaction is the increasing number of Christian converts to school prayer. It is a student movement that reclaims the public schools for God, eschewing the rebellion against a perceived hegemonic policy or force. There is a willing return to God, normative masculinity, and the heteronormative family to order the symbolic. This reflects the notion on the part of certain segments of the Right that the problems of America and violence in schools are caused by moral decay, and that a reestablishment of moral order will put America on the true path once again. It is reminiscent of Lyotard's discussion in *The Postmodern Explained* (1992): "We are in a moment of relaxation—I am speaking of the tenor of our times. Everywhere we are urge to give up experimentation, in the arts and elsewhere. I have read that a new philosopher has invented something he quaintly calls Judeo-Christianism, with which he intends to put an end to the current impiety for which we are supposedly responsible" (pp. 1–2). Webber's chapter, by examining how this movement operates, allows a space for us to consider a different dis/position to this current phenomenon. It gives us new way to look at the whole notion of the present historical conjuncture of school violence and the reactions to it.

The importance and richness of nomadic and line of flight type of curriculum research is clear in chapter 6, Marla Morris's "Stumbling Inside Dis/positions: The Un(home) of Education." She seeks to understand why traditional models of education and curriculum are less than liberatory for those whose research falls on the margins in an inequitable society. Morris takes the reader on a tour through her own personal spiritual journey to find a way into a curriculum theorizing that she could call her own. For Morris, going back to one's roots in the community and in spirituality helped her to reconceive the role of the researcher in transforming curriculum theorizing rather than simply accepting it as it has been taught to her. Again, the readers will find themselves thinking about what kind of praxis is necessary to even forge a disposition that is other than "home" and yet remain fine with it at the same time.

Between curriculum as autobiographical and theological text, between the mentors, Mary Aswell Doll's interjections, the Jewish traditions, and all just under 40, Morris has learned and tells us, "Foolishness is the key to unlocking otherness, realms of lived experience squashed by rational deliberation and mechanization. Beware the donkey driver" (p. 30). Is this the third space, between identity positions, and marked by confession? It is a line of flight for the reader to consider, and an important one at that.

In his chapter on *Curricula Vita* or course of life (chap. 7) Douglas McKnight explores the connections between the New England Puritans of 17th and 18th centuries and curriculum thinking. For the Puritans, McKnight reminds us, curriculum was the intensive and rigorous reflective process of studying and receiving a purpose and meaning in life, a vocation. McKnight explicates how these meanings have shifted in their applications in America. We again see the movement toward the discussion of the spiritual. McKnight sees the current trend in schools toward "character education" to be a misunderstanding of this reflective process, focusing not so much on the individual journey toward self-reflection, but instead as a method of instilling normative behaviors. This chapter goes on to discuss the various implications of the Puritan call to a vocation for modern curriculum thought. McKnight realizes that the present educational system with its emphasis on curriculum as a "subject matter to be mastered" is entrenched and difficult to change, but as he concludes: "Although such a state of affairs can cause one to give oneself over to dread and despair, leading to paralysis, at the same time an individual is obligated to respond, always struggling to move beyond what exists at the moment. That is *curricula vita*."

In chapter 8, Donald Blumenfeld-Jones relies on the framework of hermeneutics to discuss issues of dance curriculum. He extends on the work of both Mann (1975) and Reynolds (1989). Through the use of hermeneutics, he wishes to develop curriculum thinking and emerge with "practical wisdom." Having examined three dance curricula that dwell in the technical-rationalist way of thinking, a possible line of flight emerges through hermeneutic understanding. It is striking that one can dance a line of flight as well as write one. As Blumenfeld-Jones indicates about himself, and like many of us in the curriculum field, our thinking has changed so much over the years, and we have moved away from the straightjackets of technica–rational thinking toward the becomings of other lines of flight. As Blumenfeld-Jones, discussing the line of flight in dance, states, "They [those that rely on conventional educational slogans] have not approachepd the practical wisdom that dancers can develop when they transcend technical thinking and use theoretical understanding (such as hermeneutical thinking) to do so. They have not recognized that we dance for reasons that go beyond the rational and are no less valuable for doing so."

In chapter 9, Audrey Watkins' "Education From All of Life for All of Life: Getting an Education at Home—Precept on Precept, Line on Line" takes as its point of departure focusing on the ways in which "getting ahead" has typically been viewed as a formal enterprise that, as she says, "seeks to make us spectators to the spectacle of our own education," and the ways in which an "informal curriculum" based in life experience is more successful and important for Black women. Watkins examines the way that Black women are informally educated by their experiences in informal spaces that are often informed by a spiritual dimension and driven by a sense of moral obligation. Throughout this chapter, Watkins demonstrates that meaningful, progressive education doesn't take place where one typically expects it to—especially for Black women who are oppressed by formal education and its often irrelevant curriculum—instead, it usually happens when women teach women, mothers teach daughters, and neighbors and communities take interest and encourage entrepreneurship. What Watkins shows through interviews with Black women is that they value informal education (in the home, the workplace, the neighborhood) as having a status equal to that of the school. Furthermore, they view education in informal spaces as a powerful way of teaching the students how to survive and prevail in an inequitable society. In this way, Watkins' chapter is firmly situated within the framework of this volume by demonstrating how those who find their own way into the world, and find it necessary to eschew traditional models of research and political praxis, come to embrace curriculum as lines of flight.

Curriculum happens as an event. In chapter 10, we return to Deleuze and Daignault in Wen-Song Hwu's work. Truly reflecting the major themes of this text, Hwu wants to problematize our notions of curriculum theory and practice using the work of these poststructural thinkers. Hwu gives the work of French Canadian curriculum theorist Jacques Daignault the attention it deserves. All of Daignault's essays foreshadow by many years the type of scholarship and curriculum research that is prevalent in the curriculum studies field today (and many of the chapters in this particular text). His work, as Hwu implies, has not received the attention in deserves. As Hwu explains, Daignault and Gauthier (1982) insisted that curriculum is a paradoxical and nomadic object, which is always transient. There is, of course, within Hwu's discussion of Daignault the direct link to the writings of Deleuze, whose work has been so influential to this present text.

The challenge of Hwu's work, as well as Daignault and Deleuze's, is to challenge us to rethink curriculum and do curriculum poststructurally. Understanding curriculum as event is a nomadic way of thinking curriculum. As Hwu concludes:

> In regard to the subject of curriculum studies, he [Daignault] questions and claims that it does not exist, but subsists in things and insists in language; this questioning of curriculum as "event" gives us new understandings of curriculum and curriculum discourse.

NOMADIC MULTIPLICITIES IN CURRICULUM STUDIES

Nomadic research dis/positioned seeks lines of flight. Lines of flight can be found in the middle spaces, not in taking sides in the bifurcated opposition. We suggest bypassing these debates altogether, because they only speak knowledge to the establishment's power. Knowledge, as we understand it poststructurally, as the reduction of difference to identity, the many to the one, heterogeneity to homogeneity—is violence. The former type of violence/knowledge results from competition between ideologies or doctrines and from "the radical transformation of what exists in conformity with what we believe ought to be" (Hwu, 1993, p. 132). For Jacques Daignault, as for Michele Serres, to know is to commit a type of murder, to terrorize. Thus, we can attempt to engage in academic terrorism if we choose knowing as simply defining and objectifying. Nihilism, on the other hand, refers to the abandonment of any attempt to know. It is the attitude that says, "anything goes" or "things are what they are." It is to give up, to turn one's ideals into empty fictions or memories, to have no hope. Perhaps we should live and research in the middle, in spaces that are neither terroristic nor nihilistic, neither exclusively political nor exclusively technological.

The former leads to terrorism, because it regards education as primarily an opportunity for power to know as definition. The latter leads to technological manipulation, regarding education as primarily an opportunity for efficiency and manipulation, as we see in the current accountability, testing, and standard/canon rage. Research in the nomadic manner can avoid the dualistic dilemma of terrorism or nihilism. Much new research that has emerged with the last decade gravitates toward this notion. (See works included in this chapter's references). This new research—as evidenced in the chapters in this text and their dis/positioning—works against the bifurcations, strict disciplinarity, and entrenchment of much educational research. It is a way of the middle spaces.

Michele Serres in his text *Detachment* (1989), used farming as a metaphor to discuss the need for lines of flight:

> How can one escape totality? In the absence of roads how can one get out? Form is a prison for the head as matter has custody over the hand. How can one get out of these perfectly encircled farms? … There is not a single empty space in the loamy sands, nowhere on the ground could there be an empty nest for you, to soar vertically is the only possible direction. (Serres, 1989, pp. 13–14)

Dis/positioned research is an attempt to soar vertically. It is an attempt to get out, move through the middle, without roads, remaining undefined or defining. It is perhaps caught up in that old haunting meta-narrative of hope. However, hope keeps the field alive for us. It is part of that continuing curriculum conversation (Pinar et. al., 1995; Reynolds, 2003).

REFERENCES

Althusser, L. (1971). *Lenin and philosophy*. (B. Brewster, Trans.). New York: Monthly Review Press.

Aronowitz, S., & Giroux, H. A. (1991). *Postmodern education: Politics, culture and social criticism*. Minneapolis: University of Minnesota Press.

Barthes, R. (1986). *The rustle of language*. (R. Howard, Trans.). Los Angeles: University of California Press.

Bloom, A. D. (1988). *Closing of the American mind*. New York: Touchstone Books.

Bove, P. A. (1992). *Mastering discourse: The politics of intellectual culture*. Durham, NC: Duke University Press.

Daignault, J., & Gauthier, C. (1982). The indecent curriculum machine. *Journal of Curriculum Theorizing, 4*(1), 177–196.

Deleuze, G. (1995). *Negotiations 1972–1990*. New York: Columbia University Press.

Deleuze, G., & Guattari, F. (1987). *A thousand plateaus: Capitalism and Schizophrenia*. Minneapolis: University of Minnesota Press.

Deleuze, G., & Guattari, F. (1989). *Anti-Oedipus: Capitalism and schizophrenia*. Minneapolis: University of Minnesota Press.

Deleuze, G., & Parnet, C. (1977). *Dialogues*. (H. Tomlinson & B. Habberjam, Trans.). New York: Columbia University Press.

Doll, M. A. (2000). *Like letters in running water*. Mahwah, NJ: Lawrence Erlbaum Associates.

Doll, W. E. (1993). *A post-modern perspective on curriculum*. New York: Teachers College Press.

Doll, W. E., Jr., & Gough, N. (Eds.). (2002). *Curriculum visions*. New York: Peter Lang.

Eagleton, T. (1983). *Literary theory: An introduction*. Minneapolis: University of Minnesota Press.

Foucault, M. (1972). *The archaeology of knowledge*. (M. Smith, Trans.). New York: Pantheon.

Foucault, M. (1980). *The history of sexuality: Vol I. An introduction*. (R. Hurley, Trans.). New York: Vintage.

Foucault, M. (1982/1983). Afterword: The subject and the power. In H. L. Dreyfus & P. Rabinow (Eds.), *Michel Foucault: Beyond structuralism and hermeneutics* (pp. 208–226). Chicago: University of Chicago Press.

Gates, H. L., Jr. (1993). *Loose canons: Notes on the culture wars*. Oxford University Press.

Greene, M. (1994). Postmodernism and the crisis of representation. *English Education, 26*(4), 206–219.

Hirsch, E. D. (1988). *Cultural literacy: What every American needs to know*. New York: Vintage Books.

Hwu, W. (1993). *Toward understanding poststructuralism and curriculum*. Unpublished doctoral dissertation, Louisiana State University, Baton Rouge.

James, W. (1997). *Varieties of religious experience*. New York: Touchstone Books.

Jipson, J., & Paley, N. (1997). *Daredevil research: Recreating analytic practice*. New York: Peter Lang.

Kaufman, E., & Heller, K. J. (Eds.). (1998). *Deleuze and Guattari: New mappings in politics, philosophy, and culture*. Minneapolis: University of Minnesota Press.

Lather, P. (1991). *Getting smart: Feminist research and pedagogy with/in the postmodern*. New York: Routledge.

Lyotard, J.-F. (1992). *The postmodern explained*. Minneapolis: University of Minnesota Press.

Mann, J. (1975). Curriculum criticism. In William F. Pinar (Ed.), *Curriculum theory: The reconceptualists* (pp. 133–149). Berkeley, CA: McCutchan.

Marshall, J. D., Sears, J. T., & Schubert, W. H. (2000). *Turning points in curriculum: A Contemporary American memoir*. Upper Saddle River, NJ: Merrill.

Morris, M., Doll, M. A., & Pinar, W. F. (1999). *How we work*. New York: Peter Lang.

Pinar, W. F., Reynolds, W. M., Slattery, P., & Taubman, P. M. (1995). *Understanding curriculum: An introduction to the study of historical and contemporary curriculum discourses*. New York: Peter Lang.

Pinar, W. F. (Ed.). (1998). *Curriculum: Toward new identities*. New York: Garland Publishing.

Rabinow, P. (Ed.). (1984). *The Foucault reader*. New York: Pantheon.

Reynolds, W. M. (1989). *Reading curriculum theory: The development of a new hermeneutic*. New York: Peter Lang.

Reynolds, W. M. (2003). *Curriculum: A river runs through it*. New York: Peter Lang.

Serres, M. (1983). *Hermes: Literature, science, philosophy*. Baltimore, MD: Johns Hopkins University Press.

Serres, M. (1989). *Detachment*. Athens: University of Ohio Press.

Serres, M. (1999). *Genesis*. (G. James & J. Nielson, Trans.). Ann Arbor: University of Michigan Press.

Shor, I., & Freire, P. (1987). *A pedagogy for liberation*. Westport, CT: Bergin & Garvey.

Webber, J. A. (2003). *Failure to hold: The politics of school violence*. New York: Rowman and Littlefield.

Chapter 2

To Touch the Clouds Standing on Top of a Maytag Refrigeratior: Brand-Name Postmodernity and a Deleuzian "In-Between"

William M. Reynolds
Georgia Southern University

Thinking Beyond

In this chapter, Reynolds discusses the implications of the brand-named corporate order. The problems and concepts within a poststructural analysis of corporate capitalism is one way of understanding the expanding notions of curriculum theory. One of the problems addressed in this chapter is that oppositional politics might be approached in the postmodern corporate culture from a tactical rather than strategic manner. This chapter sets the overall milieu in which the book is situated.

Questions

1. How does Reynolds' chapter relate to the chapters by Livingston and Ferneding in terms of issues of technology, culture, and curriculum?
2. How is Deleuze's notion of the "in-between" an example of poststructural politics?
3. How does brand-named corporate culture operate? How could tactical poststructural politics operate within schools?

We're told businesses have souls, which is surely the most terrifying news in the world. Marketing is now the instrument of social control and produces the arrogant breed who are our masters. (Deleuze, 1995, p. 181)

We're moving toward control societies that no longer operate by confining people but through continuous control and instant communication. (Deleuze, 1995, p. 178)

It's not a question of worrying or of hoping for the best, but of finding new weapons (Deleuze, 1995, p. 178)

As I was driving to the university the other day, I was feeling well. I was driving my VW Jetta ("drivers wanted"); drinking Starbucks coffee (and, as the bag of coffee says, "Don't you think it's time to take this relationship to a deeper level right to our heart and soul"); and wearing a Ralph Lauren shirt (and we all know how much they cost) and Levi's jeans (of course, they are slightly uncool, considering that Pepe, Polo Sport, Nautica, and Tommy Hilfiger have more costly and much more hip jeans). I was experiencing the lifestyle and fulfillment of the brand-name corporate order. We live in the time of the looking glass:

> In another moment Alice was through the glass, and had jumped lightly down into the Looking-glass room. The very first thing she did was to look whether there was a fire in the fireplace, and she was quite pleased to find that there was a real one, blazing away as brightly as the one she left behind. "So I shall be as warm in here as I was in the old room," thought Alice: "warmer in fact, because there'll be no one here to scold me away from the fire. Oh what fun it will be, when they see through the glass in here, and can't get at me!" (Carroll, 1997, pp. 158–159)

We want to be as warm on side of postmodernity as we were before we stepped through whatever looking glass it was and away from the modernist notions of self, truth, and meaning. Perhaps we are afraid that we will find on the other side of the mirror what Neo in *The Matrix* found when the mirror covered him and there was, indeed, the matrix. So, we deal with the uncertainty of our time and theorize about the possibilities of more meaningful times ahead. That is one of the many dilemmas of postmodern existence.

Meanwhile, we live in the present historical conjuncture that is corporatized, and our cathedrals of spiritual fulfillment are the shopping malls. Families now ritually travel on Saturday or Sunday to their local malls or outlet malls to partake of not only the products of consumer culture, but also to acquire the lifestyle and ambiance that the brand names offer. The denominations of which we are members are not those of traditional institutional religion; Banana Republic, Abercrombie and Fitch, The Gap, J. Crew, and Nine West are some of the various denominations we worship, and consuming is our "religion" and our spirituality:

> From his perch as top adviser to the top media conglomerates, Michael J. Wolf observes that the theme-park-style shopping locations like Minneapolis's Mall of America maybe precursors to the live-in malls of the future. "Maybe the next step in this evolution is to put housing next to the stores and megaplexes and call it a small town. People living, working, shopping and consuming entertainment in one place. What a concept," he enthuses. (Wolf cited in Klein, 1999, p. 187)

Like the villages of premodern times with the church as the center, postmodern suburbs with the malls as their center are the present small-town life. And, similar to the premodern times, no expense will be spared in constructing these cathedrals. Like the cathedrals of old that were meant to inspire by their sheer size, artistry, and grandeur—which was in stark contrast to the everyday lives of the villagers—the malls are mega in size and contain the grandeur of the 21st century. These hold the promise of attaining the spiritual fulfillment not by tithing but by buying. It is a corporate spirituality. Arthur Miller, in *Timebends: A Life* (1987), discussed the reaction to his play *The Death of a Salesman* and this notion of spirituality in the capitalist order:

> On the play's opening night a woman who shall not be named was outraged, calling it "a time bomb under American Capitalism"; I hope it was, or at least

under the bullshit of capitalism, this pseudo life that thought to touch the clouds by standing on top of a refrigerator, waving a paid mortgage at the moon, victorious at last. (Miller, 1987, p. 184)

The corporate order has changed as well. It is now not simply a refrigerator, but a Maytag, Whirlpool, or Frigidaire. We can purchase one of those at many of the megahardware stores—alternative cathedrals for the do-it-yourselfer. They, too, sell us a lifestyle.

The brand-name corporate order and its impact on education is addressed in the remainder of this chapter. Let's first look at the brand-name corporate order.

THE BRAND-NAME CORPORATE ORDER AND CONTROL SOCIETIES

The term *corporate culture*, according to Giroux (2000a), refers to an "ensemble of ideological and institutional forces that functions politically and pedagogically to both govern organizational life through senior managerial control and to produce compliant workers, depoliticized consumers, passive citizens" (p. 41). This senior managerial control reflects Deleuze's notion of control societies run by sales and marketing: "Markets are won by taking control rather than by establishing a discipline, by fixing rates rather than reducing costs, by transforming products rather than by specializing production. Corruption here takes on a new power. The sales department becomes a business' center or soul" (Deleuze, 1995, p. 181).

Citizenship has now become a matter not of community involvement, but an individualized consumer affair. Being a good citizen means being a good consumer. Many middle-class men and women are willing to live in gated communities, surrendering individual liberties to the structures of covenants that promote feelings of safety. One example of these constructed communities is Disney's suburb of Celebration in Florida. Living in this "safe" community comes with its restrictions and rules:

The rules include not being allowed to hang the wash out to dry, keeping the grass cut, not being able to live elsewhere for more than three months at a time, holding only one garage sale in any twelve month period, displaying only white or off-white window coverings, and using only approved house-paint colors. (Giroux, 1999, p. 43)

Celebration may well be an extreme example, but there are countless suburbs in the United States in which restrictions and covenants abound—where safety and good taste are the order of the day and individual freedom takes a backseat. The encroaching predatory hoard of uneducated, low-income, non-White, and criminal "outsiders" are kept at the gate, while the suburban dwellers are "safe" in their covenant-restricted, upper-middle-class, consumer citizen, manicured environments.

Schooling at all levels is reduced to testing, standards, and accountability, preparing good consumers for the global marketplace. What is profitable in those terms is retained; the rest, much like in corporate downsizing, is eliminated. Concern for the public schools continues to be centered on control and compliance. There is a perpetual pedagogy of surveillance (Reynolds, 2002). Public education is concerned with controlling student and teacher ethical behavior, testing, and accountability in order to assuage a constructed national concern over test scores that demonstrate the ability of students to absorb and recall disparate and unconnected pieces of pre-determined information, which in many cases has nothing to do with their existence in the brand-name corporate order. Schools are operating to become less and less a primary educational site.

They are also becoming corporatized themselves. We can notice that the call for accountability and testing within the context of the ever-present calls for school reform reflect a corporate-like demand for profitable and pragmatic results. And, at the same time, this call completely ignores issues such as ethics, equity, and social justice. The intrusion of the corporate into the "business" of schooling has a long history, beginning with the industrial revolution (Pinar, Reynolds, Slattery, & Taubman, 1995; Reynolds, 1999, 2002, 2003; Reynolds & Webber, 2004).

The universities are also moving into the corporate, new world order, in some instances by hiring CEOs as presidents. James Carlin, who until recently served as the chairman of the Massachusetts State Board of Education, had a corporate agenda for the state universities.

> In his eagerness to rebuild universities in the mirror image of the mega corporation, with faculty as hostile workers and students as consumers, Carlin argues for scrapping remediation programs for students, expanding the workload of professors to four three-credit courses a semester, increasing student–teacher ratios, abolishing tenure, eliminating "public service" projects, and eradicating teacher unions. In this discourse the university becomes an adjunct of the corporation, and its historic function as an autonomous sphere for the development of a critical productive democratic citizenry is vanquished. (Giroux, 2000a, p. 53)

The corporate university functions for the bottom line. The time when universities and colleges were places for scholarly community and the last refuge of intellectual freedom is being quickly replaced by profitability figures and monitored curriculum approved by outside accrediting agencies (i.e., the National Council for Accreditation of Teacher Education, or NCATE). In *The Knowledge Factory: Dismantling the Corporate University and Creating True Higher Learning* (2000), Stanley Aronowitz discussed the corporate university:

Far from the image of the ivory tower, where, monk-like, scholars ponder the stars and other distant things, the universities tend to mirror the rest of society. Some have become big businesses, employing thousands and collecting millions in tuition fees, receiving grants from government and private sources, and, for a select few, raising billions in huge endowments. In some cities and towns, the resident private university or college is the area's largest landlord, housing students and faculty and, in some instances, collecting rents for ordinary or slum dwellings. (Aronowitz, 2000, p. 11)

The final point in this description of our corporate world is that among this movement toward a corporate, new world order, we have what Naomi Klein in *No Logo: Taking Aim at The Brand Bullies* (1999) called a "new branded world" (p. 1). Her contention was that at the present moment, corporations are not necessarily interested in producing commodities, but instead are focused on producing "concepts: the brand as experience, as lifestyle" (p. 21). One example Klein used was Starbucks coffee. Production of commodities in the branded order is relatively unimportant. The construction of identity and meaning through brands is the manner in which corporations are beginning to operate:

Starbucks seemed to understand brand names at a level even deeper than Madison Avenue, incorporating marketing into every fiber of its corporate concept—from the chains strategic association with books, blues, and jazz to it Euro-latte lingo…. The people who line up for Starbucks, writes CEO Howard Schultz, aren't just there for the coffee. "It's the romance of the coffee experience, the feeling of warmth and community the people get in Starbucks stores." (Klein, 1999, p. 20)

And, as brands such as Tommy Hilfiger (who makes nothing and brands everything) become more the trend, we increasingly see that we are living in this postmodern, brand-name, corporate order that comes precipitously close to Baudrillard's (1994) hyperreal simulacra, a copy of a copy of a copy.

"Tommy Hilfiger, meanwhile, is less interested in the business of manufacturing clothes than he is in signing his name. The company is run entirely through licensing agreements, with Hilfiger commissioning all its products from a group of other companies: Jockey International makes Hilfiger underwear, Pepe Jeans London makes Hilfiger jeans, Oxford Industries makes Tommy Shirts, the Stride Rite Corporation makes its footwear. What does Tommy Hilfiger manufacture? Nothing at all." (Klein, 1999, p. 24)

The brand-name corporate culture operates to disguise the crucial fact that much of the labor that is required to produce brand products like Nike running shoes and Tommy Hilfiger underwear is completed by workers in countries outside the United States, working for incredibly poor wages. The

workers that labor for Nike and Adidas athletic shoes (brands particularly popular with high school and college students) are produced in the Yue Yuen Factory in China, where workers are paid $0.19 and hour and work 60–84 hours a
week. Their conditions include "forced overtime, no overtime premium paid,
excessive noise pollution, fumes in the factory" (Klein, 1999, p. 474).

As I alluded to at the start of this chapter, automobiles are included in
this brand-name lifestyle order. The Saturn automobile is a case in point:

> Saturn, too, came out of nowhere in October 1999 when GM launched a car
> built not only out of steel and rubber but out of New Age spirituality and sev-
> enties feminism. After the car had been on the market a few years, the com-
> pany held a "homecoming" weekend for Saturn owners, during which you
> could visit the auto plant and have a cookout with the people who made their
> cars. As Saturn boasted at the time, "44,000 people spent their vacations with
> us at a car plant." (Klein, 1999, p. 17).

What you drive also directly impacts your feelings of lifestyle and being
hip. When discussing Benetton clothes in *Disturbing Pleasures* (1994),
Giroux alluded to the fact that one could even buy social consciousness. The
case of Saturn confirms that. In fact, there is some commodity for every political view. T-shirts, bumper stickers, buttons, and posters are all available
to allow us to advertise our beliefs.

One other area that has been branded is music. Using John Lennon's
music to hawk Nike running shoes and various other products is one example. It is significant that the music often used as advertising jingles is the
music of social protest from the late 1960s and early 1970s. The corporate
order's (read capitalism's) technique for removing any critique possibilities
from artistic creations is to turn them into commodities, thereby co-opting
them. Any creation potentially critical is made to be harmless and another
profit-making apparatus. There is also the sponsorship of rock concerts by
brand names, which is referred to as "corporate rock." And in the late
1990s, lines among advertising, music, and corporate sponsorship where
blurred when the Rolling Stones' *Bridges to Brooklyn* tour was sponsored by
Tommy Hilfiger. Both Mick Jagger and the opening act Sheryl Crow "on
stage modeled items from Tommy's newly launched 'Rock 'n' Roll' collection" (Klein, 1999, p. 47). Once a group associated with the Hell's Angels,
the Rolling Stones now wear Hilfiger. Recently there has also been the phenomenon of merging music videos and the advertising of brand names.
This skips that embarrassing intermediate process and the possibility of social critique, and thus blurs the line between advertising and music:

> The Gap launches its breakthrough Khakis Swing ads: a simple, exuberant min-
> iature music video set to "Jump, Jive 'n' Wail"—and a great video at that. The
> question of whether these ads were "co-opting" the artistic integrity of the music
> was entirely meaningless. The Gap's commercials didn't capitalize on the retro

swing revival—a solid argument can be made that they *caused* the swing revival. A few months later, when singer-songwriter Rufus Wainwright appeared in a Christmas-themed Gap ad, his sales soared, so much so that his record company began promoting him as "the guy in the Gap ads." (Klein, 1999, pp. 45–46)

Coffee, clothes, cars, and music not only commodities, they are also more than commodities. They have metamorphosized into brand names, which carry a lifestyle and permeate our popular culture, our lives, and even our identities.

Even though the simulacra of hyperreality may, indeed, present themselves, the centrality of the question of how hyperreality operates within the context of the lives of our children in pedagogically and politically significant ways deserves attention, which we attend to next.

POPULAR CULTURE AS A PRIMARY EDUCATIONAL SITE: AM I COOL?

It is time to recognize that the true tutors of our children are not school teachers or university professors but filmmakers, advertising executives and pop culture purveyors. Disney does more than Duke, Spielberg outweighs Stanford, MTV trumps MIT. (Barber, 1996, p. 12)

It is estimated that the average American spends more than four hours of a day watching television. Four hours a day, 28 hours a week, 1456 hours a year. The number of hours spent in front of a television or video screen is the single biggest chunk of time in the waking life of an American child. (Hazen & Winokur, 1997, p. 64)

Products and promotions like television, movies, the new technologies of enhanced video/computer games, and, of course, the ubiquitous Internet have transformed "culture[,] especially popular culture, into the primary educational site in which youth learn about themselves, their relationships to others and the larger world" (Giroux, 2000a, p. 108). In the struggle over the symbolic order, which characterizes our times, popular culture developed by name brands and various forms of media (including the Hollywood film industry), is crucial in creating the identities and representations that our youth embrace. Because of corporate mergers, fewer companies are determining what the symbolic order will display. Media conglomerates like Time-Warner and Disney begin to have an overwhelming influence on the symbolic order. What is represented to youth in the classroom in the form of testable, discreet forms of prepackaged knowledge becomes increasingly insignificant to them. It is only something to be suffered through, memorized, recalled, and promptly forgotten on the way to the real currency of the postindustrial, global, corporate order or, as I have called it elsewhere, *Gateism* (Reynolds, 2003), popular culture.

Popular culture is not only about media; it is also about identity and commodity (read brand) and its connection with the schools. Thus, not only do students at the primary, secondary, and postsecondary levels of education get much of their education in popular cultural contexts, but also the schools and universities in their structures and curriculums evidence the immersion into the brand-named order. Deleuze commented that this is the entry of corporate order in the schools. He believed that we should define the new sociotechnological principles and their manifestations as they emerge and how they operate within the contexts of modern disciplinary sites. In education, Deleuze acknowledged the intrusion of business (read brand-name corporate order) into the schools: "In the *school systems*: forms of continuous assessment, the impact of continuing education on the schools, and the related move away from any research in universities, 'business' being brought into education at every level" (Deleuze, 1995, p. 182).

The invasion of corporate America into public education now surpasses questions of Coca-Cola machines in the lunchroom. It has even moved beyond the insidious invasion of Channel One with its brand-name advertisements. It is the intrusion of corporate curriculum or brand-name lessons. Corporations are providing brand-name curriculum materials to schools and their teachers. Hence, not only do we have a corporate popular culture, but even the schools' uncool curriculum is receiving a dose of cool from branded materials:

> It is impossible to know which teachers use these branded materials in their class and which toss them away, but a report published by the U.S. Consumers Union in 1995 "found that thousands of corporations were targeting school children or their teachers with marketing activities ranging from teaching videos, to guidebooks, and posters to contests, product giveaways, and coupons." (Klein, 1999, p. 93)

It is not that the corporate development of curriculum materials is new (see Reynolds, 2003). The problem is that this has become accepted practice and even desired—it's cool. To fully comprehend this situation, it might be helpful to demonstrate some of this intrusion at different levels of education. There are hundreds of examples from which to choose.

In the primary grades, a level very susceptible to the incursion of branded curriculum materials, there have been a host of brand-name curricula. The Nike Corporation has an education division named, appropriately, Nike World Campus. This division has developed the clever fusion of advertising, public relations, and curriculum. They developed the "Air-to-Earth" lesson plan and materials:

> During the 1997–98 academic year, elementary school students in more than eight hundred classrooms across the U.S. sat down to their desks to find that today's lesson was building a Nike Sneaker, complete with a swoosh and an endorsement from a NBA star. The make-your-own-Nike exercise purports to

raise awareness about the company's environmentally sensitive production process. Nike's claim to greenness relies heavily on the fact that the company recycles old sneakers to recover community center basketball courts, which in a post-modern marketing spiral, then brands it with a Nike swoosh. (Feit in Klein, 1999, p. 930)

In secondary schools, there is a clever manipulation of technology, targeting advertising and curriculum in the in-school computer network *ZapMe!* This program not only sells advertising to sponsors, but also allows the tracking or monitoring of students as they surf the Web. This, of course, provides very valuable marketing research result broken down by a student's gender, age, and zip code: "Then when a student logs on to *ZapMe!*, they are treated to ads that have been specially targeted for them 'microtargeted' for them. This kind of detailed market research is exploding in North American schools: weekly focus groups, taste tests, brand-preference questionnaires, opinion polls, panel discussions on the Internet, all are currently being used inside the classrooms" (Klein, 1999, p. 94).

In 1998, Greenbriar High School in Evans, Georgia, took a Coca-Cola contest seriously. The Cola-Cola Company—a global company with its headquarters in Atlanta—ran a contest to have schools devise a strategy to promote the distribution of Coke coupons to students. The winning strategy would win $500.00 for the school. Greenbriar came up with Coke Day, in which all students were to wear Coke t-shirts. The students posed for a photograph in a formation spelling the word *Coke*. They "attended lectures given by Coca-Cola executives and learned about all things black and bubbly in their classes. It was a little piece of branding heaven" (Klein, 1999, p. 95). It was perfect except for one student: Mike Cameron, a senior, came to school that day dressed in a Pepsi t-shirt. He was suspended for his actions. The principal said it would have been acceptable, but there were Coca-Cola representatives there and that made his actions suspendible and embarrassing for the school. Apparently, the brand operates with power in the schools.

The universities do not escape the brand either. Besides the obvious intrusion of McDonalds, Wendy's, Burger King, and Coca-Cola into the various student unions, or Barnes and Noble taking or replacing campus-owned bookstores, there is more. In fact, most universities embrace the brand, especially in the area of athletics and research. In *Intercollegiate Athletics and the American University: A University President's Perspective* (2000), James A. Duderstadt reflected on his tenure as the president of the University of Michigan from 1988 through 1995. One of the many examples he cited is the involvement of Nike Corporation with the University of Michigan's football team: "Football teams at universities like Michigan, Florida and Notre Dame are now more valuable than most professional franchises" (Duderstadt in Hacker, 2001, p. 50). In what is basically a corporate brand deal, Nike pays for and supplies all of Michigan's sports equipment. In return, the University of Michigan players sport the swoosh on all of their uniforms. Another brand deal, which reverses the processes, is licensing the university name for commercial products. "One of the best sellers is a musical toilet seat that plays 'Hail to the Victors!' when raised" (Hacker, 2001, p. 50). The brand name, whether it is Nike or University of Michigan, not only invades the places of higher education but our homes as well.

Research does not escape the brand name either:

> And, in North America today, corporate research partnerships are used for everything: designing new Nike skates, designing more efficient oil extraction techniques for Shell, assessing the Asian market's stability for Disney, testing consumer demand for higher bandwidth for Bell or measuring the relative merits of a brand-name drug compared with a generic one, to name just a few examples. (Klein, 1999, p. 99)

Research funded and branded is the result.

Where are the confrontation, the protest, and the resistance? At the level of primary schools and secondary schools, there are the Parent–Teacher Organizations, and they have been vocal in their opposition. But there has never emerged a major political or policy battle on classroom commercialization. There is also a sense of frustration about opposing major brand-named corporations, and with schools so in need of financial assistance, parents and school boards are reticent to oppose funding of any kind. Objections are stifled at the university level, particularly when they conflict with the interest of the brand-name corporation. There are numerous examples of this occurring, but one example will suffice. At Kent State, one of the campuses that have exclusive vending rights, the members of Amnesty International advocated a boycott of Coca-Cola because it did business with a since-ousted Nigerian dictatorship. In 1998, Amnesty International applied for funding to bring to Kent State a human rights speaker from the Free Nigeria Movement. When it was discovered that the speaker would make critical comments about Coca-Cola's involvement in Nigeria, the funding request for the speaker was denied.

These are some examples of corporate intrusion into educational spaces, where one of the most important "legacies of American public education ... providing students with critical capabilities, knowledge and values that enable them to become active citizens striving to build a stronger democratic society" (Giroux, 2000b, p. 83) is being eroded. Brand-name corporatizing has managed to work its way into every level.

RETHINKING THE POLITICAL AND THE "IN-BETWEEN"

> *Anti-Oedipus* was from beginning to end a book of political philosophy. (Deleuze, 1995, p. 170)

They say revolutions turn out badly. But they're constantly confusing two different things, the way revolutions turn out historically and people's revolutionary
becoming. These relate to two different sets of people. Men's only hope lies in
a revolutionary becoming: the only way of casting off their shame or responding to what is intolerable. (Deleuze, 1995, p. 171)

Some work on the new emerging mystical society and all of its manifestations is being done, and as I have stated, that work is intriguing and troubling. Can we possibly address the postmodern dilemma of the branded
corporate order and its intrusion into the public schools? I do not, of
course, have the plan, the prescription, nor the answer. I believe that
Deleuze, especially when writing with his co-author Gilles Guattari in
Anti-Oedipus: Capitalism and Schizophrenia (1983) and *A Thousand Plateaus:
Capitalism and Schizophrenia* (1987), provided insight for political thought
and allowed for a space to reflect on the contours of capitalism. I recognize
that Deleuze in particular, but also his writings with Guattari, are not seen
or understood conventionally as political. But I think there is a manner in
which they are political and significant for the brand-named order. As
Patton wrote, "Despite his lack of engagement with issues of normative
political theory, Deleuze is a profoundly political philosopher. His collab-
orative work with Guattari offers new concepts and a new approach to
thinking philosophically about the political" (2000, p. 1). "Postscript on
Control Societies" (in Deleuze, 1995) is Deleuze's most overtly political essay. This essay has helped me to redefine my thoughts on the political. It
may be that Deleuze is not seen as political because he does not address issues such as "the nature of justice, freedom or democracy, much less the
principles of procedural justification" (Patton, 2000, p. 1). As well, his and
Guattari's language is not the language we typically employ when discussing politics and education. Deleuze and Guattari claimed, despite interpretations to the contrary, that their language is conceptual and not
metaphorical. But the confusion arises nonetheless. It stems from the language they use: "Deleuze and Guattari discuss society and politics in terms
of machinic assemblages, becomings, nomadism, forms of capture and
processes of deterritorialization and reterritorialization. Thus, *A Thousand Plateaus* opens with the blunt declaration that 'all we talk about are
multiplicities, lines, strata and segmentaries, lines of flight and intensi-
ties, machinic assemblages and their various types'" (Patton, 2000, p. 1).

Deleuze and Guattari were not Marxists in any traditional doctrinal
sense. Yet, an anticapitalist, antifascist thematic pervades all their writing
up to and including *What Is Philosophy?* (1994). In an interview in *Negotiations* (1995), Deleuze described capitalism as a "fantastic system for the fabrication of great wealth and great suffering" (Deleuze, 1995, p. 171). He
asserted that any philosophy worthy of being called political must take into
account the nature and evolution of capitalism. In *Anti-Oedipus*, Deleuze
and Guattari described capitalism:

What we are really trying to say is that capitalism, through its process of production, produces an awesome schizophrenic accumulation of energy or
charge, against which it brings all its vast powers of repression to bear, but
which nonetheless continues to act as capitalism's limit. For capitalism constantly counteracts, constantly inhibits this inherent tendency while at the
same time allowing it free rein; it continually seeks to avoid reaching its limit
while simultaneously tending toward that limit. Capitalism institutes or re-
stores all sorts of residual and artificial, imaginary or symbolic territorialities,
thereby attempting as best it can, to recode, to rechannel persons who have
been defined in terms of abstract quantities. Everything returns or recurs:
States, nations, families. That is what makes the ideology of capitalism a
"motley painting of everything that has been believed." The real is not impossible; it is simply more and more artificial. (Deleuze & Guattari, 1983, p. 34)

How do we address the form of capitalism I have described as the
brand-name corporate order within a Deleuzian becoming "in-between?"
Remember always that in capitalism all a body needs to do is desire—and
subordinate its desiring to earning and consuming. Corporate society no
longer requires a true correlation between interiority and its external
manifestations, or a more or less accurate correspondence of a body to its
model (its official, now residual, identity category). As Massumi noted,
"The only correlation it demands of everyone is between buying power
and image consumption. The only correspondence it requires is the credit
card company" (1996, p. 136).

Consider how Deleuze's poststructural politics would not rely on a repressive notion of power and would discard the notion of the essentially benign and cooperative character of human nature. This is a type of tactical
political thought rather than strategic: "It is aimed at particular forms of
revolutionary-becoming rather than wholesale social change. Such a political philosophy offers no guarantees: it is not a narrative of inevitable progress, nor does it offer the security of commitment to a single set of values
against which progress may be judged" (Patton, 2000, p. 8).

Is it nihilistic then, or pessimistic, or even tragic? Deleuze claimed it is not.
The notion of becoming answers this: "Becoming isn't part of history; history
amounts to a set of preconditions, however recent, that one leaves behind in
order to 'become,' that is to create something new" (Deleuze, 1995, p. 171).
Of course, brand-name capitalism limits the ability to become. A body's
transformational boundary is always already limited and indexed to its buying power. Additionally, the corporate order is recuperative of disruptions:

This means that the privilege of self-invention will never extend to everybody.
Not only do most bodies *not* have infinite degrees of freedom, alarming and
increasing numbers are starving and malnourished. Mere survival is a privilege in the brave new neo-conservative world. Capitalism's endocolonial expansion has made the law of unequal exchange that is written into is

axiomatic an inescapable and lethal fact of life. Its outward surge of expansion has nearly exhausted the earth, threatening to destroy the environment on which all life depends. Capitalism has not ushered in an age of universal wealth and well-being and never will. (Massumi, 1996, p. 137)

The "In-Between" AND

Having accounted for this, is there hope, even of a schizophrenic kind? I believe that Deleuze offered a possibility. I have previously used Deleuze and Guattari's concept of lines of flight (1983, 1987; Deleuze, 1995) as a potential way of "in-between" thinking. Thinking and working from the middle spaces between nihilism and terrorism provide potential without guarantees (Reynolds, 2002; Reynolds & Webber, 2004). Jacques Daignault (1992, p. 204) referred to this as "swirling in the middle," always remembering that the confrontation is continually tactical, not strategic. We always have to develop new lines of flight—lines of flight (becomings) that allow, however, contingently, briefly, or momentarily for us to soar vertically like a bird or slither horizontally, silently like a snake weaving our way amid the constant reconfigurations, co-optations, and movements of the brand-name corporate order. It is part of Deleuze's philosophy of multiplicities.

This multiplicity thinking helps to clarify the notion of a line of flight. It hinges on Deleuze's arguing for the priority of the conjunction *and* over the verb *to be*, multiplicity over empiricism, either, or thinking:

> One must go further: one must make the encounter with relations penetrate and corrupt everything, undermine being, make it topple over. Substitute the AND for IS. A *and* B. The AND is not even a specific relation or conjunction, it is that which subtends all relations, the path of all relations, which makes relations shoot outside their terms and outside the of their terms, and outside everything which could be determined as Being, One, or Whole. The AND as extra-being, inter-being. Relations might still establish themselves between their terms, or between two sets, from one to the other, but the AND gives relations another direction, and puts to flight terms and sets, the former and the latter on the line of flight which it actively creates. Thinking with AND, instead of thinking IS, instead of thinking for IS: empiricism has never had another secret. (Deleuze & Parnet, 1987, p. 57)

This becomes a major point in Deleuze's and Guattari's political philosophy. It is the "in-between." Becoming, new ways of thinking always proceed from the "in-between." This is where lines of flight take shape. The possibilities for creative political thought for one lie in those multiplicities, which emerge in the "in-between." This shows not what political thought should be but how AND can be productive for it:

> AND is neither one thing or the other, it is always in-between, between two things; it's the borderline, there's always a border, a line of flight or flow, only

we don't see it, because it the least perceptible of all things. And yet it's along this line of flight that things come to pass, becomings evolve, revolutions take shape. The strong people aren't the ones on one side or the other, power lies on the border. (Deleuze, 1995, p. 45)

This can reframe our thinking about the manner in which we can discuss the nature of postmodernity, poststructurally. It is not about fighting against the them, the corporate brand-name order, not about saying that they won and the only recourse, as McLaren (2000) said, is to once again storm the barricades, although there may be recurrence. The barricades just get stronger. The "struggle" is to keep on finding lines that disrupt and overturn the brand-name corporate order. An "AND, AND, AND, which each time marks a new threshold, a new direction of the zigzagging line, a new course for the border" (Deleuze, 1995, p. 45). Never resting is always being in the AND. We must see the possibilities in the space in between, because multiplicity is always in the AND.

REFERENCES

Aronowitz, S. (2000). *The knowledge factory: Dismantling the corporate university*. Boston: Beacon.

Barber, B. (1996). A civics lesson. *The Nation, 263*(14), 12.

Baudrillard, J. (1994). *Simulacra and simulation* (S. F. Glaser, Trans.). Ann Arbor: University of Michigan Press.

Carroll, L. (1997). *Alice's adventures in wonderland and through the looking glass*. London: Puffin.

Daignault, J. (1992). Traces at work from different places. In W. F. Pinar & W. M. Reynolds (Eds.), *Understanding curriculum as phenomenological and deconstructed text* (pp. 195–215). New York: Teachers College Press.

Deleuze, G. (1995). *Negotiations 1972–1990* (M. Joughin, Trans.). New York: Columbia University Press.

Deleuze, G., & Guattari, F. (1983). *Anti-Oedipus: Capitalism and schizophrenia*. Minneapolis: University of Minnesota Press.

Deleuze, G., & Guattari, F. (1987). *A thousand plateaus: Capitalism and schizophrenia*. Minneapolis: University of Minnesota Press.

Deleuze, G., & Guattari, F. (1994). *What is philosophy?* London: Verso Press.

Deleuze, G., & Parnet, C. (1987). *Dialogues* (H. Tomlinson & B. Habberjam, Trans.). New York: Columbia University Press.

Duderstadt, J. J. (2000). *Intercollegiate athletics and the American University: A university president's perspective*. Ann Arbor, MI: University of Michigan Press.

Giroux, H. A. (1994). *Disturbing pleasures: Learning popular culture*. New York: Routledge.

Giroux, H. A. (1999). *The mouse that roared: Disney and the end of innocence*. New York: Rowman and Littlefield.

Giroux, H. A. (2000a). *Impure acts: The practical politics of cultural studies*. New York: Routledge.

Giroux, H. A. (2000b). *Stealing innocence: Youth, corporate power, and the politics of culture*. New York: St. Martin's Press.

2. TO TOUCH THE CLOUDS

Hacker, A. (2001, April). The big college try. *The New York Review of Books, XLVIII*(6), 50–55.

Klein, N. (1999). *No logo: Taking aim at the brand name bullies*. New York: Picador USA.

Massumi, B. (1996). *A user's guide to capitalism and schizophrenia: Deviations from Deleuze and Guattari*. Cambridge, MA: MIT Press.

Miller, A. (1987). *Timebends: A life*. London: Methuen.

Patton, P. (2000). *Deleuze and the political*. New York: Routledge.

Pinar, W. F., Reynolds, W. M., Slattery, P., & Taubman, P. (1995). *Understanding curriculum*. New York: Peter Lang.

Reynolds, W. M. (2000, April). *Traces of the discourse of resistance: The Internet and the international student activism alliance*. Paper presented at the 2000 Annual Meeting of The American Educational Research Association, New Orleans, Louisiana.

Reynolds, W. M. (2002). The perpetual pedagogy of surveillance. *JCT: The Journal of Curriculum Theorizing, 16*(4), 31–45.

Reynolds, W. M. (2003). *Curriculum: A river runs through it*. New York: Peter Lang.

Chapter 3

Wondering About a Future Generation: Identity Disposition Disposal, Recycling, and Creation in the 21st Century

Don Livingston
LaGrange College

Thinking Beyond

In this chapter, Donald Livingston presents views of technology, cautioning us against a utopic fantasy of progress. He situates his discussion of technology and the body within the context of Deleuze and Guattari's notions of dividuals. He wants to encourage the curriculum studies researcher to decenter the body when writing curriculum theory. He maintains that asking questions in the field of curriculum studies will continue the reconceptualization.

Questions

1. What is meant by the term *dividual*? How does the dividual that Livingston discusses compare and contrast to the corporate individual that Reynolds discussed?
2. How do the views of technology, education, and identity compare with Ferneding's views of technology? What are the differences and similarities?
3. How do issues of the body (Butler, Haraway, et al.) remain central to Livingston's discussion? How does Livingston relate his theorizing to curriculum studies?

What sort of curriculum inquiry is critically important to engage in today to prepare for our future generations? James B. Macdonald was clear about this when he proclaimed that the curriculum at its heart is an ethical text (Macdonald, 1971). The curriculum should address the structural and moral concerns of today and tomorrow. If one accepts Macdonald's view of curriculum inquiry, then metaphysical questions such as "Are we still human if we do not have bodies?" are fair game for curriculum workers to ponder. But is pondering doing real research? If the wonderment is supported by an integrated analysis and interpretation of the curricular phenomena pondered, then it can be deemed research (McCutcheon, 1982).

Some in the field of curriculum studies scoffed at such a justification for research. Yet, these voices wonder too. They wonder what in the world any of this cultural studies stuff has to do with schools. Why is it that some believe that all curriculum inquiry must be directly applicable in an instrumental sort of way? Curriculum inquiry can also function to illuminate the way toward a better world. It is through this process of illumination that a cultural studies approach to curriculum inquiry creates praxis (Macdonald, 1982). It is with this spirit of praxis that I wonder about the future generation.

SHOW ME TOMORROW

Much of the science fiction that I have been reading lately is what has been called *cyberpunk*. Cyberpunk is a genre that often paints a dystopian future world that is inhabited by cyborgs and hegemonic machine overlords. This brand of science fiction disrupts my 20th-century understanding of humanness and causes me to wonder about what sort of identity humans might assume when the offspring of technology enflesh our bodies, replace our brains, and co-control our society.

I also wonder if cyberpunk science fiction is nothing more than farfetched Saturday afternoon matinee scripts or if it is a portent for tomorrow. Ray Kurzweil, author of *The Age of Spiritual Machines: When Computers Exceed Human Intelligence*, believes that much of what cyberpunk foretells will be here quicker than we might expect (Kurzweil, 1999). It is interesting to note that Kurzweil is not a science fiction writer; he is a card-carrying member of the technology community. Although I have come to understand the blurred distinction between fiction and science, Kurzweil and the extropists have embraced a realist's perspective on tomorrow. Rather than assuming a nihilistic cyberpunk view, Kurzweil described an exciting and positive future based on what is already in technology's research and development pipeline.

Kurzweil predicted that by 2009 most routine interactions, such as consumer purchases and customer service inquiries, will be performed between a human and a virtual personality. Ten years later, in 2019, a $1,000 computer will have the computational ability of a human brain. Almost everything we use will have a computer in it. Computers will be in walls, furniture, jewelry, recreation equipment, and implanted into bodies. By 2019, nearly all routine transactions will be with a simulated person. Virtual musical artists will be topping the charts, and children will be taught by virtual teachers. Many people will have virtual companions and some will routinely have sexual relationships with them. At the end of the second decade of the second millennium, it will be impossible to distinguish humans from computer identities.

The year 2029 is when a $1,000 computer will have the capacity to compute 1,000 times more than a human brain. With retinal implants, cochlear replacements, and transgenic organs and limbs commonplace, humans will be rapidly accelerating toward becoming total cyborgs. The brain will be wired to the worldwide network through neural enhancement devices. This wiring will make all knowledge instantly accessible and understandable.

By 2029, humans will be able to create multiple states of consciousness with real and virtual bodies. All sensory perceptions experienced will meet or exceed organic capabilities. The line between virtual and real will no longer be blurred; it will be erased. Virtual identities will begin to petition the government for legal rights. Because their claims of consciousness will be largely accepted as fact, machines will gain citizenship status.

At the midpoint of the 21st century, virtual bodies will be autonomous projections that will be physically materialized (Kurzweil, 1999). Materiality will be a function of machine and DNA language, 1/0/DNA.

One hundred years from today, machines and humans will have merged. There will be no distinction between humans and the technology that they have created. Multiple states of consciousness will be only temporary dispositions (Kurzweil, 1999). These dispositions will be discarded, recycled, and created in simultaneous staccato phantasms.

Most bodies will no longer be made of organic substance. Those who have chosen to retain a organic material will have been neurally enhanced with brain software. The photonic or electric software brain will replace the carbon-based brain. After this transmogrification, the brain will be able to compute a billion times faster than its meat brain predecessor. This awesome capacity will make it possible to materialize anything that can be imagined in the collective group fantasy, called the *social* (Kurzweil, 1999).

A brave new world is about to emerge. The ways in which we have defined ourselves in the past do not describe the human of the future. It is time to reconsider how we think about ourselves and how we think about our identity.

THE FASCISM OF MODERNITY'S TRUTH FETISH

Gilles Deleuze and Felix Guattari made the claim that what most people really want is fascism (Deleuze & Guattari, 1989). Their definition of fascism is not confined only to the workings of government. Rather, fascism, explicated in a broader sense, means a positivistic imposition of truths into discourse through hegemonic cultural formations. These truths are manifested in everyday discourse as binary relations such as god/man, nature/culture, mind/soul, conscious/unconscious, and so on. According to Foucault, these truths become reified in the social structure through continuous repetition of cultural practices. These historically reified cultural practices appear to be real to those invested in that particular social discourse. In this way, fascism comes to mean structuralism (Deleuze & Guattari, 1989).

The structure used to sell the truth of the self is psychoanalysis. Psychoanalysis assumes that humans are unified beings who individuate identity within the brain. Despite various challenges to its supremacy, psychoanalysis remains the dominant structuralist paradigm for the explanation of the self. Psychoanalytical theory views the body as a preontological site that serves as the vessel for identity accumulation and individual formation. Understanding identity as a process of accumulation and individual formation is referred to as *individuation* (Colwell, 1996).

INDIVIDUATION: THEORY OF UNIFICATION

Individuation is a theory that describes identity as the construction of an individual out of the prepersonal components of the individual (Colwell, 1996). Central to individuation theory is the primacy that a prepersonal component itself is the controlling mechanism in the formation of identity. Prepersonal components include psychological constructs such as superego, ego, Id, conscious, subconscious, and biological constructs such as genetics and certain aspects of personality theory. From a narcissistic position, these prepersonal controls are impediments to discovering one's identity because the individual constantly engaged in infinite phenomenological inquiries. Much like opening up the cover of a baseball and then trying to explain why each strand of string is woven the way its is, individuational inquiry can describe why some of the prepersonal controls operate the way that they do but can never quite explain all of it. In the process of searching for the essence of the self, individuals perpetually defer the formation of their identity. Thus, the individual never establishes an existential center, a position where the person is capable of understanding the standpoint of others (Deleuze & Guattari, 1989).

Rather than promote a standpoint epistemology, individual theory bifurcates the self from others. This bifurcation, in effect, erects a binary barrier between the self and the social. By viewing the self as the locus of consciousness, the social is relegated to the role of supporting the self. Historically, instruments of power have determined to what degree and in what way an individual uses the social in support of the self (Foucault, 1980). Through repeated cultural practices, those with more social cultural capital have succeeded in creating institutions, organizations, and values that perpetuate the ideal self in their own image. These repeated cultural practices have reified over time to appear to be natural occurrences.

When examined in this way, individual theory is essentially a political meta-narrative that privileges some bodies at the exclusion of others. Proponents of this naive naturalism believe that certain bodies are more privileged than other bodies because of their superior evolutionary progress (Turner, 1991). Proponents of the natural body say that social structures arise from the bodies of humans to form the organizational systems we use today. These social structures are limited only by the constraints that nature has placed on the body. The dominant culture has used naturalism to legitimate social inequalities by concretizing them as natural occurrences. Oppressed groups, too, have been known to use the same argument in order to receive special privilege, Chris Lash wrote, "Naturalistic views hold that the capabilities and constraints of human bodies define individuals, and generate the social, political and economic relations which characterize national and international patterns of living. Inequalities in material wealth, legal rights and political power are not socially constructed, contingent and reversible, but are given, or at least legitimized, by the determining power of the biological body" (Lash, 1991 p. 40). Naturalistic and sociobiology theories of individuation most certainly work against the interests of most of the world's inhabitants, yet they prevail as the dominant paradigms for identity (Lash, 1991).

DIVIDUATION: THEORY OF FRAGMENTATION

Dividuation rejects any natural notions of a preontology, presocial, or prediscursive existence. As Deleuze and Guattari stated, dividuation is desire and the social, nothing else; it is a construct that understands everything as a social machine and everything as desire (Deleuze & Guattari, 1989). Dividuation decenters the body as the locus of consciousness by fragmenting perspectives in, on, and most importantly outside of the body. Deleuze and Guattari described this fragmenting of perspectives with the metaphor of the corporation. The corporation is a body without organs that stores identity dispositions in categorical databanks. Rather than processing phenomenon from the standpoint of the self, dividuation challenges metaphysics to wonder about a noncorporeal life (Deleuze & Guattari, 1989).

The wonder of a noncorporeal life requires that the psychoanalytic theory of a centered, stable, or unified self be abandoned. Dividuation also rejects the idea of a subconscious mind and repudiates any notion that the body is the locus of consciousness. Rearticulating the subconscious as a fictive constraint, Deleuze and Guatarri offered the liberating prospect that nothing says no to you. That is, there is no psychophysical matter that controls behavior. Instead, identity is best described as a delirious phantasm that assumes its shape through desire and social regulation (Deleuze & Guattari, 1989). The body becomes matter through multiple discourses that have become reified over time. The shape of the body and all of its functions are determined by linguistic categories that define what it means to have a body. Thus, dividuation theory can be interpreted to mean that the body does not even exist as a biological phenomenon (Shilling, 1993).

Both Deleuze and Foucault wrote that the body is not a biological phenomenon. Rather, Deleuze and Foucault described the human conception of the body as a player in a phantasm, a dreamlike state. This phantasm takes shape at the point where society meets the body. Moreover, multifarious social forces compete for phantasms on the body. This competition among various societal phantasms is the cause of all bodily desire. These phantasms form the illusion of a corporeal body, which, in turn, gives rise to something that falsely presents itself as a centered organism (Lash, 1991).

When Derrida exuberantly proclaimed "the positive possibility and 'internal' structure of language" and "the possibility of extraction and of citational grafting which belongs to the structure of every mark, spoken or written," he expressed the hope that dividuals could possess the agency to act on their very existence (Nealon, 1996 p. 432). Because dividuals have no concern for internal states of the self (e.g., the notion of a core being or soul), outward manifestations of desire, will, and intention are free to emerge (Colwell, 1996). What matters is the moment, the immediate, the existential life of the person. The relationship of the dividual with respect to the social was described by Colwell as a mass within a mass while remaining unique within the mass. As dividuals act simultaneously, the single dividual is not acting as a part of just one mass, but instead of a series of masses. Although the individual assumes a singular continuous identity, the dividual is a representation of dispositions. It must be noted here that these dispositions are temporary performative actions that are used in short-term activities (Colwell, 1996). These performatives can be ameliorated into other manifestations by free will and determinism.

DIVIDUAL ESSENTIALISM?

But what sort of society will we have if dividuation takes hold? Will the repetition of temporary performative actions by the populace reify into its own sort of structuralism?

Foucault's repeated emphasis on historical reification rather than philosophical conditions of possibility as described by Derrida is an important one as we address the problem of dividual reifications. Foucault said that the body is acted on, it does not act. This idea that the body is a passive receptor and is merely the object of discourse relegates the corporeal body into a theoretical space (Lash, 1991). Although saying that everything is discursively constructed, Foucault was not saying that discourse can be a free will creation. Even in virtual reality, discursive phantasms are dependent on linguistic, institutional, and political structures of the moment. Here is where Foucault tempered the exhilarating potential that identity discourse could be a show of infinite erotic possibilities. It seems reasonable, then, to balance Derrida's optimistic notion of "discourse as possibility" with Foucault's warning that all novel discourse emerges in permitted spaces and these spaces are decided by historical forces. Foucault cautions us to beware of the emergence of a free-will dividuation meta-narrative. If Foucault's admonition of free-will dividuation goes unheeded, we run the risk of essentializing dividuation when conducting inquiry into the idea (Nealon, 1996).

IS MATTER LANGUAGE, IS LANGUAGE MATTER?

Although Derrida's philosophy of possibility and Foucault's social constructivism serve as a conceptual framework for dividuation, neither adequately addresses the question of whether the body is physical matter. Judith Butler, in *Bodies That Matter*, expanded on Foucault's position that the body and its manifested dispositions are phantasmic creations of language. Butler said that Foucault seemed to suggest that flesh is physical matter that, when acted on, produces articulable materiality (Butler, 1993). This idea—that flesh, in the form of the body, is a medium that is acted on—seems to suggest that flesh in its corporeal form preexists language. Foucault's theory that the body is cloaked until marked by language is analogous to the hoary philosopher's question, "If a tree falls in the forest, yet no one is there to hear it fall, does it make a sound?" Foucault's answer, when applied to the body, is no. According to Foucault, the body does not exist as matter until marked by language. The idea that matter is not material until marked by language describes the body as a theoretical phantasm that is subject to change. But, the question lingers, is unmarked matter still matter?

Judith Butler understood this Foucaultian idea to mean that "matter is language, language is matter." Language does not come before matter, nor does matter come before language—not a small distinction, when you think about it. Unifying these two constructs not only shatters the naturalistic, preontologic way of thinking, it also disrupts the monolinguistic idea that language alone is the source code for reality.

Understanding materiality as a group fantasy is an instrumental theory for technoscience to use as it rewrites reality with the source code 1/0/DNA. The 1/0/DNA source code is formed when information technologies merge with biotechnology (where 1/0 is the binary source code for information technologies and the letters DNA represent the source code for biotechnology). When 1/0 and DNA combine, they form a unified source code powerful enough to replicate preexisting forms of materiality as well as create novel perspectives on existence. Donna Haraway wrote that "nature cannot preexist its construction.... If organisms are natural objects, it is crucial to remember that organisms are not born; they are made in world-changing technoscientific practices by particular collective actors in particular times and places, in the belly of the local/global monster in which I am gestating, often called the postmodern world, global technology appears to denature everything" (Haraway, 1992, pp. 296–297).

The particular collective actors that Haraway named understand existence as a process of dividuation, not as a formative process of individuation. Deleuze and Guattari made this distinction in a manifesto statement in *Anti-Oedipus*:

We live today in the age of partial objects, bricks that have been shattered to bits, and leftovers. We no longer believe in the myth of the existence of fragments that, like pieces of an antique statue, are merely waiting for the last one to be turned up, so that they may all be glued back together to create a unity that is precisely the same as the original unity. We no longer believe in a primordial totality that once existed, or in final totality that awaits us at some future date. We no longer believe in the dull gray outlines of a dreary, colorless dialectic of evolution, aimed at forming a harmonious whole out of heterogeneous bits by rounding off their rough edges. We believe only in totalities that are peripheral. And if we discover such a totality alongside various separate parts, it is a whole of these particular parts but does not totalize them; it is a unity of all these particular parts but does not unify them; rather, it is added to them as a new part fabricated separately. (Deleuze & Guattari, 1989, p. 42)

Given that the source code 1/0/DNA can explain, replicate, and create matter, future generations will come to discard individuation in favor of dividuation theory. When dividuated dispositions are free to be disposed, recycled, and created within the momentary social milieu of the moment, dividuation theory will become the instrumental ontology for a fictive world. Although dividual identity might appear to be a playful interchange of temporal dispositions, we must remember Foucault's warning that there are prohibitions that regulate what sort of dispositions are possible (Foucault, 1980). Deleuze and Guattari echoed Foucault's point that dividuality will be highly regulated by society's power relationships (Deleuze & Guattari, 1989). Because dividuals openly expose their identities, social institutions that surveil such activities will have little trouble controlling dividuated behaviors. Because of this outward orientation, the regimes of truth will find it much easier to control fragmented dividuals. Power will surely rejoice when the end of the individual arrives (Colwell, 1996).

PRAXIS: SO WHAT IS THE CURRICULUM QUESTION?

N. Katherine Hayles, author of *How We Became Posthuman: Virtual Bodies in Cybernetics,* posed one perspective for curriculum studies to consider that might be interpreted by some as an idealistic, or even a romantic, position. Hayes wrote:

> If my nightmare is a culture inhabited by posthumans who regard their bodies as fashion accessories rather than the ground of being, my dream is a version of the posthuman that embraces the possibilities of information technologies without being seduced by fantasies of unlimited power and disembodied immortality, that recognizes and celebrates finitude as a condition of human being, and that understands human life is embedded in a material world of great complexity, one on which we depend for our continued survival. (Hayles, 1999, p. 5)

In the *Age of Spiritual Machines,* Ray Kurzweil presented an opposing perspective during a mock interview with Molly, a 21st-century identity, about her former job as a census taker: "We don't count people anymore. It became clear that counting individual persons wasn't too meaningful. As Iris Murdoch said, 'Its' hard to tell where one person ends and another begins.' It's rather like trying to count ideas or thoughts" (Kurzweil, 1999, p. 243).

By staking out the perceived opposite ends of the argument with these two perspectives, I am not suggesting that we begin our research with a dipolar curriculum question such as "Do we celebrate technology's wonders or do we wonder if the technology ought to be bridled?" This question obviously confines the deliberation in an either/or binary; that is, either you are a technocrat or you are a Luddite. Instead, let's examine the ontological statement, "Our machines are us; we are our machines."

A colleague recently said to me, "Well, we can just pull the plug on all of the damn things." My response was that we cannot pull the plug, even if there were just one to pull. We have always been enfleshed by our constructions and productions. Pulling the plug is tantamount to the murder of our species. As Hayles pointed out, we depend on our machines for our continued survival (Hayles, 1999).

It's quixotic to cling to the hope that the seductive siren song of the cyborg will no longer drive human invention. Extropy—the philosophy of immortality—has challenged the concept of death as a condition of being a human being, and science has embraced the philosophy of extropy as its intellectual beacon (Haraway, 1997). By the end of the 21st century, technology will have eliminated death as life's final pollution (Douglas, 1966; Kurzweil, 1999). Any nostalgia for a return to the time when humans were corporeal individuals will be lost on the crowd of thoughts and ideas. Consequently, the anachronistic anthropocentric idea that the self is the locus of identity, or that identities require original organic flesh, will not stand the test of critique from future generations.

Now is the time to ask if any of the curriculum theories proffered to date offer any insight into how we go about having a world. Perennialism and progressivism prepare the individual to succeed in society, social reconstructionism shapes the individual through service to society, and autobiographical approaches center the individual as the positions from which community connections can be formed. Although each of these perspectives offer utility for individual growth and discovery, none address the needs of a society of dividuals. Yet, when these curriculum theories are examined, it becomes evident that each of them privileges the individual as the locus of identity.

Understanding identity as a process of dividuation rather than individuation will press the curriculum to consider alternative conceptions. These alternative conceptions will encourage the researcher to decenter the body when writing curriculum theory. Because dividual identities are, more often than not, manifested in bodies without organs, the social is no longer understood as a product of corporeal beings (Deleuze & Guattari, 1989). When the corporeal body is decentered, the focus of the curriculum is on the production and construction of thoughts and ideas. If curriculum studies ignores this metaphysical shift, the field may once again relapse into a state of morbidity.

The reconceptualization of the field of curriculum over the last 2 decades has changed the way we have come to understand the purposes of curriculum theory. The primary function of the curriculum, from the re-conceptual position, is to create new realities (Macdonald, 1986). Creating new realities is not a subtle idea for future generations—it will be their primary function. The portent that dividuals will create multiple states of conscious identity positions, in and outside of the corporeal body yet within a framework of power regulations, may very well be one of the most important currents in intellectual history.

But how do we begin the process of inquiry when the future has yet to arrive? There are different ways to look at the phenomena of dividuation. We must ask what is it that is changing about our perspectives of selfhood, what constitutes an identity, and how are our machines and social structures effecting these changes in identity? Given the prospects for the future, rigorous curriculum studies research should situate the function of the body and the brain in context with the aggregate constitutive effects of bodies, brains, machines, and social structures. I realize that this is not much on which to build but, at this juncture, we are all in the nascent stage of research into this phenomenon. Thus, I am sort of wondering aloud about what the forms of inquiry might be like. Because inquiry into this sort of phenomenon has not been charted by curriculum scholars, I have no methodology to suggest.

Perhaps the questions we ask now are more important than any sort of solutions that we could offer. This is the crux of curriculum theory. Curriculum inquiry is about curiosity of the unknown, not about what we already know and hope to propagate (Macdonald, 1982). I hope that this discussion has, in some way, sparked your curiosity about the unknown, for what awaits the future generation may very well be determined by the curriculum questions we ask today.

REFERENCES

Butler, J. (1993). *Bodies that matter: On the discursive limits of "sex."* New York: Routledge.

Colwell, C. (1996). Discipline and control: Butler and Deleuze on individuality and dividuality. *Philosophy Today, 40*(1), 211–216.

Deleuze, G., & Guattari, F. (1989). *Anti-Oedipus: Capitalism and schizophrenia.* London: Athlone.

Douglas, M. (1966). *Purity and danger: An analysis of the concepts of pollution and taboo.* Routledge: London.

Foucault, M. (1980). *The history of sexuality, volume I: An introduction.* New York: Vintage.

Hayles, N. K. (1999). *How we became posthuman: Virtual bodies in cybernetics.* Chicago: University of Chicago Press.

Haraway, D. J. (1992). The promises of monsters: A regenerative politics for inappropriate/d others. In L. Grossberg, C. Nelson, & P. Treichler (Eds.), *Cultural Studies* (pp. 295–337). New York: Routledge.

Haraway, D. J. (1997). *Modest witness @ second millennium. Femaleman meets oncomouse.* New York: Routledge.

Kurzweil, R. (1999). *Age of spiritual machines.* New York: Viking.

Lash, S. (1991) Genealogy and the body: Foucault/Deleuze/Nietzsche. In M. Featherstone, M. Hepworth, & B. S. Turner (Eds.), *The body: Social processes and cultural theory* (pp. 256–280). London: Sage.

Macdonald, J. B. (1971). Curriculum theory. *The Journal of Educational Research, 64*(5), 196–200.

Macdonald, J. B. (1982). How literal is curriculum theory? *Theory in Practice, 21,* 55–61.

Macdonald, J. B. (1986). The domain of curriculum. *Journal of Curriculum and Supervision, 1,* 205–214.

McCutcheon, G. (1982). What in the world is curriculum theory? *Theory in Practice, 21,* 18–22.

Nealon, J. T. (1996). Between emergence and possibility: Foucault, Derrida, and Judith Butler on performative identity. *Philosophy Today, 40*(3–4), 430–439.

Turner, B. S. (1991) Recent developments in the theory of the body. In M. Featherstone, M. Hepworth, & B. S. Turner (Eds.), *The body: Social processes and cultural theory* (pp. 1–35). London: Sage.

Chapter 4

The Discourse of Inevitability
and the Forging of an Emergent Social Vision:
Technology Diffusion and the Dialectic
of Educational Reform Discourse

Karen Ferneding
University of Illinois, Urbana–Champaign

Thinking Beyond

In this chapter, Ferneding discusses educational reform and "techno-utopianism." She explicates the connections among a faith in technology, educational reform, and the rhetoric(s) of both. The chapter elaborates differences between a discourse of educational reform based in functionalism and scientific management and its connections to technology with a perspective that articulates social justice and equity—a discourse of possibility. The implications of the underlying meanings of the "crisis" in education are intertwined within this differentiation.

Questions

1. In what ways do the current notions of educational reform depend, according to Ferneding, on a rhetoric and logic of the "technological fix"? How does the belief in constructed conceptualizations of the power of information technologies to solve educational problems operate in reform efforts? Explain the term *mythinformation*.
2. In what ways does an unquestioning faith in the power of technology serve corporate market ideology? How does Ferneding's analysis of the corporate order compare to Reynolds' notion of the brand-name corporate order?
3. In what ways can Ferneding's discussion of technology be compared and contrasted to Livingston's portrayal of technology?

In this chapter, I examine how the narrative space of educational reform discourse has been delineated not only by a narrow vision inspired by functionalist aims and conservative ideology but also a particular techno-utopianism. It is argued that the current incarnation of a "technological fix" approach to educational reform both reflects and exploits a constructed and unquestioning cultural belief in the power of information technologies. This discursive framework is anchored by a commonsense understanding that technology exists simply as a neutral or apolitical tool/artifact. In addition, this technocentric approach to educational reform also finds expression in policies that rationalize the educational process and that further the configuration of education's purpose toward serving the ends of global corporate market ideology.

These factors are considered with regard to how educational reform discourse has historically expressed a broader social discourse or social vision that articulates social justice and similar traditional democratic ideals. Thus, the following question is posed: How has the landscape of this traditional social vision been narrowed by a "discourse of inevitability" expressed as technological determinism? This question is addressed by examining the dialectic that has existed between the traditional discourse of social justice as a discourse of possibility and a discourse of inevitability as technological determinism. It is suggested that the dominance of a discourse of inevitability reflects the general colonization of the public sphere and the lifeworld (the realm of human social relationships) by corporate ideology and technical rationalism. It is therefore recommended that to counteract the hegemony of technocentric discourse within the context of educational reform policy, educators need to implement a deliberative approach to the adoption of technological innovations that recognizes the centrality of teachers' practical knowledge germane to teaching and learning as well as broader sociocultural, economic, and environmental concerns. The adoption process of information and computer technologies (ICT)—especially as technological infrastructures—needs to embrace a broad contextual framework, because not to engage in such a practice is to both invite and sustain a state of technological determinism and further legitimize the logic of marketplace discourse to hold a powerful if not overdetermined position within the site of educational reform policy.

THE "INEVITABILITY" FACTOR AND THE DOMINANT VIEW OF EDUCATIONAL REFORM POLICY

Educational reform documents that have steered the direction of public education over the last 20 years (e.g., *A Nation at Risk, Goals 2000,* and *No Child Left Behind Act*) have alarmed certain educators for their focus on control as expressed through systems of accountability and standards. Such systems of control emphasize efficiency and thus rationalize social needs within the context of current economic utility. This condition, which Jacques Ellul (1964) called "technique," articulates a generalized "consciousness of a mechanized world" (p. 6). Specific to the realm of education, many critics have in fact characterized current educational reform discourse as being narrow in scope, reflecting instrumental rationalist and functionalist perspectives (see, e.g., Apple, 1995, 1996; Bowers, 1988, 1995; Kerr, 1996; McLaren, 1995; Purpel, 1996; Shapiro, 1996; Smith, 1995; Tyack & Cuban, 1995). In addition, the politicization of education reached unprecedented heights with the 1983 publication of *A Nation at Risk,* which sought to place the blame on public education for the diminished state of the U.S. economy (Tyack & Cuban, 1995).

At that time, a growing dependence on computer and information technologies within industry and business and the dawn of the Information Age made the production and utilization of information pivotal to the emerging globalized market economy. This factor, in turn, meant that education, because it is directly associated with the creation of knowledge and potential "knowledge workers," was moved to the center of a postindustrial culture, where it stands in parity with science and technology (Peters, 1996). Evidence for this unprecedented moment in the evolution of education—especially in the United States, Canada, Britain, New Zealand, and Australia—is demonstrated by aggressive political efforts to privatize or marketize public educational systems, policies that often reflect fundamental shifts toward market-based systems of national governance (Peters, 1996). It is true that, in the United States, public education has historically been influenced by industrialism and business through the adoption of Taylorism, vocationalist-based curriculum aims, and most recently, management techniques such as total quality management. However, the current trend of educational reforms, as evidenced in recent federal reform initiatives, indicates a repositioning of education to more directly serve corporate interests to the extent that such functional interests have superseded more traditional democratic ideals of equality and citizenship, which have characterized education's relationship to society since its inception (Apple, 1995; Goodman, 1995; Kleibard, 1992; Tyack & Cuban, 1996).

Although there exists much criticism about the functionalist aims of current reforms and the focus on accountability and standards, very few critics have been particularly alarmed by the third major characteristic of current reforms—the extensive effort to infuse electronic technologies into schools. The reasons for this are complex. Generally, technology has been socially constructed as a neutral artifact or tool and thus is considered to be apolitical (Winner, 1980). Therefore, as a culture, we rarely question actions and decisions related to technology. Moreover, technological innovation is equated to material/economic progress, and progress is synonymous with goodness (Segal, 1994). The "grand narrative" of progress (Lyotard, 1984), with which technology and science are associated, acts as a cultural myth or an uncontested commonsense social story. This social narrative is also given expression within popular culture. Therefore, technocentric reformers inspired by Information Age futurism project a techno-utopian vision of education that is both serving and being served by corporate interests.

This reenvisioning of education through a techno-futuristic corporate lens has been projected as the only solution to the current "crisis" in education. In fact, the crisis in education was defined in a rather narrow scope by the authors of *A Nation at Risk* as public education's inability to meet the needs of an Information Age. Thus, the authors of *A Nation at Risk*—the National Commission on Excellence in Education (1983)—recommended the diffusion of new electronic technologies into schools, in addition to emphasizing curriculum reforms in science and mathematics, as necessary remedies to this "crisis." This particular identification of both the problem and the solution is reflected in subsequent national reform documents (e.g., *Goals 2000, America 2000, No Child Left Behind Act*) and is related to the need to serve a globalized market economy. In effect, the naming of the problem itself and the "solution" to education's "crisis" is presented de facto. The diffusion of electronic technologies, the control of teachers' work, and the reconfiguring of public education to further a globalized market economy are "inevitable."

This situation effectively closes down the spaces for alternative perspectives, voices, and interpretations regarding the naming of the nature of public education's general condition and the imagining of its future. Indeed, Australian educational theorist Michael Peters (1996) explained that within the neoliberal metanarrative of futurism, an "enterprise culture"—characterized by a convergence of science, technology, and education—has evolved to the level of commonsense such that questions related to equity and social justice "have receded under the economic imperative" (p. 88). Thus, education has been "discursively restructured" within the context of an economic imperative characterized by the dominance of a globalized market economy and the information technology systems that support and sustain this economic and cultural hegemony. Therefore, the most profound effect of the current technology-driven reform policy is its totalizing effect through the discourse of "inevitability." Peters described this phenomenon as a "violent act of closure" that excludes "other possible stories we might inscribe on the future by arguing there is no other alternative" (p. 81).

TECHNO-UTOPIANISM AS MYTHINFORMATION

There are several complex forces involved in the current educational reform movement. Certain reforms are designed to control teachers and their work through systems of accountability and standards. In addition, educational reform is characterized by "cultural politics" where various conservative and liberal interests vie for political and ideological control (Apple, 1996). All levels of political influence, including official reform policy and various special interest factions, seem to have bought into what political theorist Langdon Winner (1986) described as "mythinformation," which he defined as "the almost religious conviction that a widespread adoption of computers and communication systems along with easy access to electronic information will automatically produce a better world for human beings" (p. 105).

In addition, mythinformation exists as a specific incarnation of techno-utopianism peculiar to the latter decades of the 20th century because it has arisen with the invention of computer and information technologies. It also seems particularly popular with those who are cynical or have become discouraged by other aspects of modern social life (Winner, 1986). Therefore, mythinformation's projected vision of the future equates the sheer momentum of the computer revolution to "eliminate many of the ills that have vexed political society since the beginning of time," whereas information itself has become "the dominate form of wealth" (Winner, 1986, p. 104).

Indeed, the proliferation of information and information infrastructures (networked systems) are envisioned to deconstruct entrenched systems of hierarchy while regenerating prospects for participatory democracy. However, empirical studies on the social effects of computers indicates that those who are privy to technical expertise seize and maintain control through that expertise (Winner, 1986). This can also be the case in educational settings (Christal, Ferneding, Kennedy-Puthoff, & Resta, 1997; Morrison & Goldberg, 1996). Although networked systems can destabilize existing hierarchical structures, this aim needs to be highly specified and articulated within the adoption process itself. Often, this is not the case in general, and within the context of educational settings it is assumed that the mere presence of such an infrastructure can generate such effects (Morrison & Goldberg, 1996). Even more disturbing is the fact that educators often reflect the impetus to infuse schools with electronic technologies simply to possess these systems—a position devoid of instructional issues and concerns related to teachers' and students' empowerment (Kerr, 1996).

In addition, although access to computer technology through the availability of low-cost computing power may "move the baseline that defines electronic dimensions of social influence," it does not, however, "alter the relative balance of power," thus making the "computer revolution" a rather conservative one (Winner, 1986, p. 112). To this end, a libertarian perspective characterized by an unquestionable faith in the computer revolution realized through market forces means that "technological determinism ceases to be a mere theory and becomes an ideal: A desire to embrace conditions brought on by technological change without judging them in advance. There is nothing new in this disposition" (Winner, 1986, p. 108). Indeed, the popularized utopian vision that such technologies will automatically create a participatory democracy relies on an ahistorical perspective that ignores the fact that technological progress has been a mixed blessing (Segal, 1994).

Why has mythinformation so captivated our social imagination to the extent that it expresses the contemporary ideology or common set of beliefs that embody the values and desires of the dominate culture? Perhaps the answer to this question can be found in the fact that the sheer omnipresence of computers and information technologies gives expression to economic and social processes while acting as "mere" tools. Winner (1986) maintained that "in our time *techne* has at last become *politeia*—our instruments are institutions in the making." Winner (1986) further cautioned us that "because technological innovation is inextricably linked to processes of social reconstruction, any society that hopes to control its own structural evolution must confront each set of significant technological possibilities with scrupulous care" (p. 54).

Thus, information and computer technologies, acting as necessary control technologies that manage the generation and processing of the new source of wealth—information—reconfigures, if not constitutes, institutions. Although this dominant model characterizes changes in business and industry, one must pause and ask if it is necessary and inherently good to thoughtlessly transfer this model to organizations that are primarily based on social relationships versus generating capital, such as education. A pragmatic perspective would respond that if these new technologies can be utilized to further general efficiency, management, and control of information (which in education would include operational data, student and teacher performance data, and instruction as a "delivery system"), then they should be infused into education. The reality is that the efficient management of information exists as the "telos of modern society" or its greatest mission (Winner, 1986). This is necessary, according to Winner (1986), because people need to be convinced that the human costs of sustaining an Information Age—such as deskilling, downsizing, the disintegration of certain social patterns, and the threat of surveillance—are worth enduring. And on a political level, this means that "those who push the plow are told they ride a golden chariot" (Winner, 1986, p. 115). Indeed, what this situation poses for educators is the possible commodification of the educational process, and thus it raises a central question in terms of what fundamentally remains in the foreground of the instructional experience—that of a delivery system or being in relation to others.

EDUCATIONAL REFORM DISCOURSE AS SOCIAL DISCOURSE

Winner's thesis about mythinformation acting as an expression of modern society's telos and the thesis that techne functions in the capacity of politeia, whereby technology expresses "processes of social reconstruction," are useful to understanding the current discourse of educational reform. However, before this relationship is examined, we turn away for a moment from the subject of technology and society to that of the politics of educational reform.

Educational historian Herbert Kleibard (1992) referred to the work of political psychologist Murray Edelman (1985) when he described educational reform discourse as "dramaturgy in politics." Edelman (1985) explained that the act of generating political discourse or "political dramaturgy" in fact embodies a society's ideological narratives. In effect, the "dramaturgy in politics" exists as an expression of a culture's social construction—how it expresses its values and social vision. Thus, political–social discourse is inherently reflexive and expresses the power of symbolic action. In addition, Kleibard (1992) noted that educational reform discourse has historically existed as a particular "social space" for political–social discourse. Therefore, educational policy discourse may be understood as "the dramatization of ritualistic myths about America and its values played out on the proscenium of the public school" (p. 186). This insight is reflected in David Tyack's and Larry Cuban's (1995) understanding of how the discourse of educational reform acts as a "dramatic exchange in a persistent theater of aspiration and anxiety," such that "conversation about schools is one way Americans make sense of their lives" (p. 42). In fact, Kleibard (1992) further asserted that educational reform discourse seems especially characterized by a struggle between interests related to equity and more pragmatic interests germane to serving national and economic needs, with the latter having secured and maintained dominance since the turn of the 20th century (p. 199).

According to Edelman, political reform narratives act on both an individual and a broad level. On an individual level, these stories are related to the construction of subjectivity and roles. On a broad, social level, political reform discourse exists as a "narrative space" where the construction of social discourse as symbolic action reflects changes in the stories we tell ourselves about who we are as a society. However, the discursive process of making and unmaking within this "narrative space" becomes delimited through the construction of "inevitabilities." Therefore, if techne acts in the capacity of politeia through the symbolic action of mythinformation and educational discourse exists as a "narrative space" where social discourse is constructed, then current educational reform discourse expresses a symbolic action characterized by mythinformation that is furthered by the logic of functionalism. Thus, the "inevitable" infusion of electronic technology into education becomes commonsense and we have our technologies expressing "processes of social reconstruction" but without much thought or reflection. The acceptance of the "inevitability factor" therefore exists as the most dangerous of assumptions that characterize the current reform movement, because it signifies consensus and closure and the unnecessity of deliberation. The symbolic action of "inevitability" dismisses the need for the public's engagement in the active creation and articulation of their social imagination while ensuring that those who hold economic power continue to do so through the naming of issues and the control of symbolic action (Eldelman, 1985). This condition, however, is not atypical. Winner (1986) explained that historically the construction of an "inevitability" argument illustrates the immense power of those who control the creation of symbolic action surrounding the diffusion of new technological innovations.

Thus, although we are told to gaze into our future through a lens constructed by a political force that depicts a confluence of a cybercultural dreamland and the hegemony of a brute global market logic, it is essential that educators ponder why access to information on the Internet has become synonymous with knowledge and education itself. Indeed, within the context of educational reform policy, an overwhelming number of educators and citizens believe that having access to information in schools can be equated to a "civil right" (Zehr, 1997). Although it is obvious that the expansion of resources can benefit both teachers and students, the growing commercialization of the Internet and the proliferation of infotainment-based resources shift the learners' experience from exploration and study to that of voyeurism and shopping.

In addition, the scarcity of resources for public schools, which arises from a general lack of political support, is a reality for many schools. Thus, underwriting the dreamscape of mythinformation demands that certain areas of the curriculum, such as the arts, as well as teachers' aides and after-school programs, be eliminated while limited resources are used to buy electronic technologies, fund endless upgrades, and hire support staff who provide maintenance for these systems. Ironically, these situations illustrate how the decision to infuse schools with electronic technologies is not an apolitical one: It is a choice with real political consequences, despite our cultural bias to construct technology as an apolitical tool. However, one important assumption that characterizes technocentric discourse is that there are no political or moral decisions, only practical ones.

QUESTIONING MYTHINFORMATION: AN EMERGENT SOCIAL VISION

There are two distinct perspectives that articulate the purpose of education within the context of educational reform policy. The dominant technocentric framework, characterized by the discourse of inevitability, is paralleled by an alternative perspective that is characterized by an "emergent social vision." The language of an emergent social vision signifies alternatives to the dominant "inevitable" social vision; an opening up of possibility toward the realization of social democratic ideals embodied within our institutional structures and social relationships through the reflective process, critical thinking, and deliberation.

In the framework of an "emergent social vision," technology adoption becomes an open question, not an inevitable fait accompli. Technology is understood as a "social process" (Schwartz & Thompson, 1990) and thus needs to be understood within a contextual framework including political factors and cultural biases about technology itself (Street, 1992; Winner, 1986). Therefore, assuming a critical stance toward mythinformation and technocentric reform policy is not a peculiar variation of technophobia but rather a call to identify priorities; create a balance between scarce resources; create a conversation about the meaning of electronic technologies as a tool, curriculum, and socialization process; and truly deliberate about what purpose public education is to serve within the context of a technological society. The glitz of techno-inspired futurism wears thin before the stark reality of the challenges of the classroom—the lack of care and social support for the majority of poor and minority children, fiscal problems plaguing public education while municipal corporate taxes decrease, the confusion and exhaustion arising from "cultural wars," the rise in violent acts in schools, and the continuous influx of official reforms that often act paradoxically to exacerbate the problems they were designed to assuage and in fact further the instrumentalization and intensification of teachers' work (Hargraves, 1994).

An emergent social vision also includes the possibility of what historians Howard Segal (1994, 1996) and Leo Marx (1994) called "technological pessimism," a particular expression within postmodernity that signifies the breakdown of the Enlightenment meta-narrative of progress. The power that sustains technological pessimism arises from the reality of technique within our social and economic systems expressed as violence, ennui, and loneliness; the degradation of our ecosystems; commmodification of social processes; and our insidiously effective and efficient systems of weaponry. These unfortunate conditions arise from human inquiry (especially science and technology), applied toward the ends of control, and sustains the foundation for what Riane Eisler (1995, 2000) described as a "dominator model" of culture.

A dominator-based culture favors the male gender and denigrates women in addition to everything that is associated with women, including issues related to children, education, and the natural environment (Eisler, 1995, 2000). A dominator-based cultural meta-narrative thus undermines the feasibility of a partnership model of culture that emphasizes sustainability with regard to technological and ecological issues, democratic and civic ideals, and a lifeworld that supports the ethic of caring and compassionate human relationships (Eisler, 1995, 2000). It is therefore interesting that it is the presence of once marginalized voices (e.g., women, people of color, and environmentalists) that have opened up the discursive landscape to include the counterdiscourse of technological pessimism (Segal, 1996). Indeed, some educators have expressed misgivings about technocentric reform policy and in fact believe that the central crisis in education today lies within systemic socioeconomic problems related to equity and social justice (Ferneding, 2003). Thus, although many teachers and administrators may perceive that students need to have some exposure to computer technologies, some believe that focusing an entire reform campaign around the demands of an Information Age and global market needs is akin to fiddling while Rome is burning (Ferneding, 2003). The 1999 incident at Columbine High School in Colorado stands as one of many unfortunate cases in point.

It is important to understand that the building of information infrastructures cannot be compared to any previous technological innovation or even to the diffusion of stand-alone computers that characterized the first phase of computer technology diffusion in the 1980s. Much like 19th-century transportation and information systems such as the railroad and telegraph, computer and information technologies have reconfigured our relationship to time and space and thus the very processes by which we experience communication and consciousness (Carey, 1989; Talbott, 1995; Winner 1996). Any system that embodies our communication process also constitutes the nature of social interaction (Carey, 1989; 1990). Because instruction is an experience based primarily on social relationships, the infusion of a techno- logical system that embodies the communication process ought to be carefully assessed. Winner (1996), for example, observed that the age of computers and cyberspace is producing a framework for individualization character- ized by crass materialism and "disposable" relationships. With regard to computer-based instruction, C. A. Bowers (1988) noted its inherent bias toward linear and logical thinking as a hidden curricular factor that acts to support a mechanistic and highly individualistic cultural metanarrative, a social framework that furthers a disregard if not an anthropocentric unconsciousness regarding our relationship to a fragile and degraded ecosystem (Bowers, 1997). Moreover, the actual instructional benefits of computer-based instruction have been questioned (Bowers, 1988; Cuban, 1997; Oppenheimer, 1997; Snyder, 1997), while negative effects on socialization and learning are also of concern (Healy, 1998; Turkle, 1997). In addition, some educators wonder how electronic technologies are reshaping the learning and instructional process itself. Educational psychologist Frank Smith (1995), for example, wondered if distance education will effectively replace teachers and fully automate the communication experience of teaching as a mere exchange or transaction, thus furthering the reductionary notion of instruction as a delivery system. But the reality is that these cautions and critical voices are few and far between. Not only is the revenue for critical approaches to researching computer and information technologies practically nonexistent, it appears that the critical language with which to express a measured and cautious approach, much less an alternative perception to techno-utopianism, remains in an emergent stage of development. In actuality, we are still deeply unconscious about our social relationship to technology. However, as an alternative to technocentrism and techno-utopianism, a discourse of possibility seeks to broaden the expression of meaning beyond that of functionalist demands. Within the context of a discourse of possibility, our understanding of what it means to live within what Neal Postman (1993) described as a "technopoly"—a state of culture that deifies technology and seeks its authorization in technology—can arise from concerns related to the lifeworld of social relationships expressed as social justice and equity.

CREATING A "POLITICS OF MEANING" AND A DISCOURSE OF POSSIBILITY

Educational theorist Maxine Greene (1986) defined social imagination as "the capacity to invent visions of what should be and what might be in our deficit society—in our schools" (p. 5). More recently, Greene (1995) described how an inability to conceive an alternative order of things can "give rise to a resignation that paralyzes people ... [and that] an accompanying effacing of the sense of personal and communal efficacy may submerge people into the given, in what appears impervious to protest and discontent" (p. 19). Thus, social imagination expresses the desire to embody human ideals of social justice within our institutions and personal actions. A social vision expresses an intention of a paradigmatic nature to see both through and beyond existing social and cultural themes and conditions that act as barriers to an idealized understanding or perception. A vision expresses deeply held values, beliefs, and personal, individual philosophies. It is inherently a reflective and an imaginative act, because it requires a comparison of the given to an idealized image. In terms of the relationship between the act of envisioning and the development of current educational reform policies, Michael Apple (1996) explained that "behind every story we tell about education—even if only tacitly—is a social theory about what this society 'really is' … these theories or social visions may be in conflict. We are in the midst of such conflicts today and education sits at center stage" (p. 98).

If we create our reality through discursive practice, then the struggle to realize our social vision through discourse is indeed an important matter. Therefore, consider the fact that the alternative social vision that stands in opposition to a technocentric and functionalist perspective arises from a discourse of possibility that expresses ideals germane to social justice, equity, and citizenship within a democratic society. In this vision, economic concerns are configured to realize equity, not the furtherance of corporate hegemony or hierarchical domination via economic class structure. A technocentric and functionalist vision contains our imagination inside a familiar but limited place of lack, fear, and construction of those living outside of our social landscape as the Other, all of which serves to rationalize greed, control, and a pervasive instrumental rationalism within and over the lifeworld. Although our present reality may be characterized by great technological feats and complex systems of control and production, the incessant marketplace kaleidoscope of mediated images and noise that characterizes our postmodern milieu belies the emptiness of our soulless and violent world and our quiet and desperate search for a deeper sense of meaning and purpose.

Indeed, educational scholar and critical theorist Svi Shapiro (1996) maintained that educators and citizens need to create a "politics of meaning" by asking questions of human purpose and vision that enable society to engage in a "cultural act" whereby society may secure "a sense of what our lives are about and what it means to live with others in community." Shapiro defined a politics of meaning to express how "at the heart of the educational enterprise are questions of human purpose and social vision—what does it mean to be human, and how should we live together?" (p. 224).

In his critique of what he termed "third wave" reformers' rhetoric, specifically the influence of futurist writers, educational historian Jesse Goodman (1995) urged educators to defend traditional democratic ideals that he perceived to express a larger "social utopian vision." David Tyack and Larry Cuban (1995) have written about the overwhelming influence that functionalist-based discourse has had on reform, and invited other educators to revisit the importance that "utopian ideals of the democratic tradition" have to the institution of education. Poststructuralist and educational scholar Peter McLaren (1995) has written extensively about the current reform movement and urged educators to engage in a "vision of possibility" and indeed seek to move beyond criticism toward the creation of what liberation theologists envision—a "theology of hope" (p. 51). Resistance to the given or "official" vision of education's future destiny and purpose has become the necessary objective for many who are critical of what they perceive to be the further colonization of educational discourse by instrumental rationality. According to Jurgen Habermas (1989), the colonization of the lifeworld by systems of economic and technical control "impedes making the foundations of society the object of thought and reflection" (p. 258). Indeed, one could say that myth-information as symbolic political action has had such an effect within the context of educational reform policy.

Thus, in the case of educational reform, the discourse of technological determinism submerges and/or distorts traditional democratic ideals. Maxine Greene (1995) asserted that the dominant reform discourse that projects an instrumental rationalist perspective has effectively narrowed our social imagination. She described this condition as "seeing schools small" and as embodied in the practices of focusing on test scores, accountability measures, and "assumes the schools' main mission is to meet national economic and technical needs … while it screens out the faces and gestures of individuals" (p. 9). What this small vision blocks out, of course, is the ability of "seeing schools big." If we saw schools from a broader perspective, the landscape of education would reveal the details and particulars of everyday social interaction that are not reducible to statistics or measurement. Therefore, we would direct our imagination toward the contextuality and lived experiences of teachers and students characterized by social interaction and the embodiment of face-to-face communication.

At this point, you may see the tension between the act of envisioning as an expression of social imagination and the characteristic of the "inevitability" of current reform measures. Existing as faits accomplis, current reform measures act in the capacity of a decree and therefore diminish if not destroy the possibility of alternative social visions. Ideally, the debate over educational reform would reflect discourse concerned with the realization of the public good and thereby could be understood as a form of trusteeship (Tyack & Cuban, 1995). It is naive to believe that futurist- and libertarian-inspired policies address a generalized concern for the public good. Although futurist- inspired educational reforms may seem imaginative, they actually reflect the status quo and further the unconscious awareness of how our techne act as politiea through the social discourse of mythinformation. Thus, as a culture, we are projecting and building the future of education without much thought, imagination, and dialogue. But the question of who has the power to speak, envision, and define the scope of the discursive landscape has always been answered by those who legitimate their own authority. This, of course, is the struggle that resistance embodies.

THE DIALECTIC OF EDUCATIONAL REFORM POLICY AND THE DELIBERATIVE PROCESS

The thesis offered in this chapter explains how educational reform policy has been historically inscribed by two spheres of discourse, a conclusion also supported by Kleibard (1992) and Labree (1987). Cuban (1997) described a similar ideological divide between those who emphasize "efficiency and preparation for a computerized workplace" versus those who believe that the aim of schools is "the social purpose of building literate and caring citizens" (p. 41). The existence of this dialectic is not the major issue, however, because both perspectives serve to articulate the competing interests of a democratic system of governance within the context of a capitalist economic system and the contradictions that arise from this set of conditions. The central issue is that the narrative space of educational reform policy has been severely delimited by the discourse of inevitability and the constituting power of electronic technologies to shape both economic and social structures. Thus, the dominate discourse reflects an amalgam of techno-utopianism and functionalism. Technocentric educational reform discourse has configured a particular social vision that has disassociated education from traditional aims related to social justice and equity. In this sense, the state of current reform discourse is not a dialectic but rather a dichotomy where the possibility of negotiation between the two spheres of discourse has broken down under the weight of the discourse of inevitability.

One can put the present into an historical perspective and hope that, as in the past, the political pendulum would swing back toward the traditional perspective, but this remains to be seen. Given the fact that the language of the market has rationalized the privatization of the public sphere and the fact that this phenomenon is supported by the dominance of a globalized market economic ideology (that is both sustained and realized or constituted through computer and information technologies), the likelihood of this ideological hegemony weakening, especially without the support of alternative public discourse, is not so good. Therefore, it is essential that conversations that arise from traditional aims in education are initiated and supported. For example, our apolitical understanding about the nature of technology as a "mere" tool needs to be revisited. If we can begin to understand that technology exists not only as a tool but also as a sociocultural process, we necessarily acknowledge both the complexity of the technology adoption process and the fact that technology is inherently reflexive. Within this framework, our conversations around technology adoption broaden and thus weaken the logic of the discourse of inevitability.

CONCLUSION

To review, it is proposed that, historically, a dialectic has existed between two distinctive spheres of discourse within the context of educational reform policymaking. The dominant perspective, which articulates a discourse of inevitability, is characterized as a fait accompli and manifests a functionalist vision that supports efficiency, technique, and "enterprise culture." Its historic antecedents are the discourse of vocationalism and functionalism and scientific management. The current incarnation of the dominant perspective emphasizes accountability, standards, and the rapid diffusion of electronic technologies. In terms of the construction of technology, it embodies a commonsense apolitical understanding in which technology exists as a neutral artifact/tool. This perspective also indicates that schools need to be restructured to better meet the needs of the Information Age and global market economy, and thus the "only" solution is to adopt a technocentric and techno-utopian vision to guide educational reform policy. This stance embodies a technological fix and techno-utopian approach to technology adoption and does not question the "grand narrative" of progress. Therefore, it supports libertarian, market-driven, and technocentric means–ends that are instantiated in the form of privatization and marketization schemes and standards and accountability systems as well as the infusion of electronic technologies. In this sense, education becomes embedded within the context of the utilitarian matrix of "enterprise culture."

The perspective that expresses a discourse of possibility arises from a sociocultural vision that embodies emancipatory ideology and thus articulates social justice and equity. This political end serves the public good and thus eschews the privatization and commodification of knowledge and the education process. A discourse of possibility questions technical rationalism and acknowledges the complexity of technology adoption, recognizing that technology is not just a tool but also a complex sociocultural process that acts to shape processes of communication and relational knowing. Thus, the technology adoption process requires negotiation and deliberation to counteract the apolitical bias that expresses the typical commonsense understanding about technology. Within this framework, mythinformation is questioned. Indeed, a particular critical approach to understanding the relationship between modern technology and society can be expressed as "technological pessimism."

A discourse of possibility furthers the understanding that if a crisis exists in education it arises not just from the economic pressures inherent in changes generated by the rise of the Information Age and a globalized market economy. Rather, an equally powerful crisis exists regarding the nature of meaning itself as well as systemic socioeconomic inequities, both of which characterize the postmodern condition. This perspective rejects libertarianism and the ideology of techno-utopian futurism but in fact recognizes the political reality of "cultural wars" and the ideological negotiation that multiculturalism poses to conservative political factions. Whereas the discourse of inevitability has constructed the crisis in education to arise from the need for education to meet the needs of an Information Age and its economic demands (and thus constructs the crisis and solution in a tautological fashion), the discourse of possibility arises from concern related to systemic socioeconomic issues. Therefore, the approach to addressing this crisis is not one of closure or to delimit the space of social discourse but rather one of opening up this space through deliberation toward the realization of traditional ideals related to social justice. The issue of technology diffusion is thus configured within a perspective that foregrounds the pedagogical and social issues that affect the physical and emotional health of children, their families, and communities.

In conclusion, in his analysis of our postmodern technological society, Andre Gorz (1989) made a poignant observation: "Technical culture is lack of culture in all things non-technical" (p. 86). If the cultural realm is characterized by the lifeworld and thus the experience of being embodied and living within the context of human social relationships, when this being in relation becomes configured through processes of functionalization and technization, something profound but subtle is lost. Thus, Gorz (1989) asked, "At what cost have we come to accept as our lifeworld, this world which is molded by the instruments of our civilization? To what extent have we, by adapting to it, become maladaptive to our own selves? ... The inability of our culture to think reality as it is lived is itself a reply to these questions" (p. 86).

In conclusion, I believe that Gorz, although writing in the context of the effects that postindustrial technology has had on labor, raised some important questions that educators as professionals and citizens need to seriously address within the context of current educational reform policy. For example, at what cost have we adopted a techno-utopian social vision of education? To what extent have we come to accept as normative this reconfiguration of education within the context of mythinformation and enterprise culture? Have educational policymakers and educators lost their ability to think reality, within the context of the educational process, as it is lived? Indeed, if we are unable to address a discourse of possibility, therein lies the answer to these questions.

REFERENCES

Apple, M. (1995). *Education and power* (2nd ed.). New York: Routledge.
Apple, M. (1996). *Cultural politics and education*. New York: Teachers College Press.
Bowers, C. A. (1988). *The cultural dimensions of educational computing: Understanding the non-neutrality of technology*. New York: Teachers College Press.
Bowers, C. A. (1995). *Educating for an ecologically sustainable culture: Rethinking moral education, creativity, intelligence and other modern orthodoxies*. Albany: State University of New York (SUNY) Press.
Bowers, C. A. (1997). *The culture of denial*. Albany: SUNY Press.
Carey, J. (1989). *Communication as culture*. New York: Routledge.
Carey, J. (1990). The language of technology: Talk, text and template as metaphors for communication. In M. Medhurst, A. Gonzalez, & T. R. Peterson (Eds.), *Communication and the culture of technology* (pp. 19–39). Pullman: Washington State University Press.
Christal, M., Ferneding, K., Kennedy-Puthoff, A., & Resta, P. (1997). *Schools as knowledge building communities*. Denton: Texas Center for Education Technology.
Cuban, L. (1997). High tech schools and low-tech teaching. *Education Week, 16*(34), 38, 41.
Edelman, M. (1985). *The symbolic us of politics*. Urbana: University of Illinois Press.
Eisler, R. (1995). *The chalice and the blade*. San Francisco, CA: HarperCollins. (Original work published 1987)
Eisler, R. (2000). *Tomorrow's children*. Boulder, CO: Westview.
Ellul, J. (1964). *The technological society*. New York: Vantage. (Original work published 1954)

Ferneding, K. (2003). *Questioning technology: Electronic technologies and educational reform.* New York: Peter Lang.

Goodman, J. (1995). Change without difference: School restructuring in historical perspective. *Harvard Educational Review, 65*(1), 1–29.

Gorz, A. (1989). *Critique of economic reason.* New York: Verso.

Greene, M. (1986). Perspectives and imperatives: Reflection and passion in teaching. *The Journal of Curriculum and Supervision, 2*(1), pp. 68–81.

Greene, M. (1995). *Releasing the imagination: Essays on education, the arts and social change.* San Francisco, CA: Jossey-Bass.

Habermas, J. (1989). Technology and science as "ideology." In S. Seidman (Ed.), *Jurgen Habermas on society and politics: A reader.* Boston, MA: Beacon.

Hargraves, P. (1994). *Changing teachers, changing times.* London, UK: Cassell.

Healy, J. (1998). *Failure to connect: How computers affect our children's minds—for better and worse.* New York: Simon & Schuster.

Kerr, S. T. (1996). Visions of sugarplums: The future of technology, education and society. In S. T. Kerr (Ed.), *Technology and the future of schooling* (pp. 1–27). Chicago: National Society for the Study of Education.

Kleibard, H. M. (1992). *Forging the American curriculum.* New York: Routledge.

Labree, D. F. (1987). Politics, markets and the compromised curriculum. *Harvard Educational Review, 57,* 483–494.

Lyotard, J. F. (1984). *The postmodern condition: A report on knowledge.* Manchester, UK: Manchester University Press.

McLaren, P. (1995). *Critical pedagogy and predatory culture.* New York: Routledge.

Marx, L. (1994). The idea of "technology" and postmodern pessimism. In Y. Ezrahi, E. Mendelsohn, & H. P. Segal (Eds.), *Technology, pessimism and postmodernism* (pp. 11–28). Amherst: University of Massachusetts Press.

Morrison, D., & Goldberg, B. (1996). New actors, new connections: The role of local information infrastructures in school reform. In T. Koshmann (Ed.), *CSCL: Theory and practice of an emerging paradigm* (pp. 125–145). Mahwah, NJ: Lawrence Erlbaum Associates.

National Commission on Excellence in Education. (1983). *A nation at risk.* Cambridge, MA: USA Research.

Oppenheimer, T. (1997, July). The computer delusion. *Atlantic Monthly,* pp. 45–62.

Peters, M. (1996). *Poststructuralism, politics and education.* Westport, CT: Bergin & Garvey.

Postman, N. (1993). *Technopoly: The surrender of culture to technology.* New York: Vintage.

Purpel, D. (1996). Education as sacrament. In F. Mengert, K. Casey, D. Liston, D. Purpel, & H. S. Shapiro (Eds.), *The institution of education* (2nd ed., pp. 207–218). Needham Heights, MA: Simon & Schuster.

Schwartz, M., & Thompson, M. (1990). *Divided we stand: Redefining politics, technology and social choice.* New York: Harvester Weatsheaf.

Segal, H. P. (1994). The cultural contradictions of high tech: Or the many ironies of contemporary technological optimism. In Y. Ezrahi, E. Mendelsohn, & H. P. Segal (Eds.), *Technology, pessimism and postmodernism* (pp. 175–211). Amherst: University of Massachusetts Press.

Segal, H. P. (1996). The American ideology of technological progress: Historical perspectives. In S. Kerr (Ed.), *Technology and the future of schooling* (pp. 28–48). Chicago: University of Chicago Press.

Shapiro, S. (1996). Memo to the president: Clinton and education: Policies without meaning. In F. Mengert, K. Casey, D. Liston, D. Purpel, & H. S. Shapiro (Eds.), *The institution of education* (2nd ed., pp. 219–230). Needham Heights, MA: Simon & Schuster.

Smith, F. (1995). *Between hope and havoc: Essays into human learning and education*. Portsmouth, NH: Heinemann.

Snyder, T. (1997, July). Presentation given at the National Educational Computing Conference, Seattle, WA.

Street, J. (1992). *Politics and technology*. New York: Guilford.

Talbott, S. L. (1995). *The future does not compute: Transcending the machines in our midst*. Sebastopol, CA: O'Reilly & Associates.

Turkle, S. (1997). Seeing through computers: Education in a culture of simulation. *The American Prospect, 31*, 76–82.

Tyack, D., & Cuban, L. (1995). *Tinkering toward utopia: A century of school reform*. Cambridge, MA: Harvard University Press.

Winner, L. (1980). Do artifacts have politics? *Daedalus, 109*, 121–136.

Winner, L. (1986). *The whale and the reactor*. Chicago: University of Chicago Press.

Winner, L. (1996). Who will be in cyberspace? *The Information Society, 12*, 63–72.

Zehr, M. A. (1997). Technology counts: Partnering with the public. *Education Week, 17*(11), 36–39.

Chapter 5

Beyond God the Unconscious: The Libidinal Politics of Spiritual Youth Movements in Schools

Julie A. Webber
Illinois State University

Thinking Beyond

In this chapter, Webber discusses the role of belief in the aftermath of traumatic events such as school violence. The theoretical picture that she presents for us is complicated; students are presented as pawns in a religious battle over the schools. The political concerns outlined in this chapter have serious implications for the future of curriculum theory and its expansion. Will curriculum expand to include religious concerns, or will it be narrowed by the traumatic political plays of factions? If we expand our reading of this chapter, and read it against other political events in the United States today (e.g., charter schools and vouchers), can we say that the way religion is exploited in the aftermath of school violence is a progressive notion or a regressive one? This chapter presents a troubling picture of school violence and the role of religion in public schools, and may be read against other chapters in the volume.

Questions

1. Webber presents the reader with a psychoanalytic reading of trauma in schools. How does this reading compare with other methodological approaches in the volume, such as Ferneding's stress on technology or Reynolds' "oppositional" approach to brand-name corporate orders?
2. Which object is more instructive to our gendered relations in schools—the "pole" or the "wound" (masculine totemic identifications or grief-laden feminine ones)? Does this mean that our gender relations in U.S. society are becoming more masculine, more feminine, or neither? Is there a way of relating to objects that moves us beyond gender?
3. Do young people of new generations have different means of voicing their opposition? Is there a direction to youth movements in the United States? If so, where are they headed? What do they want?

Only a rite, an endlessly repeated act, can commemorate this not very memorable encounter—for no one can say what the death of a child is, except for the father *qua* father, that is to say no conscious being.

For the true formula of atheism is not *God is Dead*—even by basing the origin of the function of the father upon his murder, Freud protects the father—the true formula of atheism is *God is unconscious*. (Lacan, "Tuché and Automaton," p. 59)[1]

What does belief applied to the unconscious signify? What is an unconscious that no longer does anything but 'believe,' rather than produce? What are the

---

[1]Lacan, J. (1981). *The four fundamental concepts of psycho-analysis*. (A. Sheridan, Trans.). New York: Norton.

operations, the artifices that inject the unconscious with 'beliefs' that are not even irrational, but on the contrary only too reasonable and consistent with the established order? (Deleuze & Guattari, *Anti-Oedipus*, p. 61)[2]

You *sell out* to God, and you will be *utterly amazed* at what He will do! (Student reflections from *See You At the Pole 2002*)[3]

Theoretically speaking, I have stacked the deck with the previous quotes. My starting point is Lacan, specifically his essay, "Tuché and Automation," in which he revisits Freud's analysis of a father whose son has died, and who sleeps in the room next to his dead son's body. The father has a dream in which the son asks, "Father, can't you see that I am burning?" and something occurs in this dream between awakeness and sleep that bears on the father's emotional state in the dream. As Lacan noted, "stages are organized around a fear of castration," (p. 58), by which he meant Oedipal stages of development that can be understood according to their "possible registration in terms of bad encounters," such as primal scenes and traumas. If we focus on school shootings in the United States, occurring between 1996, and April 20, 1999, we can revisit the primal scene of American culture in relation to youth at a very specific developmental and libidinal stage: adolescence. It is not merely youth who are traumatized, but also the generations before them who respond to the primal scene in accordance to their own stages of development in the libidinal milieu. Lacan further revisited Freud in this essay on other pertinent topics and themes that are applied to school violence and its reactions: unconscious states of knowledge (yes, knowledge), the role of emotion in repetition, repetitive behavior induced by traumas and primal scenes, and the objects to which humans relate, as Lacan fastidiously mimicked Aristotle, "man thinks with his object."[4] In this chapter, I attempt a broad psychoanalytic reading of the dynamics between students and the objects they choose to "think with" when they are passing through grief, fear, and politics in the wake of school shootings in the United States.

When one sells out to "God the unconscious"—that is, when religious belief becomes heavily infused with market rhetoric, faith being the militaristic justification of "just war"—one voluntarily sells out to a retrograde form of politics because one gives in to the desire to be led by negatively determined social values that aim at repressing social gestures that would disrupt the order of things. Accordingly, this chapter explores the ideological underpinnings of a counterforce that has arisen as a response to school shootings aimed at a totally different interpretation and cure for school violence. The increasing number of Christian converts to school prayer is significant when one considers that part of the reason for the popularity of God and faith among today's youth is

---

[2]1983. *Anti-Oedipus: Capitalism and schizophrenia*. (R. Hurley, M. Seem, & H. R. Lane, Trans.). Minneapolis: University of Minnesota Press.

[3]Retrieved 13 Jan. 2003, from http://www.syatp.com/02home.html

[4]Lacan, J., *The four fundamental concepts of psycho-analysis*, p. 62.

related to "the disaster," a master signifier for the effect of school shootings—indeed, of a myriad of traumas from 9/11 to the shuttle *Columbia*, including the "sniper" of Washington, DC, and the unending threat of terrorist attacks. All of these events challenge populations at the core: in their belief systems, urging them to engage in the struggle over the meaning of life itself and the way of life that should protect meaning in American public discourse.

In this chapter, however, I look specifically at the way in which belief, specifically Christian belief, has reentered the schools to engage in the struggle over meaning and the American way of life—how young people, specifically Generation Y, the progeny of the Baby Boomers, have found God as a convenient way to battle the values set forth by their parents' generation.[5] The struggle to include, or exclude, is a peculiarly American import of Christianity into the schools and curriculum of this country, but it is also related to the struggle for the cash and power that buys a "way of life" in the United States. Combine the traumas of public shootings, occurring in public spaces of assembly that are marked by what McLaren called "predatory culture," with the insight that when one is faced with this public one can "sell out to God," and you have a major set of questions on your hands: Is the United States becoming more and more religious in public spaces because of the breakdown of civil culture? Is the breakdown of civil culture producing students who are more conformist than critical, who would contribute to a diverse public discourse so necessary in an adequately functioning democracy?

The imagery of the Oedipal father haunts this religious discourse, as one can see in a thorough psychoanalytic treatment of the shooting at Heath High School in West Paducah, Kentucky, in the fall of 1997. This shooting makes a good focal point because shooter Michael Carneal chose a prayer circle in the lobby of the school as his target. All of his victims were young women. Indeed, this unconscious return of the father to say what the death of a child is, as Lacan underscored, is a fundamental strategy deplored by the Christian Right and its youth groups. Thus, it would be politically incorrect for people to say the culture needs more father outright; instead, the culture says it proleptically through other belief structures and strategies for life in a postmodern world. As we see later in this discussion, there are two competing meta-narratives for accessing wealth in the United States that are in direct competition with one another in the people's minds, but in effect form a collusion to the benefit of those already in power who seek to manipulate these meta-narratives to maintain their power.[6]

---

[5]For "the" thesis on generations and fetishism, see Morrione, D. D. (2002). *Sublime monsters and virtual children*. Unpublished doctoral dissertation, Purdue University.

[6]I would now characterize school violence as a "chronic problem" in Murray Edelman's use of the term. Edelman argued "that an explanation for a chronic social problem can never be generally supported. It is offered to be rejected as much as to be accepted. Its function is to intensify polarization and so maintain support for advocates on both sides." M. Edelman (1992). The construction and uses of social problems. In K. Chaloupka & W. Stearns (Eds.), *Jean Baudrillard: The disappearance of art and politics* (p. 266). New York: St. Martin's Press.

Generation Y is explicitly Oedipal in the sense that Deleuze and Guattari understood it. It is a generation that aims to avoid political and social responsibility in a traditional sense by holding its parents' generational values (diverse spirituality, economic equity, peace, public education, civil rights, women's rights, gay rights, and secularism) hostage, threatening to extinguish the institutional manifestations of them if it doesn't get its way. It is a repressed generation[7] in the sense that it is physically, spiritually, politically, and emotionally contained by codes imposed by legal structures, police structures, moral codes, and fears of those in power in both political spaces and in the social. First, I discuss the Christian Right and read the gendered implications of student prayer at flagpoles around the country. The flagpole is one object through which students can think through an object; the other is the wound that is created by the shootings themselves and the rupture of uncertainty they breed in American public culture and discourse. I then briefly examine "witnessing" as it impacts political participation among students in schools.

The Christian Right, as many have successfully argued, derives its power in American public discourse because unlike the Left it does not back down from questions of faith and meaning. However, this fortitude makes the representatives of this position no more honest or politically equitable than any other political-ideological movement that seeks access to capital and jobs and uses the school as a means to these ends.[8] There are the usual litany of critiques of religion in schools represented by Left groups, but they misunderstand the nature of power in this society: To have power, one must sell his or her concept of "life" itself to populations already bitterly quarreling among themselves over declining wages, prospects for career invention and advancement, and little or no public assistance for health care, child care, or job training. As Murray Edelman argued a long time ago, solving "chronic" public problems is not the business of the government because there is no way to rectify them and maintain power at the same time, because regimes would have to redistribute their own power and wealth in order to effectively alleviate problems. In the United States, access to these goods, which bring forth the "way of life" promised in the concept of "America," is virtually guaranteed through two major mechanisms: the future and education. When one is poor, or threatened with a paucity of consumer-oriented propertied "life," education and the future it promises leave the indelible imprint on the subjects' minds that they too will have free-

---

[7]See Donald Livingston's chapter in this volume.

[8]See M. W. Apple (2002). Interrupting the right: On doing critical educational work in conservative times. *Symploke*, *10*(1–2), 133–152. Apple called this period "conservative modernization," whereby political groups realize that "to win in the state, you must win in civil society." Thus, the struggle over access to capital and leisure is about finding the right answer to appease a public that is confused about how to conduct life itself, and needs confident (although not necessarily honest) answers to questions of civility. He also argued that there is a "tense alliance of neo-liberals, neo-conservatives, authoritarian populist religious activists, and the professional and managerial new middles class" that "only works because there has been a very creative articulation of themes that resonate deeply with the experiences, fears, hopes, and dreams of people as they go about their *daily lives*" (emphasis mine).

dom from earthly problems in order to purchase power and exact their own perverted repressive designs on those below them.

Americans have a long love-hate affair with youth movements, from the roving bands of boys eventually enclosed in public schools by the Women's Christian Temperance Union in the 19th century, to the barricades and tear gas that squelched those opposed to the Vietnam War. Despite the violence, the adult community has long struggled with and eventually (although reluctantly) incorporated the ideals of youth movements into the larger political structures and legal codes of the United States. They have, as I have argued elsewhere, learned to manipulate (or compromise with) the Ortegan "essential anachronism of history" that exists between generations living as "coevals."[9] However, the youth movement examined in this chapter labels itself as an exclusively "student-led" movement. It also seemingly dovetails with parental expectations, assuming a role as the alternative rebellion method for teens with no access to other social outlets for positive desires. Rebellion is no longer characterized by an organic and spontaneous gesture against a perceived hegemonic policy or force, but is instead channeled through bureaucratic procedures and parental desires, devitalizing the experience of such spontaneity and making it predictable. Instead of a *movement* that moves against a previous generation, this student-led prayer movement scripts its mission as one that reclaims the public schools for God. Therefore, it operates on a plane of reality unlike those in the past, because its power lies at the non-secular, spiritual level and is not concerned with formal political rights or equality (in fact, it fights governmental intrusion into private life even while it promotes its own lifestyle as truth), but instead with a more metaphysical and emotional program of healing.

Formerly, the school site was viewed by Christian activists as occupied by secular humanism that contributes to the devitalization of the public sphere through an assault on cherished ways of life such as family and spirituality. As James Fraser pointed out, this assumption made by the Christian right wing is the result of Reagan's unending assault on public education as a secular humanist form of mind control. Indeed, Reagan's rhetoric misinformed the public by interpreting key Supreme Court decisions concerning religious practice in schools as antiprayer. Because of this misinformation, administrators banned students from praying, even though it remained a legal activity.[10] Presently, it is a contested space where lobbying at the *meta*-physical level is conducted by proto-citizens, whose interests lie far beyond the realm of immediacy afforded by constitutional rights or rebellion/protest against an ongoing world event. With the increasing array of alternative education such as distance education, vouchers, and private religious education, the public school has lost what little symbolic power it once had to negotiate in the interests of the free and experimental

[9]Webber, J. A. (2003). *Failure to hold: The politics of school violence*. Lanham, MD: Rowman and Littlefield. An earlier (and shorter) version of this argument appeared in chapter 6 of that volume.

[10]Fraser, J. (1999). *Between church and state: Religion and public education in a multicultural America*. New York: St. Martin's Press.

public space. It is now a far cry from what progressive educators like John Dewey or, more appropriately, William James, had conceptualized as a creative and experimental laboratory, merging fact and fiction, belief and verification. James himself sought a common ground between spirituality and science more ardently than any other pragmatist. James' position matched Delueze and Guattari's imperative to root out daily fascisms in one's life, and liberate positive social desire from negative social conditions. William James, I think, would have been the first body without organs at Harvard University!

This leads to the question of what citizenship in the schoolyard looks like at present. In the next two sections, we examine two cases involving the collision of scientific monitoring, secular humanism, tolerance, and spiritual belief in public schools. First, Michael Carneal's choice of the prayer circle at Heath High School is examined, followed by a reading of a popular prayer movement directly linked to a symbol of national identity: the American flag.

CITIZENSHIP IN THE SCHOOLYARD

Michael Carneal's school shooting is perhaps the most political of events prior to Columbine. Carneal opened fire on a prayer circle in the lobby of Heath High School that included members of his own social circle. He is said to have held a contradictory position on religion. Many students at Heath High School have made claims indicating Carneal's ambivalence to the morning ritual in the lobby of the school. Ben Strong (the leader of the group) has said that Carneal hung out with other kids who openly expressed their atheism and at times would even tease members of the prayer group; yet, he and Carneal were close friends. In fact, the charges of Carneal's alleged atheism as motivation for the shootings were so prevalent at the time of the incident that several national atheist organizations issued statements in the aftermath arguing that they do not promote antireligious violence and, therefore, do not accept culpability for Carneal's behavior (*Marantha Christian Journal*, 1998). Yet, the strongest evidence that many believe the motivation was religious intolerance can be found in the community of West Paducah, Kentucky, itself. In an alluring display of evangelical patriotism, many people have incited a movement called "Prayer at the Pole," in which a prayer circle is formed around the flagpole at the school. No longer content to have the prayer sessions in the lobby, this act binds school prayer to American citizenship (and perhaps normative masculinity), at the flagpole, in the aftermath of a great social wound. The question of intent is obliterated as groups take on their own victimhood and accept that they are targets. It may even be argued that, in this case, to be targeted is the greatest victory for Christians. Therefore, Carneal's state of mind no longer matters, because his actions paved the way for a movement that bases its popularity on trauma and the wound.

These prayer sessions are reminiscent of Poland's Solidarity protests against Soviet control in the early 1980s. Members and supporters wore buttons bearing a picture of Pope John Paul II, and the Pope is known to have visited the country's religious landmarks 27 times during the height of the movement's popularity. During this time in Poland, citizenship was not only negatively formed against Soviet control, but also positively formed through identification with the Pope and Rome. This citizen-forming practice functions along the lines of Kaja Silverman's re-reading of Althusserian interpellation in *Male Subjectivity at the Margins*. Silverman argued that the funda- mental misrecognition embedded in social practice is that people continually "take as an ontology what is only a point of address" (Silverman, 1992, p. 21). This process takes place in a noncognitive manner, simulated by visual signs and emotions such as the suturing of the figure of the Pope to a political cause, the location of which is provided by the negative reaction to, in Zizek's terminology, a Big Other such as the Soviet Union and makes a momentary identification *seem* like an ontological process. Indeed, most literature concerned with understanding citizenship as formulated through a process of noncognitive identifications (as opposed to liberal experiential interpretation) assumes that citizenship is never final, but instead is a continually stimulated process of identifications that produces the simulacrum "citizen." All of this ideological work functions at the level of nationalism.

It has been intimated in the media that Michael Carneal was stimulated by the "trigger" scene in the film *The Basketball Diaries*. This passive argument indicates that he was doing nothing other than participating in a common form of citizenship that proceeds primarily through identification and misrecognition, not through participatory experience. The crucial difference is that in the former, one acts according to Hobbesian laws of motion, either attracted to or averting from an object in the world with no principle guiding the behavior nor any belief system derived from experience; whereas in the latter, one would participate because he or she experiences citizenship as connected to the object in a fundamental way that is not tied to a momentary pulsion. The students whom Carneal shot were finishing a ritual that bound them to their own form of citizenship, a form of irredentism (they claimed to be taking back "ownership" of the schools) that signified the reclamation of secular school grounds for the practice of prayer. Carneal's identification with Jim Carroll's character in *The Basketball Diaries* makes perfect sense when viewed through this political lens. Carneal's choice of the prayer circle as the object of the shooting experiment demands a reading of the function and purpose of prayer at school. In the aftermath of the shooting, prayer circlers made legitimate claims on school grounds—even as they emphatically denied that Carneal targeted them—by using the wound opened in the lobby of Heath High School to lend credence to their mission.

THE MOVEMENT

We have a flagpole, and we have Jesus! (See You at the Pole, September 16, 1998)

See You at the Pole (SYATP), a student-led prayer movement that began in Texas in 1990, saw its membership and practice increase following the Kentucky shooting's exposure in the media. In fact, the prayer group at Heath High School saw its membership increase from a mere 30 students before the shooting to 135 following the shooting (300 turned out the day after the shooting, 60 meet daily, and the national turnout in 1998 was 3 million; *Marantha Christian Journal,* 1998). Traumatized by school violence around the country, this group's central focus and purpose shifted following the school shootings, and by December 1997 was a permanent feature of school shooting coverage and public response, especially in relation to the "healing process" that begins literally minutes after news of a shooting. Originally a movement to bring prayer back into public schools, the group was controversial and troublesome to those intent on maintaining a strict separation of church and state, but following the shootings, more and more students began praying at their schools' flagpole with a resigned tolerance from school authorities.[11] Education secretary Richard Riley even announced the following message in advance of the national group's proposed meeting on September 16, 1998, to mark the students' return to school in the aftermath of the Springfield, Oregon shooting that had left the nation traumatized and afraid of what would happen when schools reopened in the fall: "Schools must give students the same right to engage in religious activity and discussion as they have to engage in other comparable activity. This means that students may pray in a nondisruptive [elsewhere cited as nondiscursive] manner during the school day when they are not engaged in school activities and instruction, subject to the same rules of order as apply to other student speech."[12]

Easily incorporated into the hidden curriculum of schools as a response to the shock experienced from the shootings, school prayer is (and has always been; this is what is erased by the movement as it accepts a societal status based on prejudice) acceptable if practiced in relative silence, in designated areas outside classrooms. As President Clinton addressed the nation at a prayer breakfast following the memorial service for the three girls slain by Carneal, he confirmed the nation's commitment to prayer as a healing practice by saying, "Our entire nation has been shaken by this tragedy. West Paducah, on the southern shore of the Ohio River, *is at the center of our circle of prayers*" (emphasis added).[13] These reactions to the shooting, especially because it appeared to target a prayer circle, gave increasing visibility to the

---

[11]Schools have the option of banning limited forums, but only if the ban is applied to all groups. It is interesting that most have chosen not to ban them in response to prayer, but when one considers the controversy surrounding gay/lesbian forums in states such as Colorado, Michigan, and Utah, it seems odd that the prayer circles gained credibility (or are at least viewed as relatively benign) after the shootings began, especially in West Paducah.

[12]Widely circulated statement given to the press by Riley for that purpose.

[13]Radio address by the President to the nation, Saturday, December 6, 1997.

SYATP movement.[14] As the school year and two more shootings passed, students around the country were ready to join in the prayer circles. With a nod from Washington and the memory of a bloody 1997–1998 school year, students needed something to suture the wounds and calm the fears that followed them to school in the fall of 1998, and SYATP supplied that for many.

The group's theme for the long-awaited day, September 16th, was "For Such a Time as This" and drew on the Old Testament story of Esther, a young woman who saved fellow Jews from death at the hands of a King who also happened to be her unwitting husband. Students in the group believe that the persecution faced by Jews under this plot created by Haman, the King's disgruntled advisor, in 437 B.C., has strict parallels with the experiences of students in schools today. Specifically, believing that as Christians and students they are persecuted by violent media and the increasing secularization of the school's curriculum, activities, and official policies, the SYATP students link secular culture with violence and a retreat from what they see as the "traditional" values of American society. In a CNN interview marking the date of school shooter Kip Kinkel's arraignment in September 1999, some students intimated that they also viewed prayer as a preventative measure, a method to block repeat occurrences of shootings.

The continuing violence reported at schools, coupled with three more extreme shootings, gave them proof of their righteousness. Increasingly, students have been called to "witness" to others, challenging the "nonsaved" to join the faith and bring Jesus into their lives at school. Witnessing takes place as students relate the specific problems they might face at their schools, such as fear of violence, guns, drugs, and "Goth" culture. They further connect these problems to the culture of the communities in which the schools are housed. In this way, they make the causal link between secular culture and violence (and, at times, pornography). For them, SYATP is a means to send a message to others that Jesus is watching over them in schools while they simultaneously argue that the fundamental problem causing school violence is the absence of God in school, which is brought about by secular culture and law. According to the National Council of Youth Ministries, the group that manages the chapters of SYATP and organizes the fall event of SYATP's national "Pray at the Pole" day, God wants to "renew and revive the nation" and the SYATP event begins a year of prayer and devotion to God that will help bring religion back into the schools. When asked in an interview what "systemic problems do members see in public schools," the Director and Promotion Coordinator responded:

---

[14]Reactions by those involved in the shooting are mixed. Ben Strong decided that "there's just no way to explain it," whereas officials who run SYATP from the National Youth Ministry argued that from their talks with prayer circlers, they formed the conclusion that Carneal's target "could just as easily have been a basketball game." Another student and close friend of Carneal's said, "Well, you'd just have to know Michael. It was just a Michael thing, I guess."

The roots of the problems in our schools—and in our culture as a whole— are spiritual in nature. When we stop following the principles God gave us in the Scripture, the results are the kinds of symptoms we see all around us: immorality, impurity, evil, hatred, murders, and other moral decay. The Frenchman A. de Tocqueville, who came to the United States in the mid-1800s to find "the source of America's greatness," stated that he found it not in our industry but in our "pulpits aflame with righteousness." The Bible says that "righteousness exalts a nation, but sin is a reproach to any people." What goes for the culture as a whole will be true in the schools as well. The solution, then, is a return to God's values.[15]

Furthermore, the group distinguishes itself from other adult mass movements, such as the Promise Keepers, by arguing that they are not redeeming themselves by making good on broken promises that might be the legacy of a traumatic family history, but instead are calling on God to come to them in times of need to instruct them at their schools. They have not forsaken God, as these adults have done, but are calling on God in expectation of further tragedy, asking for help and guidance as they confront what they perceive as the hostile culture in public schools. Additionally, they reclaim their schools in local settings, giving their mission a grassroots flavor that is more in tune with current political strategies to increase visibility and awareness through dispersion, thereby making the group's evangelical mission more effective.

These political considerations, although interesting, do not get at the belief structure that undergirds the formation of prayer circles, nor do they help sketch out the pattern of acceptance of prayer circles in public schools that can be traced from West Paducah to Littleton. What is more important is the circlers' identification with specific shootings and their use of them to exploit suffering and to authorize a political movement with an unrelated agenda. Despite their claims that prayer circles are innocent gatherings in which regular students pray for God to claim their schools, the circles can be read as a staging of what Mark Seltzer (1997) called "the sociality of the wound," (p. 3), a general depiction of the crossing of private and public desire around trauma. To get an understanding of these processes, how they function, and what they accomplish for a political movement aimed at undermining the separation of church and state in the United States, I return to Silverman's reading of interpellation. As a citizen-forming process that works *as if* to reinstate or confirm a "dominant fiction" (much like the one outlined earlier by the SYATP director concerning a return to de Tocqueville's claim about the "pulpits aflame with righteousness"), interpellation functions on the plane of ideology, not rationalism or even compromise, as in political pragmatism.

Linda Zerelli argued that quotidian politics operates out of subjective certainty; individuals know, but cannot formally validate, their actions. In this case, the fiction is not an established one, but instead is conceived as willing

---

[15]Doug Clark, e-mail interview, 12 April 1999.

the return of God, normative masculinity, and the heteronormative family to order the symbolic, or law. As willing fiction, SYATP must compete with many other fictions, but the wounds left by school shootings provide the perfect place to stage a comeback. As the membership brochure claimed, "God wants to come back and renew his Covenant with students and parents."[16] More important, God must come back to fight evil. In one article, Luke Woodham, the shooter from Pearl, Mississippi, was described as belonging to a satanic cult that worshipped the "God-killer Friedrich Nietzsche." This statement is of interest in that it signifies the Christian acceptance that God has been banished from the symbolic, even as God is always surrounded by followers. Commentary on Nietzsche from a theological point of view is lacking in the SYATP literature, but this conceptualization of God appears to confirm Nietzsche's view of the Christian God as being the one who is dependent on human worship for survival. Consider the omnipresence of billboards claiming to represent God's will and message across the country, a message that speaks directly to contemporary concerns as if it were the voice of a contemplative God: "I don't question *your* existence"—God; or "Nice wedding. Now invite me to the marriage."—God.

Unlike other Gods in Western society, the God of the proselytizing Christian can be banished (perhaps killed) if no longer allowed participation in the dominant fiction of the society. Finding ways to bring God back becomes the consuming task of students, and prayer at the flagpole is one such way to accomplish this task. Consider one description of the movement given by *Time* magazine:

> Blake Langhofer was the first to arrive. It was 6:40 a.m., and the sickle moon still hung in the dark sky over Maize High School near Wichita, Kansas. In sandals and shorts, Blake, 16, approached his school's blue flag pole. He leaned forward, placed his hands on it and bowed his head. Soon, he was joined by four friends, all jeans-clad and smelling sweetly of soap and shampoo. They formed a circle, and someone entreated the Lord aloud: "I pray you do wonders through the pole and let your wonders show through the pole." First a trickle, then dozens of students arrived; eventually more than 200 gathered in tight concentric circles around the pole.[17]

The coverage seems overtly erotic. The pole serves as a totemic marker that connects citizenship to the Christian God through an attempted re-Oedipalization of school grounds. Praying in "tight concentric circles" around the phallic object, students are revitalized by its magical tricklings. (Is this an early morning offering to help them ward off the vile and dirty images they will receive in school that day?) But it is this primitive display of patriotism that so ob-

---

[16]Web site address: www.syatp.com

[17]Van Beima, D., & Mitchell, E. (1998, Sept. 28). O, say, can you pray? A grass-roots ritual by young Christians test church and state borders. *Time*, p. 68.

viously longs for a representation of the male organ *important enough* to suture the wounds of students. I read the shootings as a wound that is formative of trauma (after all, trauma is identified by Seltzer as a category that "leaks") in the next few paragraphs (*strictly*) as it relates to the pole. Finally, leaving the pole off to the side, except where it detaches itself and reattaches itself to the trauma and shock evinced by shootings, I read the "sociality of the wound" through Jane Gallop's re-reading of Jacques Lacan's mirror phase. This reading is a bricolage of theories that pieces together some aspects of SYATP ideology in order to sketch out some of the political implications of the group's growing membership.

One way to interpret the necessity of the pole is to accept it as an uncontested symbol of authority in contemporary life. As Kaja Silverman argued, this "dominant fiction" needs the penis and phallus to line up: "Our dominant fiction calls upon the male subject to see himself, and the female subject to recognize and desire him, only through mediated images of an unimpaired masculinity. It urges both the male and female subject, that is, to deny all knowledge of male castration by believing in the commensurability of penis and phallus, actual and symbolic father" (Silverman, 1992, p. 42). The trauma of the shootings and the cognitive dissonance felt by Christians to be the direct result of secularization, as Silverman noted later, smacks of the disposition that screams "your meaning or your life," or rather, "the phallus or your life." This threat of *subjective* destitution, experienced as people believe they are living in the proverbial cultural/spiritual void of late capitalist culture, fuels the need for an authority figure to bring the representations and spiraling identifications of post-Oedipal American culture back under the control of an ordering principle that is rigidly staged in dramatic prayer.[18] What better way to recover a lost father (masculine agency) than to center libidinal energies around a phallic object and assign magical properties to it that compel believers slowly to submit to the various cultural prohibitions that, once accepted as cultural convention, will reinstate a normative masculinity?

The Covenant in the mission statement for the National Youth Ministries demands that assignees submit to "A life of discipleship which is reproducing an on-going chain of maturing believers," whose members will "in turn transfer ministry principles in such a way that they, too, will reproduce themselves." According to the group, then, the students are not yet adult citizens, but are in the developmental phases that lead to the maturity of an ego structure that is responsible and reproductive, *only when mediated through the pole*.

---

[18]The idea to read this event as a challenge to the post-Oedipal was inspired by Diane Rubenstein's unpublished manuscript "Chicks with Dicks: Transgendering the Presidency," which "questions the extent to which the phenomenon commonly referred to as 'Hillary hating/Hillary bashing' is a resentment not so much of Hillary [Rodham Clinton] (or Hillary bashers) but a referendum concerning the possibility of a post-Oedipal feminine identification" (p. 5). I want to test the notion of post-Oedipal masculine identification. This means putting the pole up against the most salient features of the wound.

Prayer circling may then be conceived of as another developmental paradigm whose desired product is the formation of a subjectivity that will enact such responsibility and reproductivity in relation to masculine identification. The egos or "souls" of students who are "saved" in prayer circles are organized around the pole that speaks the word of God. This leads to a false socialization because, if we recall Winnicott's and Klein's theories concerning the developmental role of transitional objects in the emotional lives of children, the authors take great pains to show that the object must be freely chosen by the child in relation to their facilitating environment, which houses the individuals who give them care and love, and that this environment must be consistent and free of indoctrination. It is important that the object represent a real relationship with another person whom the children know and share a bond with, not *mere* metaphysical speculation.

The next logical question is why is the ego made end-in-view? Why reconstitute, as Jane Gallop said, the tragic story of Oedipal organization when one already knows (and is luxuriating in) a culture that prefers and thrives on *slack* representation? If the story is tragic, it is because it can only end in the failure of exacting reproduction, which produces not a stable ego molded along the lines of an idealization but one that is tragic (for Gallop's Lacan), because it is propelled both by *retroactive* moves to contain a bodily image or "self" and by *anticipatory* moves to establish a foundational self from which to progress toward maturity. Working against each other, the two dispositions affect, as Gallup put it, the "violation of the very chronologies" that sustain the subject (Gallop, 1985, p. 80). This temporal disorientation is common in victims of school shootings, as evidenced by their inability to recover a complete memory of the event. Anachronisms abound in wound culture; according to Mark Seltzer, "the basic uncertainty as to what counts as the 'real foundation' of trauma is, first, the wound, it is second, a wounding in the absence of a wound; trauma is in effect an effect in search of a cause" (Seltzer, 1997, p. 9). Thus, the subject's affective history is the history of secondary identifications; the images that do "stick" with the subject must, on Gallop's reading of the mirror stage, be read as the primary ones. Thus, the mirror stage is, to borrow Thomas Keenan's term, the "conceptual hinge" on which the subject swings back and forth until a rigid conceptualization of the self is firmly rooted in an identity that allows it to believe in its totality and to disavow its psychic fragmentation (Keenan, 1997, p. 177).

The conceptualization that provides this static conception of self is the resultant ego that uses its "armor" to shield against the vision of "the body in bits and pieces" (*corps morcelé*; Gallop, 1985, p. 80). Although Lacan read bodily fragmentation as a literal and singular stage (the space in late infancy where the ego's fate is sealed), Gallop allowed for a reading that posits a plurality of stages that do not follow a rigid developmental model, but instead are contingent on "decisive" movements that "project" the subject into the future perfect (trauma?). This opening of Lacan's text by Gallop is crucial to understanding contemporary identifications; the question of the subject can be read through what happens when the subject looks into the mirror (wound), but can no longer "anticipate" a totality smiling back at him or her in the mirror; the subject instead sees only recurring images of "the body in bits and pieces." The mirror stage is, then, a returning staging base for the subject's reactions to (and projections into) historical events (school shootings), in which the body is literally rendered as "bits and pieces" whereas the mind that experiences the events also only recovers "bits and pieces" of those experiences as images. The wound that circulates back and forth among shootings, prayer circling, and witnessing acts as the reverse Gestalt (the prototype that precedes the ego) of the one in Lacan's mirror phase; that is, the wound reflects back at the subject not as an ideal ego, but as an always already-fragmented subject. The identification is primarily with the wound, whereas the pole attaches itself as a useful, but somewhat unnecessary accessory.

There is a collective wound that circulates between shootings that mirrors back at students an unmistakably fragmented subjectivity. As grief filled the first communities affected by the shootings, it soon turned into a school year that witnessed "a steady drumbeat of youthful murders [that] has been like a bandage ripped over and over again from a wound that just won't heal."[19] Beginning with Pearl, Mississippi, and ending with Springfield, Oregon, the open wounds that mark the trauma of school shootings have a discrete beginning and ending signified by the summer hiatus. Throughout the summer, parents and students nationwide lived in fear of the first day back to school. There was an unmistakable collective fear that more shootings would surely follow and, unable to make clear sense out of the incidents, most traumatized victims repeatedly asked the empty and meaningless question "Why [shooter's name]?" in an unrestrained effort to understand the impossibility that always accompanies such a disastrous event. As Seltzer argued, the usual answer to this question places responsibility on an event in the individual's past, such as abuse or neglect—forms of childhood trauma that are easy for the public to digest psychologically while also allowing for the disavowal of collective responsibility. He wrote:

> The assumption that the cause of compulsive violence resides ultimately in childhood trauma has become canonical, in criminological and in popular accounts. This is scarcely surprising. On one level, the recourse to the trauma of child abuse or sexual abuse as explanation follows from twentieth century beliefs that childhood experience forms the adult (that is, the basic premise of psychoanalysis). Such an explanation has become virtually automatic in the literature (factual or fictional) on serial killing, assuming a peculiarly a priori status, even where evidence is conspicuously absent. (Seltzer, 1997, p. 10).[20]

---

[19] Rick Bragg "Past Victims Relieve Pain as Tragedy Is Repeated," *The New York Times*, 25, May 1998, p. A8.

[20] Seltzer, p. 10. The student shooters have been labeled animal torturers and some had been previously accused of abusing other children sexually. The animal torture connection is as tenuous as the childhood experience argument when it is applied to the figure of the serial killer.

In the case of West Paducah, however, the responsibility is temporarily reversed, because Michael Carneal is "one of us." Explanations for the shooting all work to leave the wound open; interpretation is closure and this is refused by the community in order to reclaim the responsibility for a collective healing process operationalized in prayer circles. In order to have the wound, they have to assume responsibility for it, like a memorial or totem. One may read the series of shootings, up to Springfield, Oregon, as provocative, leading more students on to adopt the strategy of prayer as an attempt to formulate a collective belief structure that serves to reinforce the individual ego, or what Silverman calls the "*moi*." Reading the interpellative act through trauma, Silverman views the process as one by which a subject misrecognizes his or her "self" in the address. Like Gallop's shattering of the mirror phase into several repetitive stagings that either push the subject toward or pull the subject away from an ego, Silverman's re-reading of interpellation as failed ontological quest provokes her to question the surfacing of the ego in popular films that follow traumas inflicted on masculinity after World War II. Like Silverman's filmed analogies, SYATP acts as a restorative (curative?) practice designed by participants to remain in traumatic suspension, consulting the wounding mirror over and over again as the shootings continue to erupt throughout the year.

Until Littleton, there was no doubt that all the shootings were linked both in the media and through friendships formed via traumatic sharing sessions. Victims of the shootings became pen pals as prayer circle membership increased. Newspapers worried about the coverage of traumatic events like school shootings because they involved and affected "children," and never questioned the nostalgic binary that separates childhood from adulthood in their response. After all, such shootings are traumatic because they are about kids killing kids, or is it that the kids no longer believe in the authority and power of adults to fight them in good faith and so they turn to God for that needed containment? According to Juliet Flower MacCannell's thesis in *The Regime of the Brother*, 20th-century fascism, especially the Holocaust, eroded the confidence and trust that children had in their parents to protect and guide them. The governmental structure of fascist regimes, even fascist policies that may operate on temporary basis under democratic control, undermine the parental role in order to garner power for the regime and make all citizens dependent on it for survival. As she wrote, "[Yet] fascism had stubbornly demonstrated the fragility of the parents, their vulnerability, their powerlessness. The Holocaust structurally reversed the parent–child relation. It did so to serve fascism aggressive narcissistic ends: to be itself the survivor and the master, replacing the weak and feeble parents for good" (Flower MacCannell, 1993, p. 14). As social service and now media intrusions into the family abound and demonstrate to the public the weakness of the American family, no matter what form it takes, it continually represents this image of parental *lack*.

As SYATP's popularity indicates, students can also no longer trust public school officials (or adults in general) to take charge of either the healing or the prevention of incidents like the shooting at Heath High School in West Paducah, Kentucky. Instead, they organize their fears and healing according to the designs of youth ministers who have in turn placed trust in a God to come; no more politics, no more community. Perhaps this reaction makes a good point about schooling and politics. Jamon Kent, the superintendent of schools in Springfield, Oregon, admitted that school administrators, *because of the nature of their training*, could never imagine implementing the trauma care that other unofficial organizations contributed in the aftermath of the Thurston High School shooting.[21] The wish for authority in this country looms large on the horizon, and religion is one of the only actors capable of fulfilling it (perhaps excepting the police). Trauma victims at rallies have claimed to be reassured, even in a community church, only by targeting a police officer's uniform in the room. As they give their witnessing speeches, students affected by school shootings still long for the authority of the state to be present in a public forum to stave off the agoraphobia that sets in after having been assaulted in school.

But there are also intolerant positions adopted in relation to the government's efforts to provide protection from further public assaults, positions that are motivated by anger and hatred. In a direct move against the Clinton administration's "Zero Tolerance Policy" concerning guns, many SYATP members have claimed that the schools enact a similar zero tolerance policy concerning prayer, and some of these SYATP members even support the NRA when they make this statement. Several recent events, most notably the murder of Matthew Shepard, have brought many involved in SYATP out against hate crime legislation, arguing (in the most twisted form of logic yet) that it is a direct attack on prayer in school. Their opposition to hate crimes legislation, they claim, brings on them unwarranted oppression against their status as Christians. (Are we seeing Nietzsche's democracy at work yet?) Each time a new trauma takes place, the group resutures itself to the wound in a way that allows for visibility and coherence to support their basic practical doctrines, such as prayer, *even if the tragedy is in no way linked* to previous ones. Now in a position of semi-symbolic power, prayer groups seek to protect the gains they have made from the tragedies at schools in the last several years. They need shooters and they need the "permissive" culture that nourishes them in order to maintain a stranglehold on school policy concerning the First Amendment. Each and every time the Left capitulates to this logic of violent culture, they give the radical Right another inch from the already-open door that leads down the road to a reanimation of parochial masculinity. This movement is already reclaiming the political community and using the subjective destitution felt by students to accomplish its goals. The crowning event, however, that would open this wound completely and tear apart the idea of civil society among youth, was Littleton, Colorado.

---

[21]Kent, J. (1995, Oct. 15). *School Violence Prevention, Part 2* [video]. C-SPAN Archives.

REFERENCES

Apple, M. W. (2002). Interrupting the right: On doing critical educational work in conservative times. *Symploke, 10*(1–2), 133–152.

Barnes, C. A., & Martin-Morris, D. (1998, September). I was shot at school: Personal narrative of a school shooting incident. *Teen Magazine.*

Bartleman, B. (1999, December 2). Confessed killer can't explain deadly rampage. *The Paducah Sun.*

Belkin, L. (1999, October 31). Parents blaming parents. *The Times Magazine* (New York).

Bernstein, M. (1999, March 6). Court restricts psychiatrist's opinion of Kinkel. *The Oregonian.*

Caruth, C. (Ed.). (1995). *Trauma: Explorations in memory.* Baltimore, MD: The Johns Hopkins University Press.

Deleuze, G., & Guattari, F. (1983). *Anti-Oedipus: Capitalism and schizophrenia.* (R. Hurley, M. Seem, & H. R. Lane, Trans.). Minneapolis: University of Minnesota Press. (Original work published 1977)

Edelman, M. (1992). The construction and uses of social problems. In W. Chaloupka, & W. Stearns (Eds.), *Jean Baudrillard: The disappearance of art and politics.* New York: St. Martin's.

Flower-MacCannell, J. (1993). *The regime of the brother.* New York: Routledge.

Fortgang, E. (1999, June 10). How they got the guns. *Rolling Stone Magazine, 51.*

Fraser, J. W. (1999). *Between church and state: Religion and public education in a multicultural America.* New York: St. Martin's Press.

Frontline. (1999). The killer at Thurston High, videotape presentation.

Gallop, J. (1985). *Reading Lacan.* Ithaca, NY: Cornell University Press.

James, W. (1975). *Pragmatism and the meaning of truth.* Cambridge, MA: Harvard University Press.

Keenan, T. (1997). *Fables of responsibility.* Palo Alto, CA.: Stanford University Press.

Labi, N. (1998, April 6). The hunter and the choir boy. *Time Magazine.*

Lacan, J. (1981). *The four fundamental concepts of psycho-analysis.* (A. Sheridan, Trans.). New York: W.W. Norton. (Original work published 1973)

Laplanche, J., & Pontalis, J. B. (1973). *The language of psycho-analysis.* (D. Nicholson- Smith, Trans.). New York: Norton.

McLaren, P. (1995). *Critical pedagogy and predatory culture.* New York: Routledge.

Morrione, D. D. (2002). *Sublime monsters and virtual children.* Unpublished doctoral dissertation. Lafayette, IN: Purdue University.

Rauch, A. (1998). Post-traumatic hermeneutics: Melancholia in the wake of trauma. *Diacritics, 28*(4), 111–120.

Seltzer, M. (1997). Wound culture: Trauma in the pathological public sphere. *October, 80,* 3–26.

Silverman, K. (1992). *Male subjectivity at the margins.* London: Routledge.

Sullivan, R. (1998, September, 17). A boy's life: Kip Kinkel and the Springfield, Oregon shooting, Part I. *Rolling Stone Magazine.*

From adolescent angst to school shootings: Patterns in the rage. (1998, July 14). *The New York Times,* p. A1.

Van Beima, D., & Mitchell, E. (1999, September). O, say, can you pray? A grass-roots ritual by Young Christians Test Church and state borders. *Time, 28.*

Wenner, J. (1999, June 10). Guns and violence. *Rolling Stone Magazine,* 45–49.

Wilkinson, P., & Hendrickson M. (1999, June 10). Humiliation and revenge: The Story of Reb and VoDKa. *Rolling Stone Magazine,* 49–51.

Zerelli, L. (1998). Doing without knowing. *Political Theory, 26*(4), 435–458.

Chapter 6

Stumbling Inside Dis/Positions:
The (un)home of Education

Marla Morris (Text)
Georgia Southern University

Mary Aswell Doll (Commentary)
Savannah College of Art and Design

Thinking Beyond

Marla Morris states that she is doing curriculum in a "different key" or perhaps a different line of flight. Morris considers her curriculum theorizing heretical, because she "continually rethinks and redoes her (un)frames of reference." She, as we suggest, dis/positions herself. She terms her work in this chapter as "indirect-mystical-autotheological." She elaborates a personal spiritual journey to find a third space in which to do curriculum theorizing; a space that is other than "home."

Questions

1. In what ways is Mary Aswell Doll's commentary throughout Morris' chapter integral to creating curriculum theory in a "different key"?
2. How does Morris reconceive what it means to do curriculum theorizing? How is the working through of our traditions part of finding a third space?
3. How do Morris' conceptualizations of spirituality and autotheology compare with concepts of spirituality discussed by Webber and McKnight? How is spirituality interconnected with curriculum theorizing?

My work as a curriculum theorist has taken a turn toward what Harold Bloom (1996) called "spiritual autobiography" (p. 13). I am, however, not doing "spirituality" and I am not doing "autobiography." In *Understanding Curriculum* (1995), William Pinar, William Reynolds, Patrick Slattery, and Peter Taubman suggested that curriculum scholars may understand their work as "theological text." That is not exactly what I am doing. Pinar et al. (1995) also suggested that curriculum workers might understand curriculum studies as "autobiographical text." That is not exactly what I am doing either. I find myself undone, without a home of self. Am I (un)home in education?

Following Derrida's (1993) work in *Circumfession* (a piece that alters language in an attempt to rethink the ways in which confessionals are written), I work to undo the positioning of my self-in-the-field, to dis/position my (un)self and my (un)place within the larger sphere of curriculum work. I call my dis/position indirect-mystical-autotheology. I am indirectly speaking about stumbling against the grain of mystical heresies and against the grain

83

of my own life work in the field of curriculum studies. Through encounters with mystical heresies, the leap to the third space—the middle place, the nothingness of instability—allows questions to emerge that might loosen disciplining shackles. I am, therefore, doing curriculum work in a different key.

This chapter is an attempt to grapple with three stumblings, three kinds of mystical adventures that allow questions to be raised around curriculum dis/positioning. I examine briefly Sikhism and Sufism until I stumble toward my (un)home of Jewish mysticism. Educators curious about getting (un)framed, getting outside the frame of their discipline, might rethink and reconsider the "ways" and "whys" academics get stuck in lines of research.

STUMBLING ABANDONMENTS

I began writing this chapter 10 years ago and stopped. For some odd reason, I could not get on with the writing and I could not make connections with what I had written. I put the pen and paper down. Ten years later, the paper has actually yellowed. David Smith reminded us that "Matisse once said of his paintings: 'I never finish them, I just abandon them.' Such abandonment may be the only means through which what genuinely can find its life, but it requires very careful understanding. Certainly abandonment cannot mean a giving up of our deepest human responsibilities" (1999, p. 11). Looking back, I now understand that I stumbled into obscurities as a way to cover over my own life, or perhaps I was trying to uncover my life indirectly. But the indirect path was so deeply unconscious that I could not see what was in front of me. I was avoiding myself. Paradoxically, the deep avoidance of self has led me, 10 years later, toward my flight of heretical dis/positioning in curriculum studies, a heretical discipline within the field of education.

During the 1980s, I was the master of avoiding myself, and I avoided myself through studying—studying subject matters that did not matter to me, studying subject matters that covered over my matter, my unconscious, my screen matter, screening memories, memories still deep and buried, troubled. I studied Sikhism and Sufism. I studied William James and Mircea Eliade. I studied Hildegard of Bingen. I simply couldn't bear studying my own heretical tradition, Jewish mysticism. And I certainly did not question my own faulty education, faulty in its (un)Jewish moorings. The fault lines of a Greek, Christian, secular wandering further exiled me from an understanding of who I was as an American Jew, three generations after the Holocaust. *I began writing this chapter 10 years ago but stopped. I studied myself out of myself. I became the obscurantism I studied. I swam in the murky waters. I drowned in the murkiness of the unconscious. The three horses (id, ego, superego) led me downstream: "Oh lost, and by the wind grieved, ghost, come back again" (Wolfe, 1957, n.p.). And then the silence set in. The world came to a standstill. I read in Ezekiel that he remained silent for many years. Some say he suffered from a sort of paranoid schizophrenic paralysis.*

Studying curriculum theory and its intersections with psychoanalysis, I have been able to articulate my stumblings, at least some of them. I have written elsewhere (Morris, 2001) about these difficulties. It is much easier to study someone else's traditions than one's own. It is easier for me to study Christian mysticism or Sufism, for example, because I have little emotional stake in either. But to stumble toward my (un)home undoes my sense of self and creates an instability and anxiety about continual resistance to myself. Studying with Bill Pinar has helped me to rethink this resistance and begin to grapple with doing with what I term *indirect-mystical-auto-theology*. My encounters at the Bergamo Conference with many heretical curriculum workers, and my personal connections with intellectuals like Alan Block, have helped me to look at my own tradition, my own heresies. My encounter with Philip Wexler, his urging me on toward my Jewish sensibility, has also helped me stumble toward an uncanny no-place of the Jewish educator heretic. Mary Aswell Doll has continually urged me to think about the text of self against the backdrop of education and the mythopoetic divine. *Curriculum scholarship is not just about reading texts. If the world is truly text then our personal encounters are textual. Contextualizing our work in the face to face, is what Buber called encountering God.*

(UN)METHODOLOGICAL "QUEERIES"

There are several methodological "queeries," or puzzles, that are troubling when one attempts to think about treating different heretical traditions. Exegetical studies tend toward formalism and decontextualization. My first attempt at studying Sikhism and Sufism tended toward this kind of formalist reading. Doing a close reading has its advantages. The inquiry demands that one pay careful attention to textual matters. Close textual readings require a slowness in attention. One must attend to detail. As Jane Gallop (2000) pointed out, close readings might lend toward reading the "trivial" more carefully because worlds can be found in what is usually ignored or glossed over. In *The Journal of Curriculum Theorizing*, Gallop (2000) noted that when she teaches her students, she tells them that there are five ways to do a close reading. Much to my surprise, my reading of Sikhsim and Sufism 10 years ago mirrored Gallop's suggestions. In particular, two of the suggestions Gallop made for doing a close reading resonate with my own textual analysis. She argued that close readings might include looking for "words that seem unnecessarily repeated, as if the word keeps insisting on being written; (2) images or metaphors, especially ones that are used repeatedly and are somewhat surprising in the context ..." (2000, p. 7). Although a close reading, or a more formalist approach, may open up worlds previously glossed over, the scope of inquiry can become too narrow. In the field of biblical studies, many still treat texts in a more formalist approach. I call this methodology "spinning around the head of a pin." And decontextual studies can become problematic when the larger cultural and historical backdrop of the text becomes overshadowed. Spiders spinning in small places cannot see the larger world around them and may get squashed from oncoming traffic in culture. Surely, it becomes harder to understand what the text is saying if it is cut off from the broader horizon of culture.

If one is doing a more comparative approach, one begins to look for "this" and "that," across cultures and traditions. Comparative studies tend to lead one to conclude that similarities, archetypes, or structures overshadow differences, contingencies, and uniquenesses. Comparative studies still wedded to versions of structuralism may incorrectly assume that "this *is* that," but a more poststructural read highlights difference, paradox, contingency, and uniqueness between and across traditions. Poststructural approaches, even if comparative, may allow scholars to point out patterns—that "this" and "that" are similar. Comparative approaches that are basically structural or archetypal can become misleading and reductionistic. Bernard McGinn explained: "Those comparativists who would identify mysticism with the common core or inner unity found in all the varied manifestations of religions around the globe, as well as philosophers who debate the nature of mystical experience apart from its historical and contextual location, have contributed to this common misunderstanding..." (1965/1996). Comparative approaches can become problematic, in other words, if it is thought that mystical experience and understanding are the same for all, that there is an essence to mystical knowing.

Mystical knowing and understanding, on the contrary, are tied to historical, sociological, cultural traditions, and thus there can be no essence to mystical experience. Sikhs, Sufis, and Jewish mystical teachers crossed paths, and border crossings made these heresies possible. One simply cannot understand Jewish thinking without understanding the Muslim influence on Jewish thought or the Jewish influence on Muslim thought. Some argue that Sikhism developed out of the Sant tradition, so it is important to at least grapple with those intersections. Lines of thought are not born in a vacuum. For instance, poststructural readings foster a sensibility suggesting that "this" isn't "that" because "this" is contexualized within a unique historicity and culture and "that" is also contextualized within a unique historicity and culture.

Thus, comparisons between and within mysticisms become necessary, as long as the uniqueness of the tradition is embraced. It is a superficial treatment to suggest that at the end of the day all mysticisms are the same; clearly, they are not. Moshe Idel suggested that "Only a balanced combination of textual and comparative approaches to kabbalistic [and I would add Sikh and Sufi mysticism] material will contribute to a better formulation of the unique nature of certain kabbalistic views" (1988, p. 24). Taking Idel's lead, I suggest that doing a comparative analysis (which is poststructural) allows me to better situate myself within the broader context of Jewish mystical heresy as a curriculum worker.

I consider my curriculum theorizing heretical in the sense that I continually rethink and redo my (un)frames of reference, I continually question and (un)settle my line of re/search, to re-search again and again without falling into the trap of stuntedness. These (un)methodological "queeries" attempt to queer the boundaries between and across mystical heresy and curriculum work. Undoing my own method over the past 10 years, undoing my search for repetitions in search of sames, has been a difficult struggle. Trying to (re)write the sameness, or perhaps do a meta-analysis on what I wrote 10 years ago, is one way to question my own presuppositions. Thus, in the first section of this chapter I offer an old text as well as a text on top of that text, a midrash, a commentary that illuminates where my thinking has taken a turn via curriculum work. This is an act of schizophrenic re-reading and then stumbling into the present text, the current work of re-membering my Jewish mystical heretical curriculum work. *Reading backwards. Re-reading my mistaken presuppositions. (I wrote a short paper 10 years ago on Sikhism and Sufism that was never published.)*

SIKHISM AND MIDRASH

Noss, Parrinder, and De Barry suggested that Sikhism is syncretistic, incorporating both Hindu and Muslim beliefs (Cole & Sambhi, 1978). W. H. McLeod (1989), however, contended that Sikhism was not, in fact, intended to be syncretistic at all. Guru Nanak, the founder of Sikhism, reacted against Hindu and Muslim traditions, claiming that both were inherently problematic. McLeod (1989) argued that Sikhism may be traced to the tradition of the North Indian Sants. Nanak, noted McLeod, gave "clear expression" (p. 7) to Sant doctrine. According to McLeod, the Sants were opposed to many of the same forms of piety that Guru Nanak reacted against: "The Sant would have nothing to do with incarnationism, [the doctrine of collapsing the self with god, I-am-God] idol worship ... pilgrimages ... [b]ecause these were typically performed as exterior acts of piety.... The Sant could have no truck with the Hatha—yoga ... nor with their stress on harsh severity" (1989, pp. 7–8). Like the Sants, Sikhs do not believe in incarnationism nor idol worship, pilgrimages, and exterior forms of piety, and Guru Nanak rejected ascetic practices.

Not all scholars agree with McLeod's position, however. Karine Schomer (1987), and Nikky Singh (1993) posited that the Sikhs, in many ways, differ from the Sants. And because of these differences, it becomes problematic to trace Sikhism to the Sants (Singh, 1993). Nikky Singh claimed that Kabir, one of the most famous Sants, was misogynistic. In the writings of Kabir, one finds a deep hatred for women. Nanak, on the other hand, was in no way misogynistic. If anything, he was a fighter for women's rights. Furthermore, Singh pointed out that Mcleod was incorrect to say that Sants did not practice ascetism, because they did. And this, according to Singh, drives the wedge deeper between Sants and Sikhs. It is clear that the Sikhs did indeed develop out of the Sant tradition but, over time, changed, modified, and eventually became a unique religious tradition.

The Sikhs also seem to have many affinities with Islamic mysticism, Sufism. Certainly, Sufism was pervasive in the Punjab region during Nanak's lifetime.

Sufis and Sikhs were in contact with one another, and in some ways did influence one another. Patterns of affinities clearly exist in primary sources. Similar patterns of conceptualizations of the divine may be traced between the Sikh scripture, especially in the *Sri Guru Granth*, and the writings of a North Indian Sufi named Sharafuddin b. Yahya Maneri.

Midrash Metatext

what was I thinking?
why the obscure
references?
why such a narrow textual
reading?
A Sikh in a turban
driving a BMW
through the streets of Sante Fe,
New Mexico. Trying
to make sense
of her life, of
my connection to the
opera singer
turned Sikh. This
chapter had little to do with my own
life but more with trying to
understand how
my friend had
abandoned the world
of music and
entered the obscure life
of the Guru. This was The
generation of the Beats,
Allen Ginsberg, The Doors,
and Jimmy
Hendrix. But I was still too
young for all
of that. My friends all
40-something
abandoned
the world for ashrams
and monasteries.
Where would
I go? To the Synagogue?
Not likely.

Where do you go
when you are queer
and Jewish?
I found my (un)home
in curriculum theory,
in the academy. I
live a monastic
life in my office, studying,
like Rabbis of old
bent
over Talumudic
texts. Metatron the
Angel does
metatextual analysis
of her re-memory.

Sikh scripture, the *Guru Granth*, complied by Arjan Dev, the 5th Guru, contains writings of Ram Das, Arjan Dev, and Guru Nanak, to name a few. For Sikhs, the *Guru Granth* is the authoritative word, the Final Guru. Sikhs do not worship the Gurus, but worship the book, the *Guru Granth*. The *Guru Granth* is difficult to deconstruct because of its poetic structure. In a sense, then, the *Granth* defies classification. It is a book of the heart, not of the intellect, although it is intellectually terse. The *Guru Granth* describes God as both transcendent and immanent. On the transcendent side, God is "formless ... inexpressible" (*Sri Guru Granth*, 1988, p. 1). God is "one essence" (p. 11), "one reality" (p. 60). God is the supreme being, the timeless one. On the immanent side, God is "pervasive completely in the universe" (p. 53). God is, in fact, "ever present in the hearts of those with noble qualities" (p. 62). God is the "annuller of suffering" (p. 28).

God is called many things, named many names. "Innumerable are God's names" (*Sri Guru Granth*, 1988, p. 10). God is "holy, holy is his name" (p. 3). God is called the "immaculate" (p. 3). God is called "all dieties, Shiva, Vishnu, Brahma, the goddesses Parabati, Lakshmi, Sarasvati" (p. 4). God incorporates both female and male, yet transcends engendered creatures. Finally, God is "unknowable as the ocean" (p. 12). God is ultimately, unnameable. God is both "unattributive" (transcendent) and attributed"/immanent" (p. 203).

Mid(rush)

Marla, Mary here.
What are you Seeking?
Where is the Sikh?
I'm 60-something and
your Granth God is

driving me m.a.d. (My
initials). God: Where's my Groth? My holy, holy
white wine. You make me
Whine.

Like the God-of-process theologians in the West (Whitehead, Cobb, Griffin, Hartshorne), the God of Sikhism is a dynamic God, a process moving within humankind, pervasive within the hearts of people, yet transcendent and eternal. The Sikh God is one with whom devotees become wholly absorbed: "As the fish, I find the life of absorption in the water that is God" (*Sri Guru Granth*, 1988, p. 166). As the fish is absorbed in the water that is God, the soul is absorbed in the lightness that is God. The fish, even though absorbed in the water that is God, does not lose its fishness, its fish identity-formation, even though absorbed in the light that is God. A pan*en*theistic system, such as Sikhsim, allows the soul to retain its soulness while merging with God. The soul, in other words, is not identical with God, even after merging with God, but one might say God is part of the soul. A strict identity soul = God is incarnationism and this is considered anathema in Sikhism. The *Granth* uses the beloved/lover metaphor for the relation of the self to God. God is the beloved and the devotee is the lover. The lover retains her identity yet merges with her beloved.

Contrasted to the Vedantic theological writings of Hindu writer Shankara, one notes the difficulties of collapsing self and God. Pantheism troubles the waters. Shankara described the *Atman* (soul)/*Brahman* (God) relation as a strict identity, *Atman = Brahaman*. When Shankara says "*Atman = Brahman*," is he not saying "I am God?" If the only reality is *Atman-Brahman*, the phenomenal world, strictly speaking, does not exist. My body is an illusion if I am the body of God. Furthermore, if *Atman = Brahman*, is *Brahman* evil? Accounting for evil in pantheistic systems becomes problematic. If *Brahman* is evil, who needs a God like that?

Unlike Vendantic theology, Sikhism, by maintaining a pan*en*theistic system, safeguards against these problems. The soul retains its aloneness, yet it is webbed within the larger ecosphere and sphere of the divine. The phenomenal world exists, although it is difficult to say what it feels like to live in the middle of phenomena. The problem of evil is humankind's problem because God gives us free will. Therefore, God is not evil. Human beings make choices and those choices can lead to good or evil.

Midrash Metatext

Continually bogged down
in texts. That is where I would
like to stay. Lost in the struggle
to understand density. To remain
in the marsh. Mary is annoyed

at the density and must rush
through it. Where is the space,
the breathing space? I can't
stand the heavy spaces.
But we are different, I am lost
in the density but reader you
might want to rush through, cut
to the chase. Sinking, though,
is where work gets worked
through.

The soul in the realm of the phenomenal must proceed with caution. The world is mired in a "marsh of illusion" (*Sri Guru Granth*, 1988, p. 30). The *Granth* suggests that one must not get bogged down in the phenomenal realm and became attached to material objects and worldliness. One must continually struggle to extricate one's soul from marshiness. However, this detachment does not mean abandoning responsibility in the world. One foot must remain worldly. What is bad is attachment to worldly things. If one gets stuck in worldliness, "sinking" (*Sri Guru Granth*, 1988, p. 60) is certain. Instead, "dying to the world" (p. 30), dying to worldly things, becomes the path, the process out of transmigration. Transmigration for the Sikhs is not the goal. One does not want to be reincarnated, one does not want to have to do it over again, because one wants to finally merge with God. Thus, "Thoughtless it is to settle down in the world" (*Sri Guru Granth*, 1988, p. 133). Rather, one ought to settle down in God, because God is the eternal, whereas the world is "A dream … in an instant it is over" (p. 43).

Settling down in God, attaining unity with God, may be achieved by contemplation, meditation, and devotion. Contemplating the words of the *Guru Granth* leads one closer to God, Sikhs tell us. Taking in, psychologically, the words of holy scripture illuminates. By "absorbing holy teaching" (*Sri Guru Granth*, 1988, pp. 5–6), one dwells in the presence of the divine. By absorbing holy teaching, one becomes filled with "truthfulness, contentment, and spiritual fulfillment" (pp. 5–6). Contemplation, although an intellectual function, is ultimately a loving contemplation. A loving knowing, then, is centered within the heart. Attachment to overintellectualization becomes disastrous. Intellectualization, as Anna Freud pointed out, serves as a defense mechanism and may cover over the uncanny feelings one has in the face of the divine.

Mid(rush)

Marla, Mary here. Are
you in the marsh? Still?
Moving or still in the

marsh? That must be
awful. To be bogged
down is awful. Full of awe.
Divine.

   Meditation on the name of God is one of the most powerful experiences of
dwelling in God's presence. *Nam Simran*, or remembering the name of God,
by repetition of God's name, is the path toward the divine. By meditating on
God's name (*Nam Simran*), one becomes absorbed in God entering "the supreme state" (*Sri Guru Granth*, 1988, p. 141). Here one experiences "unity"
and "bliss" (p. 139). A higher state of meditation *Ajapa japa* (spontaneous
meditation), allows one to achieve a lightness of being in unity with God.
Spontaneous meditation is done effortlessly and is "rare" (p. 30). Not many
can reach this advanced stage of meditation. What makes spontaneous meditation difficult is the ego. The ego tends to get in the way of one's relation with
the divine. Thus, it becomes important to work on the "malady of egoism" (p.
67): "In egoism … is the world robbed of devotion to God" (p. 45).
   It is not enough to meditate on God, one must be completely devoted to
God—"Devotion to God is love for him" (p. 64). As the lover is devoted to
the beloved, so too is the devotee devoted to God. Sikhism is a religion of
the heart. God's presence must be felt within the heart. Devotees, however,
must be graced by God to escape transmigration. It is ultimately only by
God's grace that "some are exalted" (p. 1)—"Some by God's ordinance are
whirled around in cycles of births and death" (p. 1).

Midrash Metatext

Sounds like Double
Predestination. Why
would I bother with this?
Why was I hiding in this
close reading, this painful
exegesis? While living in
the French Quarter I
bought a long black robe
which I wore around my
pathetic apartment.
Reading sacred texts and
vampires novels, I was
trying to forget my past.
I was trying to forget.

   Those who do not do good deeds, act, in a sense, against God. Sikhism,
thus, has an action-centered ethic: "With good acts alone is wisdom per-

fected" (*Sri Guru Granth*, 1988, p. 56). Although attachment to the world is bad, one must not renounce the world either. Renouncing the world is, in essence, fleeing social responsibility. Underlying all virtuous activities, said Guru Nanak, are "sweetness and humility" (*Sri Guru Granth*, 1988, p. 470). Nanak noted that sweetness and humility are the greatest of all virtues. Compassion, modesty, and contentment flow from sweetness and humility. It is not enough to be lost in God, one must also do good deeds to become what the Sikhs term "God-filled."

SUFISM AND MIDRASH

Trends in early Sufism (690 CE) tended to be contradictory. Some trends stressed severe asceticism, fasting, abandoning the world and seclusion; other trends suggested love and devotion; still others focused on ethics (Nurbakhsh, 1983). One of the most famous Sufi masters, Muhad-Bin ebn Arabi, stressed unity of being (Nurbakhsh, 1983). Later Sufis, like Nizam Ad-din Awliya (1292–1325), focused on renunciation of attachment to worldliness, but without renouncing the world per se (Nizam, 1992).

Different orders of Sufism presented puzzling differences. For instance, the Qadiriyya order emphasized purification of self, whereas the Chistiyya order stressed love, devotion, and ethics (Valiuddin, 1988). The Naqshbandiyya order is famous for its emphasis on *Yad dasht,* or spontaneous remembrance of God (Valuiddin, 1988). Although trends vary much within Sufism, there are also some common themes running throughout. Generally speaking, Julian Baldick noted that Sufism "emphasizes love of God. The Sufis are … perpetually engaged in remembrance (dikhr).… Sufism also constitutes a path (tariga) which begins with repentance and leads through … 'stations' … [that] culminate in 'passing away'; (fana) of the mystic … the survival (baga) of the … transformed personality" (1989, p. 3). The goal of the Sufi is to attain unity with God (*Tawid*).

Mid(rush)

> *Mary here. The*
> *names, naming. Naqshbandiyya,*
> *Muhamd-Bin ebn*
> *Arabi. I could write*
> *a poem. Names. I*
> *am lost in the*
> *naming. Hour*
> *divine!*

Doing a close reading of *The Hundred Letters* of Sharafuddin Maneri, (1283/1980), the famous North Indian Sufi mystic, I have come to find many patterns of images of the divine that echo the texts of the *Granth*. Maneri's descriptions of God are many. Most fundamentally, however, he described God as both transcendent and immanent. On the transcendent side, Maneri suggested that God is the creator of all, "eternal in both his essence and his attributes" (1980, p. 175). God is the "unique being" (p. 13). Because God is a unique being, he is "infinitely greater than any man" (p. 13). The creator God, who is a unique being, is eternally greater than humankind, transcending our horizon. However, God is also immanent, pervasive within the world, within human hearts. God is everywhere: "As a notable Sufi has said: I have not looked at anything without seeing the Lord in it" (Maneri, 1980, p. 57). God is immanent, pervasive in the world in the form of a "dazzling divine light ... that exists within every particle" (pp. 12–13).

Midrash Metatext

> *Holy sparks. It was my encounter with*
> *Philip Wexler at*
> *the University of Rochester*
> *that made me stumble toward*
> *the (un)home of*
> *Jewish mysticism.*
> *His text Holy Sparks*
> *sparked my interest in*
> *the intersections of*
> *Jewish mystical*
> *heresy and*
> *curriculum theorizing.*
> *Reading backwards, I*
> *see that my work*
> *on Sufism already*
> *began the discussion*
> *on dazzling divine light....*
> *That is what holy sparks are.*
> *Jews live in*
> *a broken world,*
> *always already exiled.*
> *Exiled inside and outside*
> *of the academy.*
> *At the time I wrote*
> *this brief essay on Sufism*
> *I had no idea of the*
> *connections*
> *with my own*
> *heretical tradition.*

God moves through the hearts of Sufis who become "absorbed in God" (Maneri, 1980, p. 67). Like many passages in the *Granth*, romantic imagery (lover/beloved) also runs throughout Maneri's letters: "Everyone who would penetrate further into the wall of love and will receive great delight and preeminence from the face of the beloved ... for he is the beloved of souls and the desired of hearts" (Maneri, 1980, p. 109). Maneri stressed that Sufis must be careful not to fall into the trap of incarnationism. He wrote that the "I," although a part of God, is not identical to God. The self is the "microcosm" of the "macrocosm" (p. 175). Furthermore, Maneri noted that "it is not true that a person becomes God, for God is infinitely greater" (pp. 12–13).

Maneri's brand of Sufism teaches that the phenomenal world is real but dangerous if one becomes attached to it. Attachment to the phenomenal realm only distracts the self from attaining unity (*Tawid*) with God. Maneri provided counsel: "Those immersed in the affairs of the world should not sink lower into them, but rise to the pinnacle of detachment" (p. 16). Like the ethical teachings of Guru Nanak, Maneri taught that detachment from the world does not mean indifference to the world. Detachment means not getting wrapped up in material pursuits and ambitions. Maneri's ethic, like Nanak's, is action centered. A Sufi must be capable of applying "truths to real life situations" (Maneri, 1980, p. 105). Thus, in one sense, a Sufi lives in the world as a social activist, yet is detached from worldly things. Sufis, like Sikhs, generally do not stand for oppression. Both are fighters for social justice: "A Sufi is impelled to action by his heart" (Maneri, 1980, p. 99).

Tawid, or unity with God, may be attained by mystical knowledge (gnosis) and meditation. Gnosis, in this sense, is a secret knowing opened to Sufis and is "the very essence of the souls of believers" (Maneri, 1980, p. 175). Gnosis, however, is not completely intellectual; it also involves the heart: "O Brother, mystical knowledge is the seed of love!" (Maneri, 1980, p. 105). Moreover, mystical knowledge is dependent on God's grace. It is by God's "ordinance" (Maneri, 1980, p. 167) that some will attain *Tawid* whereas others will not.

Another path toward God is found in meditation on the divine name of God, *Dikhr*. The concept of *Dikhr* is quite similar to the Sikh concept *Nam Simran*, remembrance of the divine name. Both Sufis and Sikhs engage in repeated chants to become one with God. Advanced Sufis "exert themselves so in meditation ... nothing else finds access to their hearts" (Maneri, 1980, p. 69). Higher states of meditation are considered to be spontaneous. *Yad dasht*, then, or constant remembrance, is the higher path to *Tawid*, unity. Similarly for Sikhs, *Ajapa japa*, or spontaneous remembrance, is also an advanced type of effortless connection to the divine. Again, we find that one of the difficulties in becoming completely absorbed in God is egoism. Maneri noted "Verily, it is important to clear one's ego out of the way" (1980, p. 53). An emptying out of the ego is referred to as a "passing away of the ego." The transformed person, the one who remains, becomes filled with God.

Midrash Metatext

> *Mirroring texts is one way*
> *to read. Looking for*
> *patterns. But these two*
> *traditions are vastly*
> *different from each other.*
> *Sufi Muslims are Muslim.*
> *Why couldn't I see that*
> *before? Why is it so*
> *hard to understand*
> *difference? Why work on*
> *Sufism? Perhaps the*
> *attraction to social justice?*
> *This has always already been*
> *part of my heretical backdrop.*
> *Perhaps Sufi texts were just*
> *sitting there in the library waiting*
> *for me to pick them up and begin*
> *browsing. I had made*
> *a methodological error in my*
> *close reading. I framed these*
> *lines of thought as mirrors.*
> *Now I must shatter that mirror,*
> *undo my methodology, and*
> *admit that this has been a failed*
> *attempt at understanding the*
> *Other.*

JEWISH MYSTICAL HERESY

Scholars argued that there are indeed connections between Sufism and Jewish mysticism, as well as other modes of thought. Whose mystical heresy was first? Gnostics, Jew, Christians, Muslims? Who influenced whom? Harold Bloom suggested that Jewish mysticism is webbed in a "tangle" of influences: "Kabbalah, with all its speculative grandeur, nevertheless, could not resolve its tangle of curiously mixed sources: ancient Jewish theurgies, Neoplatonism, Gnosticism, Sufism, and perhaps Christian elements" (1996, p. 215). Z'ev ben Shimon Halevi stated, "This system [Kabbalah] is an amalgam of ancient Jewish teaching, Babylonian and Persian cosmology, and many other influences such as the gnostics and Sufis. The strongest outside factor is neo-platonism ..." (1985, p. 38). Daniel Matt (1996) commented that it was Abraham Abulafia, a Jewish mystic associated with what is called the "ecstatic strand" of Kabbalah, who "may have been influenced by Sufism and yoga" (p. 13) and injected traces of Sufism into Kabbalah in the 13th century. Perle Epstein argued the reverse, she claimed that Abulafia "influenced the Moslem Sufis" (1978, p. 85). Moshe Idel (1988) posited that during the 13th century an "encounter took place between the ecstatic Kabbalah of Abraham Abulafia and Sufi elements, apparently in Galilee" (p. 15).

Mid(rush)

> *Marla, Mary here. This*
> *webbing, confusing*
> *though it is, is not as*
> *tangled as I first thought.*
> *First thoughts come out*
> *of linear readings. Ego*
> *readings. But what*
> *threads to tangle.*
> *Nice webbing!*

Although there may be connections between these various traditions, as early as 1843 Adolphe Franck remarked that "The truth is that Arab mysticism and the principles taught in the Zohar strikes us by their differences rather than their similarities" (1843/1995, p. 49). A reading of the Zohar, a Kabbalistic text, convinces that this mystical heresy is vastly different from Sufism, Christian mysticism, gnosticism, Sikhism, and neo-Platonism. One of the reasons it is different is that it is attached to the Jewish tradition—it is part and parcel of the larger Jewish culture. This is the lesson that scholars have learned from Gershom Scholem, who (1954) taught that "There is no mysticism as such, there is only the mysticism of a particular religious system, Christian, Islamic, Jewish ..." (p. 6). And these particular religious systems, although influencing one another, differ when studied contextually, historically, and culturally. Their brands of heresy differ.

It is also interesting to note that among the traditions of mysticism, Jewish mysticism has always been marginalized. Moshe Idel pointed out that "Kabbalah does not yet enjoy the same degree of honor as Islamic, Hindu, and Buddhist mysticism. Only rarely are Kabbalistic concepts or ideas mentioned in comparative studies" (1988, p. 17). One thing is clear, however. Within the Jewish tradition, Kabbalah has been seen as Other. Scholem noted that, historically, Jewish scholars have trashed its significance. Scholem wrote that "The great Jewish scholars of the past century whose conceptions of Jewish history is still dominant in our days, men like Graetz, Zunz, Geiger, Luzzato and Steinschneider, had little sympathy—to put it mildly— for the Kabbalah" (1954, p. 1).

Midrash Metatext

> *Approaching 40. Forbidden*
> *to read, to study Kabbalah.*
> *Forbidden to include this*
> *study in academic journals.*
> *People are not interested in*
> *Jewish educational difficulties.*
> *Excluded from canons of all*
> *sorts. Identity crisis approaching*
> *40. Feeling grey and blue.*
> *Blue and white, the color of the*
> *Israeli flag. Exiled in America.*
> *In Ezekiel two images: blue*
> *stones and linen clothes. Sign-*
> *acts of schizophrenia or the*
> *divine. If you haven't become*
> *schizophrenic by the time you*
> *reach 40 you are probably over*
> *the hurdle. Hurdling toward the*
> *Divine. Rushing toward God is*
> *a stumbling into madness.*

Men under 40 have been forbidden to study Kabbalah (Matt, 1996), and women have always been forbidden to study it (Idel, 1988). Because I am under 40 and a woman, I guess I am committing double heresy. Not only is studying Kabbalah "scandalous," as Scholem (1965/1996, p. 97) pointed out, it is dangerous. In the Kabbalah, we read: "Whoever delves into mysticism cannot help but stumble, as it is written: 'This stumbling block is in your hand.' You cannot grasp these things unless you stumble over them" (Zohar, in Matt, 1996, p. 163). What is it one stumbles into or over? It could be ghosts, resurrections, transmigrations, voices, sparks, instability, foolishness, visions, weeping, angels, and what some might term "psychosis" (Afterman, 1992, p. 71) or "insanity" (Franck, 1843/1995, p. 17). Studying Kabbalah might open up a space for understanding what cannot be represented in rational discourse. The leap is reflected here: "The sky talks fast, asking one to reply. If one talks back just as fast, one can get into the sky.... Every created thing has a 'mouth,' everything in the world is 'talking' very fast, inviting you" (Afterman, 1992, p. 77).

Psychosis or wisdom? There is nothing new about irrational modes of thinking. In fact, the history of Jewish mysticism can be traced back to the Hebrew prophet Ezekiel.

Ezekiel is the most bizarre book in the Hebrew scriptures. We read in the first chapter that "the hand of the Lord was on him there" (*Holy Bible*, p. 791):

As I looked, a stormy wind came out of the north: a great cloud with bright-
ness around it and fire flashing forth continually, and in the middle of the fire,
something like gleaming amber. In the middle of it was something like four
living creatures. This was their appearance: they were of human form. Each
had four faces, and each of them had four wings ... they sparkled like bur-
nished bronze. Under their wings on their four sides they had human hands.
(1989, p. 791)

Hallucination or a vision of the divine? Voices from God, or schizophrenia? Perhaps both. An early version of Jewish mysticism is termed
"Merkabah mysticism" and can be traced back to Ezekiel and *3 Enoch*, an
apocalyptic text. Harold Bloom (1996) commented, "As an apocalypse, 3
Enoch belongs to the pre-Kabbalistic tradition of Hebraic gnosis called
Merkabah mysticism, the Merkabah being the prophet Ezekiel's term for
the chariot that bears the enthroned Man of his vision" (p. 48).

The Merkabah mystics believed that if they covered themselves literally
with the names of God, they would experience something similar to Ezekiel.
Perle Epstein (1978) explained, "The ritual called 'putting on the names'
literally consisted of clothing oneself in a robe inscribed all over with sacred
names of God. The Merkabah mystic used the external reminder to induce
in himself the absolutely undistracted meditation on the names that would
carry him toward visionary experience" (p. 39).

Later trends in Jewish mysticism are associated with the Jews' exile from
Spain in 1492. The Kabbalah, a generic name for different versions of Jewish mystical thought, developed during the 12th and 13th centuries especially in Spain. Scholem pointed out that Merkabah mysticism and
Hasidism (which developed later in Eastern Europe), although falling under the broader rubric called Kabbalah, are vastly different. He stated
"There is little resemblance between the earliest mystical texts in our possession, dating from Talmudic and post-Talmudic days, the writings of the
ancient Spanish Kabbalists, those of the school which flourished in Safed,
the holy city of Kabbalah in the 16th century, and finally the Hasidic literature in the modern age" (1954, p. 19).

Generally speaking, there are three kinds of texts associated with
Kabbalah: Bahir, Zohar and Lurianic texts. The Zohar, especially after the
Jews were exiled from Spain in 1492, became what some term "the Bible" of
Kabbalah (Matt, 1983, p. 11). This book was written by Moses de Leon, although there have been many squabbles over the authenticity of author-
ship. Daniel Matt commented that the "Zohar refashions the Torah's
narrative into a mystical novel" (1983, pp. 8–9). And this is what some rabbis thought was so scandalous. Fictionalizing biblical truths? Oy.

Many Kabbalistic ideas have gotten squashed over the years or have been
completely marginalized because the rabbis thought them to be heretical.
Most of these ideas are paradoxically tied to yet alien from traditional Jewish
thinking: resurrection, metempsychosis or reincarnation, notions of *Ein Sof*

(the infinite), *Ayin* (nothingness), three souls, enclothement, the shattering of sparks in a broken world. Kabbalah teaches that three garments cover the souls (because there are three souls, not one) of the righteous, the unholy have holes in their garments. For traditional Jews this is certainly (un)holy!

Mid(rush)

Mary here. Between the holes
and the garments lie the holies
which, because they are ciphers,
cannot be read in whole, only in
the holes.

The Kabbalah teaches that the world is created in a void. Sparks fly out of the void and are shattered as they plunge to earth. God is both Ein Sof, the infinite and a transcendent being who is beyond names and is ultimately a mystery, and God is also reflected as sparks of light emanating out of the darkness through levels of what is called "Sefirot": "Emanating from Ein Sof are the ten Sefirot. They constitute the process by which all things come into being and pass away" (Zohar, in Matt, 1996, p. 29). The Sefirot are thought of as numbers, "ciphers" (Matt, 1983, pp. 20–21). Whatever they are, they are not things. Scholem (1954) commented that "The Sefiroth of Jewish theosophy have an existence of their own; they form combinations, they illuminate each other, they ascend and descend" (pp. 224–225). Stephen Sharot noted that the Sefirot are also translated as "successive manifestations of divinity" (1982, p. 32). The first Sefirot is Ayin, or nothingness, and it is said that great Jewish teachers, Tzaddiks, dwell in nothingness, by losing their egos (Scholem, 1962/1991). "Think of yourself as Ayin and forget yourself totally. Then you can transcend time, rising to the world of thought, where all is equal: life and death, ocean and dry land. Such is not the case if you are attached to the material nature of this world. If you think of yourself as something, then God cannot clothe himself in you" (Zohar, in Matt, 1996, p. 71).

Growing up in the reformed tradition, I can tell you that I have never heard of any of these things. Resurrection? "The 'righteous' clothed in that garment, they are destined to come back to life. All who have a garment will be resurrected" (Zohar, in Matt, 1996, p. 94). Is that not a Zoroastrian notion that got smuggled into Christianity? Reincarnation?? One of the most bizarre images in Kabbalistic thought is Metatron. Adolphe Franck (1843/1993) wrote that "The angel, or rather the hypostasis called Metatron plays a very great part in the Kabbalistic system. It is he, properly speaking, who governs this visible world; he reigns over all spheres suspended in space, over all the planets and celestial bodies" (p. 18).

During the Enlightenment, when rabbis were attempting to assimilate into the larger cultural scene of rationality and scientism, the mystics were calling for a more irrational and mythological mode of thinking, and hence, "In the revaluation of the Enlightenment, it [the Zohar] became the 'book of lies'" (Scholem, 1949/1977a, IX). Adolphe Franck commented that the Zohar is "irrational, rude" (1843/1995, p. 149). The Zohar is downright queer. The difficulty of reading the Zohar is that it is not systematic. Scholem claimed that this is not unlike traditional Jewish thinking: "The Zohar remains true to the tradition of Jewish speculative thought which ... is alien to the spirit of systematization" (1954, p. 205).

Ah, that is why Derrida is so difficult to read?! Read his *Circumfession* (1993). Confessional fox or hedgehog? Clearly fox. Jewish fox, that is. Moshe Idel (1988) claimed that "historical Kabbalah represented an ongoing effort to systematize existing elements of Jewish theurgy, myth, and mysticism into a full-fledged response to the rationalistic challenge" (p. 253). I do not believe that Western culture has ever left behind the scars of rationalism. Rationalism keeps us from thinking the unthinkable. Philip Wexler, however, asserted that cultural trends are slowly moving in a less mechanized, rationalistic manner. Wexler (1996) noted, "There is some evidence for a move toward a culture with a different set of assumptions than those that have prevailed since at least the Renaissance: less rationalist, scientific, materialist and mechanical, and instead, more spiritual, ideational, vitalist and transcendent" (p. 74).

Getting outside the frame of rationalistic and mechanistic modes of thinking can be traced to Kabbalistic thought. Consider the following passage:

> All the time I was on my way here, I had to suffer the annoying chatter of the old man who drove the donkey. He bothered me with every kind of foolish question, for example, What serpent flies in the air with an ant lying quietly between its teeth?... What eagle has its nest in a tree that does not exist and its young plundered by creatures not yet created, in a place which is not? (Zohar, in Scholem, 1949/1977b, p. 61)

Foolishness is the key to unlocking otherness, realms of lived experienced squashed by rational deliberation and mechanization. Beware the donkey driver.

MIDRASH: STUMBLING INSIDE THE (UN)HOME OF EDUCATION

Daniel Matt pointed out that "The root of midrash means 'to search.' Midrash is the ancient technique of searching for the meaning of passages, phrases, and individual words.... It includes philology, etymology, hermeneutics, homiletics, and imagination" (1983, pp. 7–8). Midrash is commentary. Jews love to comment, then comment again, countercomment and overcomment, commenting more, meta-commenting. Commenting across heresies helps me stumble backward toward my (un)home of education. Education as a discipline, disciplines. What counts as educational theory and curriculum studies? Ellen Messer-Davidow, David R. Shumway, and David J. Sylvan commented, "Socially and conceptually, we are disciplined by our disciplines. First, they help produce our world. They specify the objects we can study" (1993, p. vii). Scholars outside the field of curriculum studies might suggest that my work is not related to curriculum at all. What do heretical rantings have to do with curriculum? Everything. William F. Pinar pointed out that "the effort to understand curriculum as theological text is not a separate specialized sector of scholarship; it is the call to live with others morally and transcendentally" (1999, p. xxiv).

This chapter has been an attempt to try to cut across the "basic borders" (Pinar, 1998, p. ix) of curriculum theorizing. Following Pinar's urging, I am trying to get outside the frame of curriculum understanding to dis/position myself. Pinar (1998) wrote, "There are individuals ... who are working on the edge and perhaps even outside contemporary curriculum discourses" (p. ix). What I have learned from studying these various heresies is to continually try to overturn my own presuppositions. David Smith (1999) argued for the embracing of "mutations" (p. 18). He taught that "Every identifiable 'thing' [or I would add way of thinking] is itself in a condition of constant mutation, completely infused with everything else, never 'this' for more than a moment" (p. 18). Ghostly apparitions, voices, sparks, broken vessels, and unnameables undo, place us on the edge of thought. Mary Aswell Doll called for "what dwells within and between oppositions and contradictions ... a ghostly 'third'" (1987, p. 146). In the (un)place of the third, curriculum sensibilities can shift, can become more open to otherness, the otherness within. Drawing on the work of Henry Corbin, Harold Bloom (1996), like Doll, urged that one enter that third or middle place, the place where mystics dare to go. Bloom remarked that "Between the sensory and the intellectual world, sages always have experiences an intermediate realm, one akin to what we call the imaginings of poets" (p. 5). Perhaps, Wexler (1996) was right to point out that it is through the psychoanalytic notion of regression that one may experience this middle place that might inform our pedagogical practices. Wexler stated that "The interpretation of the regressive process as one that enables expression and experience of the sense and communion that gets suppressed in the individuating path of autonomous ego development is especially relevant for a cultural, historical or contextual understanding of teaching" (p. 141).

As Wexler pointed out, the middle place between this and that, that liminal space opens up the possibility of relationality between teachers and students. The mystical pedagogue is not up in the clouds somewhere, but instead is grounded in the place of no place, in the space where the ego dissolves. We learn from mystical heresies that heretics are not escapists. Many, historically, have been social activists and fighters for social justice. Skihs,

Sufis, and Jewish heretics, generally speaking, have considered action and doing to be primary.

The odd thing about doing an indirect-mystical-autotheology is that, after all, the stories I have just commented on are not about me. To get dis/positioned is to undo the notion that my work is about me and that I am I. Perhaps I have stumbled too soon and should wait until after I reach the age of 40, as the Jewish heretical tradition teaches. But I cannot wait any longer. Perhaps I have come belatedly to my (un)home by getting (un)framed.

Lines of re-search, should serve to re-search, redo midrash, to search and search again, to desearch, to dis- the search, dis-the-sertation, to start over again or not start at all. The paradox of thinking myself out of the category of curriculum as theological text and out of the category of curriculum as autobiographical text is that I always seem to come back to my (un)home of thinking theologically and autobiographically but never really doing either. My students asked me the other day if I thought that my work around curriculum was theological, and I surprised myself by saying no. Why the no? I don't know!! It just came out of my mouth. (The sky has a mouth and it talks fast.) But then I told them about my next book project. The next step is a step back to Ezekiel, prophetic discourse, otherness, curriculum studies as … confessional, heretical discourse … lifework. I stumble at calling myself an indirect-mystical-autotheological curriculum worker, because although dis/ positioned I am in position to do some kind of work that is carved and crafted in between spaces. Stumbling to keep up with the fast-talking sky is the work of this curriculum worker.

REFERENCES

Afterman, A. (1992). *Kabbalah and consciousness*. Riverdale-on-Hudson, NY: Sheep Meadow Press.

Bloom, H. (1996). *Omens of millennium: The gnosis of angels, dreams, and Resurrection*. New York: Riverhead.

Cole, W. O, & Sambhi, P. S. (1978). *The Sikhs: Their religious beliefs and practices*. Boston: Routledge.

Derrida, J. (1993). *Geoffrey Bennington (Derridabase) and Jacques Derrida (circumfession)*. (G. Bennington, Trans.). Chicago: University of Chicago Press.

Doll, M. A. (1987). The temple: Symbolic form in scripture. *Soundings: An Interdisciplinary Journal*, *LXX*(1–2), 145–154.

Epstein, P. (1978). *Kabbalah: The way of Jewish mysticism*. New York: Doubleday.

Franck, A. (1843/1995). *The Kabbalah: The religious philosophy of the Hebrews*. New York: Carol Publishing.

Freud, A. (1966/1993). *The ego and the mechanisms of defense*. Madison, CT: International University Press.

Gallop, J. (2000). The ethics of reading: Close encounters. *The Journal of Curriculum Theorizing*, *16*(3), 7–18.

Holy Bible: New standard revised version. (1989). Iowa Falls, IA: World Bible Publishers.

Idel, M. (1988). *Kabbalah: New perspectives*. New Haven, CT: Yale University Press.

Maneri, S. (1263/1980). *The hundred letters*. (P. Jackson, Trans.). New York: Paulist Press.

Matt, D. (1983). *Zohar: The book of enlightenment* (D. C. Matt, Trans.). Mahwah, NJ: Paulist Press.

Matt, D. (1996). *The essential Kabbalah: The heart of Jewish mysticism.* San Francisco: Harper.

McLeod, W. H. (1989). *Who is a Sikh? The problem of Sikh identity.* Oxford, UK: Clarendon.

McGinn, B. (1965/1996). Forward. In G. Scholem, *On the kabbalah and its symbolism* (pp. vii–xviii). New York: Schocken.

Messer-Davidow, E., Schumway, D. R., & Sylvan, D. J. (1993). Preface. In D. R. Schumway & D. J. Sylvan (Eds.), *Knowledges: Historical and critical studies in disciplinarity* (pp. vii–viii). Charlottesville: University Virginia Press.

Morris, M. (2001). *Curriculum and the Holocaust: Competing sites of memory and representation.* Mahwah, NJ: Lawrence Erlbaum Associates.

Nizam, A. D. A. (1992). *Nizam ad-din Awliya: Morals for the heart: Conversations of Shaykh Nizam ad-din Awliya recorded by Amir Hasan Sijzi.* Mahwah, NJ: Paulist Press.

Nurbakhsh, J. (1983). *Sufi women.* New York: Khaniqahi Nimatullahi.

Pinar, W. F. (1998). Introduction. In W. F. Pinar (Ed.), *Curriculum: Toward new identities* (pp. ix–xxxiv). New York: Garland.

Pinar, W. F. (1999). Introduction. In V. Hillis & W. F. Pinar (Eds.), *The lure of the transcendent: Collected essays by Dwayne E. Heubner* (pp. xv–xxiv). Mahwah, NJ: Lawrence Erlbaum Associates.

Pinar, W. F., Reynolds, W., Slattery, P., & Taubman, M. (1995). *Understanding curriculum: An introduction to the study of historical and contemporary curriculum discourses.* New York: Peter Lang.

Scholem, G. (1949/1977a). Introduction: Historical setting of the Zohar. In G. Scholem (Ed.), *Zohar the book of splendor: Basic readings from the Kabbalah* (pp. VII–XVII). New York: Schocken.

Scholem, G. (Ed.). (1949/1977b). *Zohar the book of splendor: Basic readings from the Kabbalah.* New York: Schocken.

Scholem, G. (1954). *Major trends in Jewish mysticism.* New York: Schocken.

Scholem, G. (1962/1991). *On the mystical shape of the godhead: Basic concepts in the kabbalah.* (J. Neugroschel, Trans.). New York: Schocken.

Scholem, G. (1965/1996). *On the kabbalah and its symbolism.* (R. Manheim, Trans.). New York: Schocken.

Schomer, K. (1987). Introduction. In K. Schomer & W. H. McLeod, (Eds.), *The sants: Studies in a devotional tradition in India* (pp. 1–5). Motilala: Banarsidass.

Sharot, S. (1982). *Messianism, mysticism, and magic: A sociological analysis of Jewish religious movements.* Chapel Hill: University of North Carolina Press.

Singh, N. G. K. (1993). *The feminine principle in the Sikh vision of the transcendent.* New York: Cambridge University Press.

Smith, D. (1999). *Pedagon: Interdisciplinary essays in the human sciences, pedagogy, and culture.* New York: Peter Lang.

Sri Guru Granth Sahib, vol. one. (1988). (G. S. Talib, Trans.). Patiala, India: Punjabi University Press.

Valiuddin, M. (1988). *Contemplative disciplines in sufism.* London: East/West Publications.

Wexler, P. (1996). *Holy sparks: Social theory, education and religion.* New York: St. Martin's Press.

Wolfe, T. (1957). *Look homeward angel: The story of a buried life.* New York: Collier Books.

Chapter 7

Curricula vita as a Call to a Vocation: Exploring a Puritan Way

Douglas McKnight
The University of Alabama

Thinking Beyond

In this chapter, McKnight provides an examination of the curriculum thinking of the New England Puritans of the 17th and 18th centuries. He makes a detailed comparison between the notions that the Puritans had for curriculum and spirituality and the manner in which those ideas and theories have been remolded in the present American educational context. McKnight emphasizes the Puritan notion of reflection and spirituality. He discusses how reflection has been misunderstood, and the manner in which spirituality has become a normative experience through school programs.

Questions

1. How is the present focus on character education in schools a misunderstanding of the reflective process that McKnight describes as integral to the Puritan concept of spirirtuality? How does McKnight's discussion of spirituality compare to Webber's and Morris' conceptualizations?
2. How can an analysis of the Puritan notions of curriculum assist curriculum theorists in their move away from contemporary functionalist/modernist ideas of curriculum and schooling to discover lines of flight and multiplicities?
3. How does McKnight's concept of *curricula vita* allow for the space to struggle and to create lines of flight within the current educational moment?

> How can one talk about education, specifically curriculum, and also talk about the spiritual? (Huebner, 1993/1998, p. 401)

> Because conventional education neglects the inner reality of teacher and students for the sake of a reality "out there," the heart of the knowing self is never held up for inspection, never given the chance to be known. (Palmer, 1993, p. 35)

Recognizing that some very old Puritan bones will rattle and disrupt my every word with their trembling jeremiads and sermons, I acknowledge their presence and risk considering a present condition that concerns all who have invested in education, specifically curriculum, a purpose beyond the means by which we sort out social classes, warehouse students, or train them for jobs and consumerism.

The beyond of which I speak is cradled within a very old notion, that of *curricula vita*, literally translated as "course of life." The term *curricula* is a

Latin root form of the modern definition of *curriculum*. However, *curricula* as a concept was flattened out by 19th- and 20th-century educators to mean a grouping of discrete subjects and competencies to be mastered. John Calvin sponsored the Latin phrase *curricula vita* in the 16th century as a description of a journey that began with a summons, a call to depart by an absolute other, which for Reformation Christians was God. It is important to note here that I am not pursuing the notions of vocation and calling purely in theological terms of Judeo/Christian orthodoxy. These concepts spill over any such legalistic boundaries and wash over the individual who senses something beyond him- or herself, nothing less than a surplus that no form of knowledge can check or control. It is within the context of one who possesses a visceral impulse to investigate life and the inherent mystery within that leads one to listen, hear the calling of something absolutely other, and engage in a spiritual and temporal voyage.

For Calvin, and for the colonial Puritans of the 17th and 18th centuries, this journey was to reveal one's gifts for a life task, a vocation that embodied both spiritual and mundane obligations. Curriculum was not a part of the process. It was the intensive, rigorous, reflective process of studying and receiving a purpose and meaning in life. "Call" (or "calling") and "vocation" are significant in a discussion about perceiving curriculum as something beyond, because each generates obligations and responsibilities on the individual's part, as well as on the cultural institutions within which people dwell.

I would like to ruminate on these notions as alternative means of interpreting and approaching the predominate understandings of curriculum as practiced in schools. I approach the issues first from an etymological standpoint, which should provide a context by which to trace how these historical meanings have shifted in their applications in modern America, with grave consequences to the notion of the "individual." I then conclude with a narrative of how colonial Puritans in early America utilized the notions of *curricula vita*—calling and vocation as means to relate the individual to society, to his or her interior existence and to a spiritual absolute other that infused meaning to one's everyday activities. Such an examination should present the benefits as well as potential pitfalls of applying such powerful notions to modern schools and curriculum in general.

ETYMOLOGICAL PERSPECTIVE

Both vocation and calling are sewn from the same historical seeds. *Vocation* comes from the Latin terms *vocatio* ("a bidding or invitation"), and *vocare* ("to call to"). *Vocation* is linked with *vox*, or *voice* and *vocal*. In this sense, a vocation is something one is called to or invoked to (invocation) by another, as well as a condition in which one is given a singular voice. The term *calling* or *call* encompasses both the actual invitation from something that is wholly other, and thus not able to be articulated, as well as the process one chooses to enter into to infuse mundane existence with spiritual meaning.

In this call toward a vocation, one is compelled to travel through a life's course (re curriculum), with an ambiguous gesture, literally stepping two different ways at once. One trajectory directs the individual to meditate on and embody received cultural institutions—family, school, civil/state society, work, and church, and the cultural artifacts produced by each. An effect of this motion is to understand and relate to any meta-narrative (cultural themes and assumptions) that may stitch institutions together. At same time, the individual, with an inherited map and language of interpretation in possession, departs on a spiritual, interior campaign. A spiritual quest binds one not only to existing institutions, but also to a state of absolute otherness, a theological or philosophical other that issues the original call. Crucial to this cultural process is the embodiment of how to listen for the call, how to recognize the message as a summons, and how to respond and submit to its direction—a gesture that generates and stirs one beyond any immediate condition. Out of this spirit of seeking (sometimes torture, sometimes grace), a method of interpretation surfaces, a means by which to understand how one's singularity unfolds in the everyday world and to advance a spiritual relation that gives meaning to existence beyond "objective facts." This is curriculum as *curricula vita*; a course one runs in life. Understanding curriculum as *curricula vita*, as an ambiguous labor first given to the American consciousness by the colonial Puritans, has been lost in the modern discourse of curriculum, except for occasional voices in the wilderness (e.g., Huebner, 1993/1998; Macdonald, 1995; Pinar & Grumet, 1976).

MODERN CURRICULUM AND THE LOSS OF INTERIORITY

The void left by the collapse of *curricula vita* language, an effect of the mid- to late 19th-century institutionalization of mass public schooling, has been filled by a technical curriculum discourse that treats individuals as economic resources, far past even what the worldly and practical colonial Puritans would consider appropriate. Students and teachers have become pliable materials to be exploited for social/economic utility (Palmer, 1993). Individuals are expected to accept curriculum, now associated almost solely with schooling, as a disparate grouping of subjects. Each subject field has its own closed discourse, without any explicit means to guide the individual in crossing disciplinary boundaries so that he or she could have insight into how knowledge is produced, or how each field shares similar metaphors and ways of understanding. The individual is given no "time" to explore temporality, no moments of recursion to draw relations between exterior and interior existence. An effect is the lack of any greater purpose attached to that life (Palmer, 1993). The student (knower) is separated from what is known (the exterior world), and what is unknown (the interior worlds of a living being). No tools are given for the individual to build an interchange between the two. Without such interpretive appliances, a rupture occurs and the idea of moving beyond one's present condition collapses into dust and fades from any discussion of education and curriculum. Parker Palmer (1993) addressed the issue this way:

> In the conventional classroom the focus of study is always outward—on nature, on history, on someone else's vision of reality. The reality inside the classroom, inside the teacher and the students, is regarded as irrelevant; it is not recognized that we are part of nature and of history, that we have visions of our own. So we come to think of reality as "out there," apart from us, and knowing becomes a kind of spectator sport. (p. 34)

This perception of curriculum as thoroughly "objectivist" assumes that "facts" need little explanation and mediation by the teacher. The student knower is not expected nor encouraged to interpret. Such means of transmitting received knowledge operates from the same logic that manufactured standardized tests as the means to evaluate students' mastery of information. In fact, as national standardized test scores continue to waver, as more and more money is tied to such "measurements" to determine the success or failure of schools, few policymakers apprehend such a technical notion of curriculum as the problem. Instead, administrators, politicians, and national accreditation groups impose on college education departments hundreds of pages of step-by-step instructions—loaded with rubrics, measurements, and evaluations—on how to do more a "rationalized" job of "training" students to become more "effective" teachers. An effective teacher is one who can "prove" or show "evidence" that learning (i.e., knowledge mastery) has taken place.

Although this language often professes an interest in the individual, it is a highly selective interest. The interest extends only so far as this paradigm can demonstrate predictable and measurable effects on external behavior and academic achievement. A concrete example of this is the recent accountability discourse adopted by both Democrats and Republicans in setting federal educational policies. The culmination of this discourse has been President George W. Bush's educational map, attached to the mantra "No child left behind." This plan is based on the notion that if students at a school do not score well on state-chosen achievement tests, then the school will be publicly denounced. President Bush would institute annual standardized achievement tests to measure whether teachers have been able to impose on students certain basic skills and memorization techniques, the type of "learning" that can be measured by such tests. Schools doing poorly will be given some extra federal funds to improve the test scores. If these scores do not rise, then the teachers and administrators in the school will suffer the ultimate punishment: The school will be closed and students will go elsewhere.

Due to all of the federal funds tied to test score improvements, the obvious outcome of this, if states agree to accept the money and, hence, all of the accountability measures that go along with it, will be that the daily school experience will be drastically constricted and controlled. Whereas schoolteachers already complain about having to halt their teaching of state curriculum each year to prepare students taking other state-mandated exams, this annual federally funded exam would enforce an even more restrictive environment through annual testing for each grade. Teachers will be compelled to become ever-more didactic as more emphasis (due to the correlation of money to test scores) is placed on external measurements and control of student "learning." In other words, a teacher's and a student's worth will be based on these accountability measurements. The value of one's educational experience will be tied to achievement scores. Less and less space in the classroom will be given to individual exploration of how the curriculum affects a student's identity and understanding of the world. Students will be even less encouraged to engage in a personal relation with the curriculum in an effort to create meaning, and more encouraged to ignore the internal machinations at work when one interprets and ruminates on how the texts or classroom dialogue affects one's ethical and moral existence.

In other words, what will be lost here is the inward turn, a rigorous process of experiencing and exploring one's interiority to transcend an immediate condition in a way that gives life meaning beyond conspicuous consumption. Curriculum theorists William Pinar (1995) and Madeleine Grumet (Pinar & Grumet, 1976) developed somewhat of a similar process, called *Currere*, a Latin form of curriculum that translates as a "course to be run." For Pinar, the path of this course to be run is revealed and understood as one engages in lifelong self-analysis through a complex combination of psychoanalysis and autobiography. Curriculum theorist Dwayne Huebner (1993/1998) described this act of going beyond as the experiencing of "moreness"—all that overflows any category to which objectivism attempts to pin down the individual. Technical curriculum cannot contain nor measure this surplus.

If a person has no means by which to conceptualize, thematize, and hence give meaning to the complex and often swirling and contradictory impulses (which will certainly be the effect of new federal and state educational policies across America), then any "knowledge" that falls outside of the realm of predetermined facts will fade into irrelevance. Experiences become fleeting and without lasting effect, leaving the individual without an intellectual anchor. The other political response to this sense of the individual floating along, which is translated as not having a strong "moral" compass to guide his or her thoughts and actions, has been to ignore the singularity of individuals and impose certain "normative" behaviors based on social scientific categories.

For instance, during the last few years, nearly every state and local government has gotten involved in the morality business by creating a curriculum of "character." In almost every case, a familiar logic was followed:

1. Test scores are down or flat; individual behavior is terrible.
2. If individual behavior is improved, silence will ensue and concentration (memorization skills) will improve.

3. The result will be higher test scores, and thus America will be able to compete on a world scale and remain a great nation.
4. Therefore, develop what moral characteristics are most basic to being an American (generalized Protestantism).
5. Develop a method, a program, by which to transmit those characteristics.
6. Enter into the schools and "teach" the administrators and teachers how to impart these characteristics most effectively.

From this logic have come city, state, and national programmatic solutions, including such ones as "Character Counts," "Character One," "Character Education Partnership," and so on. In Baton Rouge, Louisiana, the mayor and a committee of community leaders decided on a page-long list of "good" moral attributes that should be taken to the schools. The list trotted out the usual suspects: punctuality, respect (of authority), sobriety, obedience, self-discipline and honesty. Each of these notions was believed to be self-evident and easily transmitted without historical explanation or cultural analysis. There was no dialogically arrived-at meaning by students and teacher. The perception was that the students would somehow "naturally" understand these terms, memorize them, change their behavior according to this mastery, and then enter into American institutions as productive citizens.

My question to the mayor when he presented this list to our faculty at the time was: "What do you mean with each of these words and what cultural definition did you take into consideration? … It appears that understandings of such terms are situated differently within each culture." His response, which drew applause from most of the teachers, was that everyone knows what *respect* means, that it has been lost by the youth of today, and that in order to save our kids we must instill respect in them. This response is problematic. I decided to test the mayor's assumptions. In one of my literature classes, I handed out a *Sports Illustrated* article concerning the Latrell Sprewell incident. Sprewell was the NBA star who got into an argument with the head coach, left the court, came back a couple of hours later, and confronted the coach. A shouting match ensued, and Sprewell proceeded to choke the coach. Sprewell stated that the coach yelled at—and thus humiliated—him too much.

After reading the material without commentary or questions on my part, I introduced the notions of courage and respect as moral attributes to the students. We discussed if Sprewell could be characterized as having courage or understanding respect. Following the mayor's logic, one would assume the students would relay that Sprewell did not possess these characteristics, because he immediately resorted to anger and violence based on what appeared a minor insult. However, my students did not agree. Almost to a one (these were mostly African-American inner-city youth, mostly poor, living in Baton Rouge, Louisiana) they responded that not only did Sprewell demonstrate his courage, but also his understanding of respect and the consequences of someone else not showing a "man" proper respect. Sprewell had no choice but to teach the coach a lesson. The coach had no right to yell at him, because, for these students, to yell at and expect someone to listen to you just because you are in a position of power is the opposite of courage. To strike back and show physical dominance is the definition of courage. To prove that he could physically master the coach meant that the coach had to respect Sprewell and not the other way around.

These students had a very clear understanding of what they meant and how they acted on these notions in the world. It was their reality. To tell the students that these words could actually—according to the moral powers that be—mean just the opposite made no sense to them, nor were they interested. The voice of institutional power poured right past them, leaving no conscious marks. Yet, at no time has it been recognized that the very institutions that are trying to transmit obedience and usefulness to the individual are no longer in a position to speak to the individual. Imposition and not recognition of the nature of the calling to a vocation has marked the 21st-century technological mind. Modern rhetoric still speaks of curriculum as preparation for institutional life, which translates as preparation for serving an economic function.

Institutional life no longer can promise to deliver any sense of greater purpose or meaning to the individual, who, despite still possessing the impulse, has no clue of how to locate such a design. The spiritual sense of the individual relating to cultural institutions, as developed by the colonial Puritans, has been discarded. Confidence in institutions as providing meaningful vocations and individual purpose has crumbled.

This fragmentation has left the individual alone, separated, left to his or her own devices at a very early age. Experiences are supplied cheaply and quickly, from which the individual receives titillation but does not connect the individual to either his or her own interior being, nor to others around him or her, nor to things that are spiritually oriented. The only lasting effect is dread, alienation, and an intense longing to consume more in the hope that somehow the hunger will be satiated and something meaningful will emerge from the modern feast.

Without such ingredients, the inward turn to contemplate and ruminate on his or her existence and purpose, crucial to the responding to the call and finding one's vocation, are improbable. In a time when the modern individual is appreciated as an autonomous and unhindered subject, free to pursue all desires, it seems paradoxical that the individual also appears most helpless to institutional forces shaping his or her choices and means by which to fulfill desires. An indicator to understand what appears to be a paradox may emerge from exploring, briefly and broadly, how the very concept of "individual" has changed over the last few centuries. This change in perception of what constitutes an individual provides a context by which to discuss how the notion of the calling functioned in American society at one time.

CALL TOWARD INSTITUTIONAL INDIVIDUALISM

In *Institutional Individualism*, Walter Kaufmann (1999) traced the fluid nature of the word *individual*, less a change in definition than in emphasis on how one relates to cultural institutions. The etymology of *individual* begins with the Latin root *dividere*, meaning to divide, and prefaced by *in-*, translated as "not," giving *individual* a meaning of "not dividable," or "indivisible," which strikes the modern sensibility as strange. As Raymond Williams (1983) explained, the term *individual* is usually perceived as something separate from, whereas *indivisible* is something necessarily connected to. However, Kaufmann (1999) pointed out how the word came to mean its opposite:

> Before the seventeenth century, the dominant meaning indicated something or someone that could not be separated or distinguished from the group. To be an individual in the modern sense of the word would mean that you were eccentric, incomprehensible, because you did not take part in the "common sense."
>
> By the ... nineteenth century (i.e., rugged, self-reliant, Emersonian individualism), the dominant meaning of individual came closer to how we now think of the word: something or someone that is unique, special, distinguishable from commonalties. This individual too is indivisible—but only from himself or herself; he or she can be divided from the group but cannot be further divided. Modern individuality is the irreducible unit of identity. (p. 18)

In effect, the 17th-century individual would identify him- or herself in terms of how he or she resembled others, whereas the modern individual derives a sense of self from how he or she is different from others within shared cultural institutions. Colonial Puritans demonstrated the relational sense of individual most obviously in America.

For the colonial Puritans, who provided a powerful cultural framework for a beginning American "identity"—especially through the spread of their cultural texts and institutions (Bercovitch, 1975, 1978, 1993)—an individual was not perceived as a discrete entity struck deaf and then told to listen for his or her calling. The Puritan system provided a cultural, although heavily patriarchal, constraint system that gave contour and voice to one's possible identity (Kaufmann, 1999). The cultural paradigm worked in this way: A Puritan network of institutions was patterned from the filial arrangement, because a child naturally made acquaintance with the world through a family. Due to the Puritans' inheritance of an English patriarchal system and a theological system that constructed the absolute other as the ultimate male authority figure, the father was responsible for these relations. However, it was recognized that the child had to move beyond the immediate family and enter into social and spiritual affiliations. The impetus for this cultural trajectory was basic human desire, which for the colonial Puritans was a factual state of existence, neither good nor bad but instead neutral.

Colonial Puritans firmly believed that individuals possessed some natural desire to relate with a paternal ideal, with the ultimate affiliation being the absolute other (Kaufmann, 1999). A child would begin by idealizing the immediate father, but then soon recognize weaknesses or moral cracks, and seek a better father and embody that person's traits. In each institution was presented some leader who was to represent the more ideal father. The child was to be "naturally" drawn to imitation, with each successive paternal figure presenting a more pure ideal, until the child finally recognized the experienced a conversion to the "original" father, the absolute other. Only then in this spiritual relation did one become an individual. Despite our modern awareness of the problematic and even oppressive nature of such paternal relations guiding one's *curricula vita*, colonial Puritan male and females did not perceive such analogies and institutional structures as being oppressive.

In fact, the first filial arrangement was the only institution in which this "creature" did not voluntarily submit (Greven, 1977; Kaufmann, 1999; Morgan, 1944). Through interaction with the family, in terms of direct and indirect instruction, the child embodied as natural the filial cultural arrangement that shaped one's identity (Kaufmann, 1999). However, by the age of 14, a child began acting on the impulse toward affiliation by rejecting the immediate family in favor of more ideal affiliations. The boy or girl would often then turn his or her attention and behavior to other institutions, such as school and scholarly study if the boy decided to become a clergyman, or to an apprenticeship if he or she wanted to become a craftsman, handmaiden, or seamstress. An apprenticeship would last up to 7 years. Once a decision was made, rarely could the child turn back (Morgan, 1944).

As a colonial Puritan moved from one institutional sphere of existence to the next, he or she experienced a shift from filial to affiliate relations. In this process, the previous arrangement was rejected in a cultural desire to locate a more ideal relation with a paternal other. Significant for the individual, then, was not to discern differences between he or she and another being, but instead to identify and appropriate the differences among cultural institutions, each one promising a different paternal appeal (Kaufmann, 1999). After this decision, the individual affiliated with the community at large, which later developed into an affiliation with a national identity—an American—and then the congregation at church, or more accurately, the minister himself as next ideal father. Finally, in the act of *Christi imitatio*, one became a complete individual and chose willingly to submit to and identify with the absolute other. Although this took literally years of study and interior reflection, colonial Puritans actually perceived this as a motion back in time to reunite with the original ideal father.

In the network of these affiliations, the individual was not expected to eradicate all differences and only resemble one's immediate family. To deviate was the human soul's natural state, for it no longer dwelled as one with the absolute other. However, this deviation was connected to sin, and sin took on forms unique to each individual. Puritans desired to return to a moment without sin, which, in a true Puritan paradox, was never fully possible while living on earth. To return to the original absolute other was to have the effect of wiping away all differences, all sin, and experiencing the absolute other as no longer other, but one in the same. The only differences expected to survive in the individual were the differences among institutions, as well as those practices that distinguished Puritans from Catholics or other denominations that were not Congregationalist.

Although this process strikes the modern sensibility as an act of submission—and thus anathema to one's personal freedom of expression—for the Puritans it was rather an act of volition. A choice to surrender to something beyond one's own self was freely made, demonstrating a strong "devotion to the purest institutional authorities" (Kaufmann, 1999, p. 3). As Kaufmann further proposed, "Following the logic of affiliation, to strengthen these institutions was also to strengthen, not diminish one's sense of self.... To exist without an institutional affiliation was to be abandoned to one's corrupt and degenerate self" (p. 3).

However, the responsibilities and obligations did not flow one way. If the institutional leaders failed to elevate their actions to communal standards, specifically in terms of visible sainthood, Puritan congregations revoked all power. The institution—meaning those leaders who represented the sacredness of each institution—had to adhere to the paternal ideal of guiding and serving the collection of individuals to justify each individual's willingness to embody institutional identity (Kaufmann, 1999; Stone, 1979). Simply put, a father had to take care of and guide his children.

Significant is that a cultural framework existed to help one develop a "lens," to use an anthropological term. An individual would assume this lens to determine his or her calling, his or her lifetask through a search of the interior and exterior known and unknown. From this perspective, the institutional structure of colonial Puritan society was not set up to oppress one's free will, but actually made one's individuality and identity possible. Without it, no spiritual or mundane life had any meaning, because it was believed that the person could not transcend his or her condition without a social form or language of interpretation and institutional guidance.

Only when possessive individualism emerged with capitalism as the privileged meta-narrative were institutions perceived as something to hinder and control the individual's desire for "personal expression." The mass school system was not excluded from this shift, and quickly embraced and institutionalized these assumptions of what it meant to be an individual, as well as what kind of methods were necessary to control and direct the individual. In effect, the bureaucratic structure of public schools adopted an understanding of curriculum that treated the individual as an economic resource, little different than a piece of raw material to be molded into a refined product (Cuban, 1971; Kliebard, 1971). The sense of a human being as more than something to be externally manipulated was lost. The interior world of an individual was actually let loose and set afloat without a lifeline. For some, this meant freedom of the self. However, the spiritual sense of the individual as having a purpose beyond earning good grades, getting a job, becoming a "good" consumer, and in return receiving titillating sensual experiences and possible material wealth, was displaced. A call remained, but only in the form of urging one to choose a job or profession or become a clergyman, nun, or monk. The process of the calling as *curricula vita*, a cultural and spiritual course one has to undergo, was trivialized in education. One was now called to go to "job fairs" and to take national standardized exams that demonstrated in which field of work, each with its own curriculum subjects to be mastered, the individual appeared most likely to succeed.

It would be beneficial to the effort to retrieve *curricula vita* in curriculum studies as some sense of a calling toward a vocation by exploring how it operated in the lives of colonial Puritans. This is not to say that I am engaging in a nostalgic operation in which I believe America should return to some idealized past. Institutional structures based on some patriarchal ideal are neither desired nor possible due to informed critiques coming out of the many different feminist camps over the last 30 years. However, although the notions of *curricula vita* and calling and vocation certainly emerged out of a generalized paternal belief that a child must forever seek something more and engage in some spiritual journey toward an absolute other, this does not preclude its value.

It is beneficial to ruminate on Puritan perceptions and language, metaphors, and ways of understanding at play then, all of which infused the American psyche with a powerful sense of energy and cultural purpose (Bercovitch, 1978). To look at *curricula vita* as calling and vocation again will open a window to see what began for the Puritans as productive and pregnant notions have been reduced to a linear enumeration of facts and not one that envelops the fullness of living beings. Colonial Puritans accepted Calvin's notion of *curricula vita*, which coupled not only the external course of study one had to go through for an earthly vocation and institutional life, but also the interior, much less linear process necessary to generate meaning and spirituality.

PURITAN CALL: INTERIOR SEARCH
AND ARCHETYPAL GUIDES

Sacvan Bercovitch (1975), in his discussion of Puritan leader John Winthrop and the duties of a social ruler as visible saint, interpreted the significance of the twofold concept of calling—the inward call to redemption and the summons to a social vocation—imposed on man by God for the common good: "In keeping with their militant worldliness, the Puritans laid special emphasis on vocation.... Invoking various scriptural models, they distinguished the merely good ruler from the saintly ruler, and insisted that the saintly ruler reflect his inward calling in his social role.... As his vocation was a summons from god, so his belief led him to do well in public office" (p. 6).

This concept of the calling, then, placed not only demands on the social institutions to care for and watch over the individual, but also expected the individual to serve the Puritan institutions as a visible saint, no matter the vocation. However, service was not possible unless one was attentive to a particular voice. One listened for the call of the absolute other. This listener strained to catch the summons, most audible when one was deep in study, reflecting on and praying for guidance through the internal wilderness, where the soul dwelled.

For the Puritans, however, the soul had lost its original identity. Because of the biblical fall of Adam and Eve, the dwelling no longer was a transparent pool reflecting God's light, but instead an overgrown and opaque wilderness that had to be eradicated and given order (i.e., institutional individualism). The Puritans, strict Calvinists, refuted the notion that one could go at this exploration of, or better, campaign against, the interior wilderness without a spiritual sense of method. For any hope of achieving transcendence, one had to have a lens, a language by which to articulate one's findings.

Although it was believed that each individual's inward turn had different tones, textures, and types of dark creatures to be eradicated—the worst being any residue of an unencumbered self—the Puritans brought with them from Europe an empirical, experiential approach to understanding the world and the self. With this paradigm came the assumption that not only could one locate God in the external world through the objective study of nature, the same would hold true for the inner life of mankind. The individual's interiority was an object subjectively analyzed, studied, and reflected on, even though the outcome often could not be articulated in the language of science or reason (Greaves, 1969). Humans needed mediation. God provided language as a means to understand and articulate, although it was an imperfect tool, often as likely to create pitfalls and ambiguous signposts as to explain with clarity. But for the Puritan mind, this was not an undesirable condition. Language was given to slow humans down, because the journey to the absolute other needed time for reflection and deep understanding, neither of which could or should happen immediately. According to Puritan belief, if God was experienced too quickly, it would ruin the individual, overload him or her with too much before enough maturity of flesh and thought could control the spiritual knowledge. In other words, time was needed for an individual to work through his or her unique although sinful state, as represented by the metaphor of the wilderness, as well as through a linguistic means to begin understanding what was happening during this internal pilgrimage.

For the Puritans, this was a recursive activity, because one did not move in a linear from Step A to Step B of salvation. The individual revisited every doubt and concern and moral action to think about, pray about, and interpret again the meaning of each situation and how it affected his or her life's course. For the recursive journey of interiority, a particular kind of language—something between science and poetry—appeared to provide a means of mediating the complexity of understanding the experience of "knowing one's self" and giving it articulation. Meaning emerged out of the act of articulating. Articulation followed a narrative form.

Puritan leaders, such as Cotton Mather, penned individual expressions of *curricula vita*—spiritual autobiographies, treatises, jeremiads, and biographical books and sermons—intended to map out the stories of those Puritans deemed visible saints. These examples followed a specific literary form in which the individual heard and responded to the call, worked through the interior wilderness, and imitated the story of Christ (*Christi imitatio*). This result became externalized in a choice of vocation:

> The Reformed alternative was the *exemplum fidei*. Formulated by Luther in the course of his attack on the Catholic saints, it proposed a mode of *imitatio* that emphasized the spirit rather than the letter of the deed. In this view, the miraculous pattern of Christ's life unfolded in organic stages of spiritual growth. The anomaly did not matter, only the common truths that the anomaly signified in context: the process of calling, temptation and salvation share by all believers. (Bercovitch, 1975, p. 9)

The figures of these stories about a visible saint's journey through the exterior and interior wilderness became archetypes, figural/historical representations of spiritual transcendence. Although the happenings and the individuals were real (and thus historical), every action, thought, and temptation each experienced was written in a way that moved them in conjunction with Christ's journey, or the journey of some other biblical character also imitating Christ (thus figural). The one responding to the call, then, had an interpretive framework by which to understand how to traverse the interior path, how to give the desires, temptations, and tribulations symbolic significance. This narrative means of interpreting the interior response to the calling satisfied the empirical sense of reality as well as the spiritual sense of temporality. Each visible saint had to hear the calling, respond to it, enter into a wilderness, fight temptation of sensual existence, and be given grace. Out of the interpretation of cultural texts, one arrived at a destination and, thus, vocation:

> In Cotton Mather's (1702/1977) work, *Magnalia Christi Americana*, he portrayed Puritan Governor John Winthrop as the first American archetype or representative saint, calling him Nehemiah Americanus, in reference to the biblical Nehemiah, who led the Israelites back from Babylon to their promised land. As the first governor [Winthrop] restored theocracy, he inspired them to take up once again the burden of their covenant. He revived their sense of destiny, ensured their protection against heathen neighbors, organized further migrations from Babylon to Judea, reformed civil and religious abuses, and directed the reconstruction of Jerusalem from a wasteland into a city on a hill. (Bercovitch, 1975, p. 1)

In these narratives, the individual did not attempt to escape the darkness of the interior wilderness, but instead tried to cut out an opening that would allow the light of the absolute other to filter in and cleanse the self. The consequence of a Puritan individual not responding to this call was grave. The individual would succumb to the interior thicket, which would in turn infiltrate the congregational/institutional identity, invite the rule of ignorance, and devastate the colonial Puritan project of creating a "city upon the hill" (Bercovitch, 1975). Colonial Puritan leader John Winthrop employed the phrase "city upon the hill" not only as a promise of what might happen if they were successful, but also as a warning to reflect the seriousness of each individual's obligation to respond to the call. If each individual did not engage in the Calvinist sense of *curricula vita*—of charting out a course of life that generated an identity of institutional individualism and a relation with an absolute other—all would be lost. This ideology placed a heavy burden on each individual, despite the notion that an individual self as having priority over or separate from the Puritan project as a whole was loathed by these early Americans. This was an interesting bind for a Puritan, because one had to concentrate, often to the point of obsession, on one's self to make the necessary affiliations and relations to institutions and the absolute other. This is a significant juxtaposition to another ideology of self-identity that was spreading across Europe, that of the humanist celebration of the self as autonomous and unhindered by history or existing institutions.

Both humanists and Puritans professed interest in the world, but they differed on what kind of emphasis should be placed on the individual. Both worldviews had perceptions that unleashed an intense impulse toward self-study, demonstrated in resurrection of the old Socratic adage, *Scito te Ipsum* (know thy self). However, for the humanists, this command had the effect of celebrating the notion of an autonomous, secular self, and the "primacy of the single separate person, and justifies his self study on its intrinsic merits, without pretense at religious or even moral instruction. He assumes that what he has thought and done will interest others because it is authentically his, the product of his own personality in all its rich uniqueness. The mode of identity he offers posits that no two selves are alike" (Bercovitch, 1975, pp. 11–12).

However, colonial Puritans appeared to interpret this command with a different lens. One did not find glory in his or her individual self, only greed, pride, and a thicket of sin. The impulse was to analyze, examine one's interiority through the use of cultural texts in order to weed out the iniquitous self and transcend to a spiritual self. During the Renaissance, when mirrors became popularized, many sought within the reflection a glimpse of their true inner selves. However, Puritans looked for just the opposite: "Puritans felt that the less one saw of one's self in that mirror, the better; and best of all was to cast no reflection at all, to disappear" (Bercovitch, 1975, p. 14). A reflection of one's self without the absolute other shining through or at least looking over his or her shoulder was but an image of personal failure.

The interior self blocked true spiritual effervescence due to its state of darkness and guilt. This was an interesting dilemma, because the desire to annihilate one's interior self and replace the empty reflection with an image of God actually had the effect of celebrating an obsession with the self. The proliferation of spiritual autobiographies (which became narratives of one's journey toward conversion and were used as the resource for public testimonials before the congregation), as well as diaries and letters speak to the significance Puritans placed on maintaining a record of one's earthly and spiritual self. In other words, the harder he or she worked to become more Christ-like, the greater was the desire to impose one's self on the world and display visible sainthood. The interior search was useless if it did not result in a vocation in which one could exercise his or her will in the world and demonstrate saintly attributes.

CALLING TO A VOCATION: EXTERIOR CURRICULUM

As discussed before, the call to a vocation, spiritually infused by the interior dialogue with the absolute other, operated within the structure provided by Calvin's *curricula vita*. Thus, his notion of *curricula* obviously was not situated only within schools. Calvin's notion of curriculum encompassed that of one's whole life. Due to the nature of the calling toward a vocation, his *curricula vita* also emphasized study of the natural world and the words and philosophical theories of humankind. Such subjects were not only important in that they pointed toward the message of the absolute other, but they also were necessary for intelligent action in the world. Schooling, and the curriculum that encompassed the different subjects, was immensely important for the Puritans. When the Puritans organized Harvard into a college (the first in the nation), they developed a curriculum in which textual studies—based on the findings of philosophy, science, and rhetoric—were coupled with theological studies of faith.

However, the preconditions for entering into that level of study were just as important for the Puritans. Learning the mechanics of reading, learning a trade or entering the ministry were all preconditions—pieces of the structure of good habits—necessary for the individual to have the slightest chance for grace to cascade down on him or her (Morgan, 1944). For the colonial Puritans, schooling, especially in terms of rudimentary literacy, was a serious, legal requirement. It provided the basic tools by which not only to answer the interior call but also to become a capable, worldly individual with craft and intelligence to understand the full meaning of world activity. A Puritan parent's first and foremost responsibility was to provide and care for the family, under the threat of harsh penalty.

In 1641, John Cotton wrote of a type of formal education for children that exacted from the father a heavy investment of time and money: "According to law every father had to see that his children were instructed in some honest lawful calling, labour or employment, either in husbandry, or some other trade profitable for themselves, and the common-wealth if they will not or cannot train them up in learning to fit them for higher employments" (p. 439).

Crucial to the process of revealing one's vocation was the obligation to gain knowledge of the world, because God was in all things and the one able to "read" the text of the world enhanced his or her chances at salvation. Ignorance of world knowledge—as opposed to truth revealed to an individual by God—threatened one's salvation and the perpetuation of the Puritan errand of creating a city on the hill: "Truth which came by ordinary means, as in science, philosophy, and the arts, would not contradict but enhance revealed truth.... At best human erudition was so full of God's truth that its only enemy in Puritan eyes was ignorance; it was so closely related to God as the author of all truth that it tended toward the perfection of the human mind" (Greaves, 1969, p. 121).

Morgan (1944) explained the significance of this fear of ignorance and the need to educate, especially children, into the various ways of knowing different from interior faith:

> The Puritans sought knowledge ... not simply as a polite accomplishment, nor as a means of advancing material welfare, but because salvation was impossible without it.... They retained throughout the seventeenth century a sublime confidence that man's chief enemy was ignorance, especially ignorance of the scripture.... The Puritans rested their whole system upon the belief that "every Grace enters into the soul through understanding; and since children were born without understanding they had to be taught." (p. 46; quoting Mather, 1702, p. 34)

To understand was to have inherited cultural ways of knowing, a map that was then individualized into a method by which one could navigate his or her course in the world. It is no coincidence, then, that Puritans appropriated the literal academic curriculum maps created by Peter Ramus. Although the Puritans provided archetypes, typologies, spiritual autobiographies, and figural histories of visible saints to help guide the interior struggle, in the end it was still an individual journey, each different, although all with the same end in sight. The goal was the same, because the journey was individual. However, when it came to the textual study of the external world, science and theology had to work together much more explicitly. In the Puritan perception of life, because the interior world represented a wilderness, the external world was to represent order and predictability. However, both realities were to be broken down, analyzed, and put back together—a highly empirical approach (Greaves, 1969). As Mages (1999) explained about Ramus, "Employing this Ramean method, one first identified the concept to be investigated then divided it into halves, halved these again in turn, and so on until all the components were established. Once all the reasons or concepts were laid out, then an individual could start combining them to form arguments" (p. 97).

During the 16th century, Ramus developed for university education (although primary and secondary schools quickly adopted his structure; Ong, 1971) a map that attempted to codify knowledge and present the reader with a linear process by which to attain that knowledge. His textbooks, encyclopedic in form and content in that they were believed to provide information to the student in systematic and efficient ways, spread all over Europe and America (Ong, 1971).

Just as the printing press standardized the means by which to spread the content of one's thought throughout Europe, Ramus created a way to standardize knowledge to be included in these texts, as well as to how those texts should be taught.

Ramus' maps were wildly popular in Calvinist universities throughout Europe. When in the mid-1600s the Puritans developed Harvard's course of study, the leaders adopted Ramus' logic and curriculum maps. Puritans subscribed to Ramus assumptions that nothing was usable in any text or object of study, including one's interior self, unless first analyzed. Also, whatever information was discerned from the analysis had to have some "utilitarian" function in the world. Knowledge for knowledge's sake was useless to the Puritans and to Ramus. Puritans believed that the maps proved well suited to rationalize and order the integration of the Christian view of revealed truth and the language and knowledge of the new learning, specifically the scientific and philosophical paradigms arising out of the renaissance: "Hence, there was an affinity between the discipline, order, and control Calvin [Puritans were strict Calvinists] felt all Christians should bring to their lives and that which Ramus brought to pedagogy" (Doll, 1997, p. 11). Ramist methods emphasized control and predictability in the world, which acted as a counter to the wilderness within. The effect was that the "knowledge" put forth in these maps became perceived as static, or better, as a "commodity rather than as wisdom "(Ong, 1971, p. 175).

And it was partially due to this adopting of the Ramus view of knowledge that has led to the loss of interiority in curriculum in the present age. The Puritans for a short while struck a balance between the narrative course of the interior struggle and the mastery of cultural knowledge as a means to operate intelligently (i.e., usefully) in the world. However, the individual's sense of struggling with the texts as a means to work through one's calling was reduced to knowledge consumption as the Ramus view took hold during the emergence of mass public education in the late 1800s. The presentation of what constituted knowledge had a new clientele in mind, not just the clergymen and monks of the scholastic era, but the merchants and artisans of the burgeoning capitalistic era (which included a majority of practical-minded colonial Puritans). Simply, this clientele saw the world with different eyes:

There is an obvious relationship between this mentality and the mentality of a commercial, merchandising world, where good had to be thought of in terms of operations with a view to possible users or consumers. Ramist "methods" makes it possible to think of knowledge itself in terms of "intake" and "output" and "consumption"—terms which were not familiar to the commercial world in Ramus' day, of course, but which do refer to realities present within that world. (Ong, 1971, pp.173–174)

However, in the beginning, Ramus mapping was just part of the colonial Puritan sense of external curriculum. It was much more involved in terms of attempting to strike a balance or show how the knowledge of science and knowledge of experiential faith were not in opposition, but both announced the truth in different language. For the colonial Puritans, scholarship not only led to one becoming a clergyman or civil leader, because these were just a couple of possible vocations; curriculum also had to prepare the vocations of the "working" world.

However, as Puritan Congregationalists dispersed into denominationalism—a fragmentation of one Protestant theology into a variety of subtly different ones, each forming its own group consciousness but each adhering to certain generalized Protestant beliefs—the notion of the calling shifted. A balance within the notion of curriculum between the individual struggling to understand his or her interiority as a means toward finding a vocation and the body of cultural knowledge and narratives with which one interacted was lost. Instead, when education became a reality during the late 1800s under the wishes and efforts of the White, urban, Protestant middle class, living in the large Midwest and Northeast cities, curriculum became perceived as a tool to "Americanize" immigrants and "train" children to serve secular society. One was still called to the clergy or to the church, but one was "trained" for work or profession, not a vocation.

Ramist maps of grouping knowledge and discipline fields, linked with his method of transmitting that knowledge, became the privileged form of curriculum development. Curriculum as the broad operation in which one took a spiritual *curricula vita* journey in response to a calling toward a vocation was trivialized and dismissed without discussion, until the fairly recent reconceptualization of curriculum during the 1980s. This led to a break in the technical discourse's stranglehold on the possibilities and purposes of curriculum. However, although such a reconceptualization has found a home in certain intellectual circles of education departments in higher education, no such shift has taken place in the institution of schooling. The challenge for those interested in developing a discourse of *curricula vita* seems overwhelming, due to the incorrigible fact that bureaucratic institutions, which work in tandem with the technical sense of curriculum, will not willingly change. The system of curriculum as subject matter to be mastered is so embedded that nothing less than a complete implosion or meltdown by mainstream schools across the country will open up a moment in time for radical change to occur.

However, in true Kierkegaardian fashion, although such a state of affairs can cause one to give himself or herself over to dread and despair, leading to paralysis, at the same time an individual is obligated to respond, always struggling to move beyond what exists at the moment. That is *curricula vita*.

REFERENCES

Bercovitch, S. (1975). *The Puritan origins of the American self.* New Haven: Yale University Press.

Bercovitch, S. (1978). *The American jeremiad.* Madison: University of Wisconsin Press.

Bercovitch, S. (1993). *The rites of assent.* New York: Routledge, Chapman and Hall.

Cotton, J. (1641). *Way of life.* London.

Cuban, L. (1971). Teaching the children: Does the system help or hinder? In V. F. Haubrich (Ed.), *ASCD yearbook* (pp. 147–160). Washington, DC: Association for Supervision and Curriculum Development.

Doll, W., Jr. (1998). Curriculum and the concepts of control. In W. F. Pinar (Ed.), *Curriculum: New identities in/for the field,* (pp. 295–324). New York: Garland.

Greaves, R. (1969). *The puritan revolution and education thought: Background for reform.* New Brunswick, NJ: Rutgers University Press.

Greven, P. (1977). *The protestant temperament.* New York: Knopf.

Huebner, D. (1993/1998). Education and spirituality. In *The lure of the transcendent: Collected essays of Dwayne Huebner* (pp. 401–416). Mahwah, NJ: Lawrence Erlbaum Associates.

Kaufmann, M. (1999). *Institutional individualism: Conversion, exile, and nostalgia in puritan New England.* London: Wesleyan University Press.

Kliebard, H. (1971). Bureaucracy and curriculum theory. In V. F. Haubrich (Ed.), *ASCD yearbook,* (pp. 74–94) Washington, DC: Association for Supervision and Curriculum Development.

Macdonald, J. (1995). *Theory as a prayerful act: The collected essays of James B. Macdonald.* New York: Peter Lang.

Mages, M. (1999). *Magnalia Christi Americana: America's literary old testament.* San Francisco: International Scholars Publications.

Morgan, E. (1944). *The Puritan family: Essays on religion and domestic relations in seventeenth-century New England.* Boston: Trustees of the Public Library.

Ong, W. J. (1971). *Rhetoric, romance, and technology: Studies in the interaction of expression and culture.* Ithaca, NY: Cornell University Press.

Palmer, P. (1993). *To know as we are known: Education as a spiritual journey.* San Francisco: Harper/Collins.

Pinar, W. F. (1995). *Autobiography, sexuality and politics: Essays in curriculum theory, 1972–1992.* . New York: Peter Lang.

Pinar, W. F., & Grumet, M. (1976). *Toward a poor curriculum.* Dubuque, IA: Kendall Hunt.

Stone, L. (1979). *The family, sex and marriage in England, 1500–1800* (abridged). New York: Harper and Row.

Williams, R. (1983). *Keywords: A vocabulary of culture and society* (rev. ed.). New York: Oxford University Press.

Chapter 8

Dance Curricula Then and Now: A Critical Historical–Hermeneutic[1] Evaluation

Donald Blumenfeld-Jones
Arizona State University

Thinking Beyond

In this chapter by Donald Blumenfeld-Jones, the theoretical world of hermeneutics and the world of dance intertwine. Blumenfeld-Jones indicates that even an activity as fluid as dance has succumbed in many of its curricular manifestations to technical-rationalist models. He employs hermeneutics as an avenue for dancers to use theoretical thinking to achieve a line of flight away from or a way to transcend conventional educational thinking. Blumenfeld-Jones demonstrates that the reasons dancers have for dancing go beyond the rational and that those reasons are valuable.

Questions

1. How is the combination of hermeneutics, dance, and curriculum theory an example of the type of research that this book advocates?
2. This chapter is content-oriented, specifically focusing on dance curriculum. How does the emphasis on the curriculum content benefit from historical analysis? How does the historical analysis that Blumenfeld-Jones uses compare to the historical analysis used by McKnight? Can historical analysis be part of the multiplicities that this book describes?
3. In what ways can the multiple readings of hermeneutical analysis that Blumenfeld-Jones applies to dance be used in multiple disciplines?

Conventionally, curricula are thought of as plans or frameworks for educational action, a species of policy directives to be implemented. This narrow conventional view hides the fact that curricula are also evaluations of previous curricula and imaginative texts that are produced by people living in the midst of a field of endeavor with a history and a context to which they are responding

---

[1]Jurgen Habermas, in *Knowledge and Human Interests*, offers a three-category division of the human sciences: empirical–analytic, historical–hermeneutic, and critical–emancipatory. Particular projects tend to be one or the other of these kinds. Each category has associated with it particular human interests, even though, at least in the empirical-analytic category, the quality of "disinterested" inquiry is central to notions of good practice. According to Habermas, such disinterestedness can also be found in historical-hermeneutic inquiry, although not so stridently defended. Historical–hermeneutic inquiry is primarily concerned with understanding, in an either omniscient or partial, but always descriptive, way. No judgments are made. Only with critical–emancipatory inquiry do we have explicit ownership of an interest: greater freedom for all through a critical project. In this present study, I adopt Habermas' historical–hermeneutic label but would argue that my project is critical, emancipatory, and political. My intention is to offer a critical historical–hermeneutic analysis designed to persuade others that the usual ways of thinking about dance education are flawed and/or regressive and lead to less freedom for all who experience them.

through the creation of new curricular initiatives. When we image curricula in this less conventional fashion (not seeing them as practical policy directives), they become historical documents that speak of their times, their makers, and the conditions of their production. They become personal documents as well, speaking of individual responses to those situations. Additionally, for those of us who read these texts, we need no longer treat them as authoritative directions for actions but instead as documents that we may interpret in order, perhaps, to better understand ourselves and our own place in the field of endeavor that has a history and a context to which we, too, are responding. In short, from these texts we can learn who we are as historical beings living in the onflowing stream of thought that comprises our particular field of endeavor, and we may learn of the implications of our own curricular decisions.

It is with this in mind that I launch this project, which I characterize as hermeneutic. I argue that each of the dance curricula are grounded in both implicit evaluations and images of desired worlds (the curricula point the reader toward a better world than the present one) arrived at (unconsciously) through an hermeneutic process: The curricularist interpreted particular conditions and expressed those conditions (and that unconscious process) in the writing of the curriculum. My task is to make that process apparent through my own hermeneutic analysis of the curricula. In so doing, I also attempt to show how the curriculum design process, were curricularists to consciously practice it as an hermeneutic process, could become educational in character. That is, the designers could learn something during their design practice while they are, simultaneously, creating plans so that others might learn.

The genesis for this project is multiple and, given that this is a critical historical-hermeneutic study, its genesis constitutes part of what we hermeneutically name the horizon of the project and, thus, needs some explication. This, in turn, reveals some of my own prejudices and expectations that inform my thinking about these curricula.

My thinking about this project began when I read John Mann's essay (1975) calling for a new language for talking about curriculum. His call for what he named "curriculum criticism" dovetailed with my own interest in literary criticism and hermeneutics as a way to think about human experience while experiencing curriculum. In describing curriculum criticism, Mann stressed the "aesthetic elements" of language (p. 133) and wrote, "To regard a curriculum as a literary object … means first of all to think of it as a set of selections from a universe of possibilities … the function of the curricular critique is to disclose its meanings, to illuminate its answers" (pp. 135–136). This resonated with my approach of examining the specific language that curriculum designers use to express their curricular ideas (Blumenfeld-Jones, 1995). In this present project I am adding to Mann's ideas the notion that the curricular answers of which he wrote are responses to explicitly stated and implicit, unstated questions. These implicit, unstated questions animate the positive prescriptions of policy directives as much as the explicitly stated questions that the curriculum is answering, and help to reveal more of the history to which the curricularist is responding.

Later on I read William Reynolds' work (1989), in which he utilized hermeneutics as a form of curriculum evaluation. Reynolds drew on Paul Ricoeur's work to develop what Ricoeur called a "hermeneutic arche." The hermeneutic arche is tripartite: It begins in a naive reading of a text; is followed by an examination of the structures of the text, because these position the writer and reader vis-á-vis the world and each other; and finishes with querying the text's relationship to the world as the text's referent, and what the reader of the text may gain in her or his understanding as a member of that world. Reynolds applied these ideas to two particular curricular approaches (Mortimer Adler's *Padaiea Proposal* and Pinar's & Apple's work in reconceptualist curriculum theorizing).

My work both partakes of and extends Mann's and Reynolds' thinking. In terms of consonance with their work, I, like Mann, focus on curricula as literary objects. I want to develop the idea (and practical methods for realizing this idea) that attention to the actual language in use provides insight into the historical content of the text. I am also drawn to Reynolds' naïve reading through which, by delineating the surface of the text, we can see how a deeper reading provides a more complex shape to the text where previously it may have appeared as just one thing after another. Reynolds' notion of relating the text to the world is also central to my own thinking, and it is in this perspective that my work extends the work of both Mann and Reynolds. I want to develop an approach that reveals the historical characteristics of curriculum and their direct, material presence in the curriculum text itself. This means that all curricula are representative of a particular response to a particular historical moment, and that to understand them we must see them as sociohistorical products. Finally, like Reynolds, I am interested in the educational character of hermeneutic thinking and want to extend that notion. Shaun Gallagher, in *Hermeneutics and Education* (1992), argued strongly that the practice of hermeneutics is educational because it functions from question posing and subsequent question resolution, which lead to new questions on the part of the learner, eventuating in what Gallagher termed *practical wisdom*—a way of living morally on a daily basis. Can curriculum thinking, if practiced in a hermeneutic fashion, also be educational in character and develop such practical wisdom? These are some of the issues I hope to be able to address through this study.

THE PRACTICE OF HERMENEUTICS IN THIS STUDY

My hermeneutic practice proceeds through a series of simultaneous questions to which I seek answers. In my approach, as I have indicated, I seek to understand a curriculum text in its own time by asking, "What is there in the text that can reveal the circumstances within which the text was created?" These circumstances may be revealed in a number of ways. We may ask, "What are the explicitly stated reasons for producing the curriculum, and what issues has the curricularist raised about the field in question?" I term answers to this question the "ostensive motives of the curricularist." Through explicating these ostensive motives, we come to understand the curricularist's notion of the history and traditions of the particular curricular field. He or she may adopt an objective stance toward these conditions, meaning that he or she does not necessarily acknowledge the effect of these conditions upon his or her own curriculum work: They are objects outside the self of the curricularist. In such a stance, although curricularists may examine, probe, and critique the field, we may not detect their own direct involvement with the dilemmas. They are merely stating the case as it is and providing the appropriate response to that case. In short, curricularists may not notice the political character of their own work—may not notice their implicit answer to the basic curriculum question, "Who should decide?" Rather, they are only delivering answers to the other basic curriculum question, "What shall we teach?"

Second, we can ask, "What are the specific, individualized issues that curricularists have with the field that moves them to conceive of new curricula?" I consider these to be the personal motives of the curricularist. They might be revealed in tone or content. They may be different from ostensive motives, thereby creating tensions within the text that may reflect tensions within the lived experience of the curricularist. Although we cannot speculate psychologically, we can note that, in these situations, the text reflects unresolved conflicts and tensions. Third, we may ask, "What are the general historical, sociocultural conditions that create a context for the text?" The curricularist and curriculum are inevitably ensconced in such historical motives. By historical motives, I mean the surrounding conditions that affect curricular decisions. Of the three motives (ostensive, personal, historical), this last is the most difficult to explicate, but in some ways it is the most significant. Although a curriculum may be the product of the curricularist's imagination, no curriculum emanates idiosyncratically from the person's mind or responds to an isolated tradition. The multiple contexts of the curricularist's decision making not only affect decisions but must find a material presence in the curriculum.

The reader's role is central. Readers bring their own ostensive, personal, and historical motives (all of which hermeneutics names "horizon") to bear on a text, constraining possible readings of the curriculum. There can never be an univocal reading of a curriculum, because there is never a readerless curriculum. If tensions are discovered within the curriculum between the layers of motives I have outlined, this reveals as much about the reader who discovers them as it does about the author and curriculum under question. I do not mean to argue that there is, therefore, never a valid reading of a curriculum. Rather, the reading is always situated and tentative while being simultaneously suggestive of new possibilities heretofore not apparent because this particular reader had not yet read the curriculum.

A number of simultaneous events must occur within an hermeneutic reading. The traditions (as the hermeneut understands them) that ground the curriculum must be explicated. The particular conditions that surround the curriculum must be elaborated. Anomalies in the curriculum must be analyzed. These anomalies are the location of both the author's personal intentions and the tradition's assertion of its own prerogatives over and above the immediate and practical reasons for the author's choices in creating the curriculum. Readers who perform the interpretation must reveal their own prejudices and positions vis-à-vis the curriculum and tradition as the horizon of their understanding of the text. This fourth dimension does not invalidate the interpretation, but locates it carefully. The warrant of interpretations can only be founded upon this fourfold frame because, otherwise, the curriculum is used as merely an excuse for the interpreter to forward particular agendas. This approach to reading demands a certain fair-mindedness toward curriculum evaluation and yet does not eschew a critical reading of curricula. The distance between what is there and what we believe is there is bridged, and particular curricula are not turned into mere objects of contempt or approbation—they become the situated documents that they are.

AN INITIAL READING OF THE CURRICULA: HORIZONS

Before embarking on the curriculum analysis, I want to tell you something about my choices of these three texts. There are not many available dance curricula that are sufficiently textlike that an hermeneutic analysis may be performed. Many are simply lists of objectives and activities, organized in a particular order. I sought out curricula that contained, beyond such pedagogical instructions, explication and rationale. Such curricula could function as a framework off of which specific curricula and daily events might be constructed, and are more in line with how I think of a curriculum, as a source or plan for planning specific educational events. When curriculum is looked at in this way, texts not ordinarily thought of as curriculum become available for examination. The three following texts, therefore, all can be understood as curricula, even though they may not appear in the guise of conventional curricula.

The first book is Alma Hawkin's *Modern Dance in Higher Education* (1954). Hawkins wrote this book to aid in rethinking the place of dance in general education. She proceeded to critique her era's conventional thinking and suggest the kinds of activities and events that are appropriate for dance when thought of in general education terms. Thus, she outlined a general plan for dance education practice. The second book is Margery Turner's *Modern Dance for High School and College* (1957), written to aid in teaching people how to teach dance. In this text, as with Hawkins, we are given the reasons why dance ought to be taught in a particular way and the actual processes through which this way can be realized. Turner also outlined a general plan for dance education practice. The third book is James Penrod's and Janet Plastino's *The Dancer Prepares* (1990). Penrod's and Plastino's book was designed to be used as a textbook by teachers of introductory college dance classes. Although it does not lay out how dance ought to be taught, it nevertheless can be used by individual instructors to construct a curriculum for an introductory college dance class. As with the Hawkins and Turner texts, many reasons are given as to why dance should be approached in the way that these texts do, thus also potentially functioning as a curriculum planning guide.

More specifically, all three curricula presented themselves, in one way or another, as answers to dilemmas of dance education of their specific times. Hawkins (1954) addressed dance educators and her perception that they needed to understand their project in the light of educational issues and theory, rather than in the professional, vocational dimension, that they had previously used. The history of dance education constitutes Hawkins' horizon. In a similar fashion, Turner (1957) couched the discussion in terms of the perception of others as to the character of dance education. Dance education is seen as "play and must be recast, to validate it, as work" (p. 3). Like Hawkins, Turner used certain educational language and concerns to align dance with education. Her language, however, differed from Hawkins'. (Later in this chapter I detail these differences.)

For both Hawkins and Turner, the audience appeared to be twofold. Hawkins addressed dance educators of her day and Turner addressed future dance educators. Obliquely, they both addressed educational policymakers. By providing present and future dance educators with better arguments for the educational value of dance, both authors answered critics of dance education and attempted to place dance in a more solid educational position. For both Hawkins and Turner, an improved education of dance educators solved the problems of dance education.

In contrast, the audience for Penrod and Plastino (1990) is beginning dance students, with dance educators as a secondary audience (here's how to teach beginning dancers; here's what they need to know). Despite this difference in audience, however, certain similar characteristics may be noted. Although there appears to be no concern with placing dance in a good educational light, the authors made an effort to describe the educational benefits of studying dance. Considering that authors of introductory sociology or biology textbooks do not include arguments as to the educational benefits of studying sociology or biology, the fact that such arguments appear in this text suggests that the problems confronted by Hawkins and Turner had not departed from the scene by 1990. Although the emphasis on persuading the reader as to the educational value of dance may have receded to the background by 1990, the necessity of that persuasion still exists. Penrod and Plastino had an additional purpose, explicitly stated: They sought to foster an educated dance audience that can support professional dance. The students in this course are not expected, for the most part, to aspire to the life of a dancer. Rather, they are gaining valuable knowledge whereby they will be able to appreciate and become supporters of more sophisticated forms of dance.

In all three cases, the general educational setting defines the horizon of the decisions made by the authors. Additionally for Penrod and Plastino, the professional world of performance constitutes another aspect of their horizon.

Situating these curricula in particular curriculum design movements (in a historical motive) reveals something of the historical/political contexts within which these curricularists were working and the ways in which they thought. This analysis utilizes Kliebard's curriculum history (1995) and set of varying curriculum approaches.

Hawkins aligned extremely well with the "life-adjustment curriculum" movement of the late 1930s and 1940s. Hawkins created a text at a time when the Korean conflict had placed us on a war footing redolent of WWII, even though there was more ambivalence around the country about this conflict, which had not even been designated a war. Hawkins' prescriptions offer an ameliorative adjustment of people to a somewhat unstable social circumstance. The people who would experience her curriculum were those who were making the transition from war to peace as people returned home from this conflict to confusing times. We can see that the conditions under which she was writing may have directed her attention in these ways, even though she did not reference WWII or the Korean conflict. Rather, her prescriptions were set at a time when social adjustment was still of some concern.

Although Turner's text appeared a mere 3 years later than Hawkins', much seems to have changed. She utilized a mélange of arguments. First, she appeared to be responding to critics of the life-adjustment curriculum who wanted a return to rigor in schools by calling for a focus on "work" rather than "play" in the dance curriculum. This aligned well with the critics of life-adjustment who declared that the curriculum was rampantly anti-intellectual and soft, and that schools had abandoned their traditional function. Kliebard informed readers that "the counter-attack of the intellectual community reached a sympathetic public" (p. 225), stemming from the ways in which FDR's "brain trust" had been so successful at bringing about an end to WWII. If the critics were seeking a stronger, more rigorous curriculum, Turner was willing to oblige. Kliebard pointed out that, with the launching of *Sputnik* in 1957, the life-adjustment curriculum was "already in steep decline" (p. 264). It seems of some significance that Turner's book was published in 1957. As with Hawkins, I am not arguing that Turner was directly aware of the changing mood of the country, and she was obviously not aware of the launching of *Sputnik*, but, given her possible alignment with the life-adjustment critics, it may be that she was presciently aware of coming change during the writing of her book.

Turner also argued for associating her call for "work" in dance education with problem-solving education, a progressivist notion. Ironically, such an argument makes her ideas a poor response to life-adjustment education critics of the early 1950s, many of whom also branded progressivism as an educational evil, which had led us away from sound education practices. Turner's invocation of democracy, although it might seem strategically wrong given what I have just written, did stem from a dance education tradition. By asserting that her version of creative dance education would enhance the development of good democratic citizenship, she joined dance educators from the late 1930s and early 1940s who also made such arguments. However, its reiteration here may also be taken as a sign that dance educators lagged in developing their educational thinking, because such justifications were made in the presence of a then-past world war and had fallen out of favor with the public. At least, such arguments were not substantive answers to the critics of progressivism or life-adjustment.

Penrod and Plastino (1990) also revealed an alignment with general curriculum practice and social conditions of their time. They addressed their text to the beginning dancer, but they couched the whole in terms of professionalism. That is, they argued that although not every student would become a professional, every student should have a professional experience. Furthermore, this professional experience was to be built around the demands of the marketplace. This approach aligns well with the present strong emphasis on making school experience relevant to the workplace, especially as found in the current "school to work" movement. The fact that they were writing during the Reagan–Bush presidency years only strengthens our understanding of why they would focus on the creation of markets, given that era's focus on an entrepreneurial spirit. However, this emphasis on professionalism is ironic, given that it is exactly this approach that was criticized by Hawkins in 1954, an approach that she noted had been in place for many years prior to her writing. We may notice, therefore, an historical circularity in dance education thinking.

In sum, these alignments between curricular prescriptions and historical curriculum design constitute some of the immediate historical motives within which the writers were working. They are useful to the extent that we can make judgments about the relationship among dance educators and their social, institutional, and tradition settings. Apparently, and not surprisingly, dance educators appear to be constantly seeking validation in terms of dominant educational trends, although in some cases their choices were already passé. An alternative might be for them to have sought the uniqueness that is dance, and have addressed important educational questions in new ways. They did not choose to do this, however, but rather chose to feature those aspects of dance that, whether or not they were aware of it, may have found favor with the perceived powers of the time.

We still do not know why these curricularists make particular decisions, especially, as I shortly note, some decisions that appear to have undercut the general thrust of the argument. These contradictory moments in the curricula reveal something else at work, and perhaps hidden aspects of the curricula. What is revealed is, of course, not only a function of the curriculum but, also, a function of myself as the reader. This is not to say that the hidden aspects are not part of the curriculum, but, rather, their significance is a function of the relationship between me and the curriculum. Therefore, it is necessary to understand my horizon from within which I am reading.

MY HORIZON IN RELATION TO THE TEXTS

I have danced professionally since 1970. My finding of dance as a life's work was one of those extraordinary moments in a person's life that it is a privilege to have experienced. This is not to say that the ground was not prepared by many disparate events and experiences over the course of my life. However, in the moment of taking my first dance class, in the very opening 10 minutes of that experience, my life's course was set. These previously uncoordinated events and experiences came together in that one experience. I now made sense of them as a confluence of interests and desires. The essential understanding of that moment, however, is not a rational clarity of purpose but the powerful pleasure through which, in the words of Lina Wertmuller's film, I was "swept away." Something had happened to me and for me in a way I had never experienced. It might be characterized as a "conversion" experience in that I had previously shunned dance because of homophobic attitudes. Now I had attended a dance class for I knew not what reasons.

I had chosen to go to that first dance class on a whim. A male friend asked a group of us sitting in a crowded lecture hall if anyone would join him, because he was going with his wife to a dance class and he didn't want to be the "only guy" there. "Yes" just popped out of my mouth. I was utterly surprised at my response, but felt an obligation to fulfill my promise. I went, and had this extraordinary experience. Afterward, I had to decide whether or not to go again. Making this decision was more serious, because my friend was not going to attend this second class. I was, now, not fulfilling an obligation, but making a personal choice based on my own desires. By attending that second class, I acknowledged that there was something there for me. During that second class, I was invited to participate in the spring concert. Dance was suddenly a wholly different affair. I needed to think about the idea of public performance (although I had, for many years, participated in theater). My first dance class experience was something purely personal, and now I was being asked to transform the personal into the public. I did not immediately say "Yes," but asked to think about it. Two or three weeks later, I agreed to perform.

Performing is a very different experience from dancing for oneself. The whole purpose of dancing had to change. No longer was it a personal experience of joy and pleasure, but now was a measured experience of what the audience might see or not see, how to communicate to the audience whatever it was that I wished to communicate. No longer was dancing just for me.

As I proceeded into the profession, a new sort of tension arose. The German Expressionist tradition in which I learned to dance was analytic in character. We learned that all dance, at its base, was concerned with four fundamental categories (space, time, shape, and motion), which were interwoven in all dance moments, even if the dance was ostensibly about a story of social interaction. We learned how to recognize, improvise, choreographically shape, and perform these four categories and their details. At my very first encounter with these ideas I was immediately captivated, and it was this encounter that solidified my intention to become a professional dancer (by studying with the people who had developed these ideas and the accompanying art). Although I was encouraged to use my intellect in dance (which greatly appealed to me), I was simultaneously berated for being too "heady" while I danced. I had originally begun with a nonintellectual experience which took over my imagination, was attracted to an intellectually intelligible system of dance (my first, university dance classes), gravitated to an intellectual system, and, subsequently, told I was being too intellectual. When I eventually pursued my doctoral studies in education but continued to teach and study dance at the university, dance students would say to me, "You think, we move."

I relate these stories for purposes of situating two tensions that exist, for me, in thinking about dance education. First, there is the unresolved tension between intellect and motion. It is unresolved in that I have not yet fully understood how they are appropriately related. There is a certain irrational explosiveness to dancing, a certain powerful need that some of us experience, which cannot and will not be denied. Merce Cunningham, one of the 20th century's most notable and influential choreographers, called this an "appetite for motion." This appetite must be sated. It is not a public appetite; it has nothing to do with public performance. Instead, it has to do with an ineffable urge that I cannot explain but that I hope for you to understand. Some people are always in motion; they find themselves moving unthinkingly and then realize that they are moving. Their moving is pointed out to them by others and then they say, "Oh, was I doing that?" or "Oh, I'm moving, aren't I?" The moving is not aimless, but neither is it aimed for particular expressive purposes. Rather, it may be thought of as the way some people think. They are not thinking about something else through movement. They are thinking in movement.

A second tension exists between this appetite and the kinds of arguments made by Hawkins, Turner, and Penrod and Plastino. None of these thinkers discussed this appetite, nor did they reference the need for a thinking dancer (which provides its own kind of pleasure). Dance was never justified on pleasurable terms or on personal terms that are irrational and ineffable. Rather, as I shortly describe, dance as an educational endeavor is justified in either rational (Hawkins, Turner) or vocational terms (Penrod & Plastino). Such approaches do not match my phenomenological experience, do not match what brought me into dance (both motion and intellect), what disallows me to stop dancing. If I describe this in a way that appears to place me in the sway of a power greater than my rational decision making powers, it is because I willingly allow this affection I have for motion to be an unquestioned part of my life. I can make, as I have done (Blumenfeld-Jones, 1990), sociological arguments for my involvement in dance, but these do not suffice to explain my continued involvement, because they outline the possible reasons why I became professionally involved but they do not explain why I dance.

Given my own experience, I am often mystified by the arguments made for dance and education. How could these thinkers have missed these powerful dimensions? Have they missed them? If not, do they appear in their work somewhere? Would they understand me were I to communicate this to them? Thinking in this way brings me to another reading of these curricula, seeking dimensions of these curricula that might call into question their ostensive motives and might more closely match my own sense of reasons for dancing, which might, to use more hermeneutic language, provide the message in the text that motivates my reading and answers my personal questions of existence and practical wisdom.

ALMA HAWKINS: *MODERN DANCE IN HIGHER EDUCATION*

Alma Hawkins was very clear about what problem she was addressing in her curriculum. She was working to resolve the tension that existed between dance as it had been taught and as it should have been taught. She wrote:

> This study is concerned with the role of modern dance in present higher education. More specifically, it is the purpose of this study:
>
> 1. To develop a concept of modern dance as education.
> 2. To identify specific contributions of modern dance to the goals sought through education.
> 3. To determine principles that should guide the teaching of modern dance.

The need for these determinations arises from the fact that:

> During the years when modern dance was establishing itself in education, very little sober consideration was given to the educational purposes of dance and the teaching methods that would achieve them ... A real solution to the problem of defining the proper approach to dance in education will be attained only as dance educators acquire a true understanding of the potential contribution of dance experiences to the growth of an individual and establish a philosophy of dance and guiding principles in conformity with the goals of education. (pp. 1–2)

She also noted that dance education thinking had been dominated by "professional dance [which] has exerted strong influence on, and in a sense pointed the direction for, dance in education. This no doubt partially explains why the major emphasis has been on activity and not on the purpose of dance in higher education" (p. 3). It was her contention that "even though the purposes and needs of the students in [the college class and the professional studio] differed greatly, the teaching procedures were similar … as … college teachers pattern[ed] their teaching after that of the professional artists with whom they studied" (p. 19).

Hawkins used a suggestive series of words (*sober, proper, conformity*) that stand in contrast to her description of a new kind of dance that is now generally called "modern dance" (p. 3). This new dance "is the expression of the dancer's feelings and ideas through the conscious organization of movement" (p. 3). Such dance is based on "feelings" but when thinking educationally we must think in a "sober" manner. It is not that these two terms are antithetical per se but, rather, that there is a certain freedom of imagination associated with modern dance that could hardly be called "sober." Indeed, when she recounted, later on, the history of modern dance, it was in terms of an expressivism, which moves audiences well beyond being "sober" or "proper." In other words, there is a tension in her curriculum created by trying to think about a more or less free-form experience flowing from feelings and ideas within a sober setting.

Hawkins was able to set this tension aside by distinguishing between educational dance and "perfected dance," the latter being the art form with its emphasis on beauty, harmony, and grace as well as meaningfulness. She described "perfected dance" in terms of particular social relationships (the hierarchical relationship of choreographer to dancers in which the dancer makes no artistic decisions but instead is a tool of the choreographer), a dedication to technical skill, the dancer's dedication to the "mere acceptance of another's point of view," (p. 2) and a career only available to a few. Educational dance, on the other hand, should not focus on achieving good dance but, rather, should focus on contributing to the growth of the individual qua social human being. Educational dance can lead to "more mature and effective behavior" (p. 35). Furthermore, such dance is for everyone rather than the select few who demonstrate ability. Hawkins wrote that this is the essence in "our democratic society" (p. 34). She also noted, "That essence finds fulfillment when each student [is helped to] discover and develop his power of expression … to grow in his understanding of self and in his relationship to others and these gains will, in turn, contribute to his progress towards total development" (p. 108). Hawkins understood development in terms of specific human needs that educational dance can help students to fulfill: "an adequate body, satisfying expression, and effective human relations" (pp. 108–109). Attending to these needs will lead to "[c]hanges in understandings, attitudes and behavior … [dance education making] particular contribution to the development of the individual in the area of self-real- ization and human relations" (pp. 108–109). These three needs became the organizational structure for the curriculum, as she devoted one chapter to each need.

In each chapter, the goal was to adjust the student to particular parameters. In her "adequate body" chapter, Hawkins characterized the student as a "biological and social ... organism ... in interaction within the organism and between the organism and its environment" (p. 39). Interactions come in the form of adjusting the person to be effective within various circumstances. There are two kinds of adjustments that people make; involuntary adjustments, biological in character, over which people have no control; and voluntary adjustments that are under a person's conscious, learned control. Adjustments are made in order to accommodate to changing circumstances. Only voluntary adjustments are amenable to educational effort.

Why might one wish for adjustment? Hawkins wrote that "the desire for an effective body" is a response to "developmental needs and ... social pressures" (p. 39). Developmental needs are biological and inevitable as one seeks "total fitness ... the functioning of all parts of the body in such a manner that the organism makes satisfactory adjustment to its environment" (p. 41). Education supports and enhances the inevitable biological need for fitness: "Man is meant to be an active animal [manifested through] the significant role that movement plays in the functioning of the organisms [that] makes the human being's need for activity apparent" (p. 41).

Social needs are no less inevitable than biological ones. For instance, in arguing that people possess a need for acceptance, Hawkins noted, "Remember that man is a social animal ... constantly striving to maintain a satisfactory relationship with this social environment" (p. 47). A biologically effective body aids in a social acceptance, making the social and biological a single unit. In more overt terms, she wrote that "physical skills have high status value," that the college student "attaches great importance to his performance in certain [popular] physical activities" (p. 48). The "natural" body with its origins in biological necessity is transformed into a social body, which is altered to enhance social acceptance but is no less determined by innate needs.

Hawkins moved beyond calling for mere adjustment to inevitable circumstances. Although she critiqued "perfected dance" for its emphasis on perfection, she reinstated a form of idealism in the educational arena. Kliebard informed us that the life-adjustment curriculum was, in part, a response to the return of the soldiers after WWII, designed to ease their transition back into a peacetime society and to aid all Americans in a return to stability. This curriculum also implicitly posited a good life toward which to educate people after the horror of war and its disturbance to the appropriate social order. Hawkins' notions of both a biologically fit body and a highly skilled body (read beautiful and athletic) posited an image of the ideal body that would fit into the new peacetime situation. As she wrote, "Adolescents ... constantly measure themselves against the prevailing norms of feminine and masculine attractiveness.... Girls feel great pressure to be 'good looking and graceful,' while boys want to appear 'strong and manly.' ... Physical appearance is more important for women than for men in most modern cultures and is codified to a large degree with social status ends" (p. 49).

The second need posited by Hawkins is "satisfying expression" that she, again, clearly linked to adjusting people to the present situation. She averred that "satisfying outlets for expression which do not result in irreconcilable conflicts with onself or with one's environment are essential to mental health" (p. 60). The arts release tension in a "mature [way thus] avoiding less desirable emotional reactions," which leads to emotional release and, thus, "effective functioning ... and good mental health" (Prescott in Hawkins, p. 69). Hawkins sought, through dance, "integration of personality" that occurs through the "logical arrangement of ideas ... [dance is] a means by which personal experience may first be clarified and then expressed ... repeated creative efforts ... increase understanding ... such appreciation also helps the individual identify himself with his contemporary culture and to understand something of the flow of culture throughout the years" (pp. 71–75).

Because Hawkins was dealing with an art form, she had to find a way to link these general notions with it. She did so by using biological and body metaphors to connect self-expression with aesthetic and creative expression. Aesthetic expression "affords rich sensory stimulation and produces a feeling response that is satisfying to the individual.... [Aesthetic expression is] as essential ... as food and drink.... [T]he desire for aesthetic experience [is] related to the needs of man's nervous system" (p. 61). She then pointed to psychological force, describing aesthetic experience as "the need for a specific form of experience ... the most delightful organization ... organizing experiences into satisfying wholes" (p. 62). Note the term "delightful." This is anomalous, considering that she had not previously alluded to what the experience of dancing might be like, only what its biological, social, and psychological outcomes might be. We might ask ourselves: Is it important that the organization be "delightful"? Is such delight merely functional within her overall scheme, or is it not absolutely necessary (delight is a side benefit rather than central)? What if "delight" were not forthcoming? Would the adjustment that she seeks still be obtainable?

We can answer these questions through a look at her discussion of aesthetic, creative experience. When we undergo such "expression of ideas and feelings ... progressive symbolization ... the consolidation and integration of day-to-day experiences ... a harmonious relationship with the various aspects of life as he experiences them" is achieved (p. 60). Aesthetic ends become transformed into psychological ends. Hawkins continued that creative experience proceeds through tension. She wrote that a "stimulus ... produces tension within the organism to which the individual responds with his feelings and ideas or concepts," which are then "shaped" and "reshaped" to produce a formed response to the stimulus (pp. 63–64). This response resolves the tension. If a need is biological and must eventually be resolved (because if biological needs such as eating and breathing are not met, the result is death), then it ceases to have anything to do with delight. It would not matter whether or not it was delightful because, delightful or not, it must be met. This possibly underlying logic is supported by the complete absence of such language in her discussion of aesthetic experience. Hawkins seems only to have mentioned delight in passing.

"Effective human relations" constitutes the third need to be met through educational dance. Here Hawkins effected a strange turnabout. Previously, her curriculum privileged accommodation to the status quo (through her emphasis on adjustment). Here, she wrote that "existing cultural patterns tend to stifle the free expression of feelings" and that the arts do not (p. 69). Nevertheless, she still understood the dance education mission as attention to "the problems of human relations" (p. 86). In fact, creative and aesthetic experience should lead toward the ability to work creatively to solve social problems (p. 76). "[Educational] experiences ... become meaningful only as they are related to the learner's aspirations, interests and present stage of living" (p. 38). Fulfillment of the three needs is best accomplished "through teacher–student planning, a process through which members of the group clarify their individual goals and together determine group goals and directional plans for activity" (p. 54). The teacher contributes from his or her "large ... familiarity with certain kinesiological factors ... understand[ing] about behavior and the individual's response to activity" (pp. 55–56).

Dance teaching is characterized by a focus on developing "a sound body ... for future dance experiences," (p. 56) an "enlarged ... understanding of dance as an art form" (p. 37) as the student becomes "increasingly proficient in technique and creative expression" (p. 37). Dancing directly contributes to general physical fitness; improvement in conscious physical control and physical appearance; improved self-regard that leads to improved social acceptance and, simultaneously, good social relationships; and, finally, the ability to solve problems, a transferable skill that meets the general social need for good problem solvers.

Hawkins' prescriptions are paradoxical. On the one hand, she attempted to escape from professional dance influence by focusing on dance as an education tool for all of the previously cited outcomes. On the other hand, she continued to talk about good-quality dance, developing choreographic skill, and technique proficiency. She used the word *delight* but only once. Her educational values were clouded by professional dance thinking. Where she had previously strenuously argued against the professional dance values, here she made them part of her goals for educational dance.

Why do I write "clouded"? They can only be "clouded" if I agree that the distinctions she drew were valid, and her educational values had become compromised by the incursion of professional dance values into the education arena. A great deal depends here on what is meant by "professional." We have seen that Hawkins characterized "professional dance" as socially hierarchical, and not focused on the people who dance but instead on the vision of a single person for whom the dancers labor. This was and remains a reasonably accurate image of professional modern dance. However, there are other ways to construe the term *professional*, as in "profess" for something in which one believes. Such "profession" is serious and dedicated and does not, by definition, exclude a concern with the individuals with whom one works. It does not exclude attention to the needs of those individuals. Neither must we accept the behaviorist, deterministic cast of Hawkins' descriptions of people. When we step beyond such thinking, there are many other ways to construe dance and the arts in general as educational (see Blumenfeld-Jones, 1997, 1998).

She consistently used language redolent of needs and drives and links— thereby, biological, social, and psychological in a seamless web of inevitable linkage and support. This coordinated well with the modern dance attitudes of the time. Martha Graham's work dominated the modern dance world, and Graham was strongly interested in delving into the deep psyche of human beings to get at what is essentially human, transcending time and space as well as founding an entire motional vocabulary on the basis of one bodily function, breathing (the Graham contraction-release approach). The Humphrey-Weidman approach, which also had widespread influence, posited the principles of human movement based on fall and recovery, which, so they argued, informed all human movement. The entire mood of dominant modern dance was to put forth a grand system. No matter that the systems theorized throughly different bodily behaviors as the basis for human movement; both approaches posited a dyadic answer to the issue of how human movement functions. Little wonder then that Hawkins, despite her rejection of the dance art as a basis for dance education, nevertheless adopted the same sort of mood, positing a fundamental set of tenets based in biological, social, and psychological inevitabilities. She, of course, marshalled many nondance education scholars to support her claim, placing her in the mainstream of academic thinking.

Hawkins' deeper motives are difficult to discern, because she consistently stood outside the curriculum. Was she an academic seeking legitimation among her peers? Was she encouraging the dance people who would read this curriculum to think and speak as she did? I am trying to show that it is through an accomodationist stance toward standard educational thinking of her time that she hoped to solidify the position of dance in higher education.

MARGERY TURNER: *MODERN DANCE FOR HIGH SCHOOL AND COLLEGE*

Margery Turner's book, although it only followed Hawkins' text by 3 years and preceded Penrod and Plastino by 33 years, offers a bridge between the two texts. Turner began her book by sounding very much like Hawkins but, in the final analysis, she focused on developing dancers and those who can appreciate the art of dance, sounding very much like Penrod and Plastino. This is not to say that Penrod and Plastino referenced Turner in any way, nor does it suggest that Turner influenced them without reference but, rather, that if we look at the historical hermeneutic flow of the tradition, there must be ground prepared for later events even if that ground remains subconscious background.

Because most of Turner's text is devoted to specific activities for the dance teacher to use, rather than moving from chapter to chapter, as with Hawkins, I write briefly about the general flow of the text. I point to the bridge capacity of the text. I also, however, develop a specific argument about the text that shows how the text may stand in opposition to Hawkins and Penrod and Plastino, which are, themselves, and perhaps curiously, quite similar in character if not in agenda. I begin with a general textual exegesis.

Turner presented a very clear agenda for writing this curriculum. In her preface, she wrote of the needs of dance education. It requires "higher standards of work," must not be considered as recreational activity at which one plays for a season, "must function in the lives of people" and become "a dynamic part of their experiences," and must "at least ... [en]able them to understand dance as spectators" (pp. 3–4). When dance becomes an accepted part of education, it will fulfill the educational purposes of problem solving: "[L]earn how to get at the root of a difficulty ... how to meet barriers and conquer them; how to think logically, so that her idea will be communicated clearly, how to work with other people and share ideas; and how to evaluate creative projects that will benefit others as well as herself. All of these values will aid the student in understanding herself and others" (p. 2). Additionally, the student "develops ... kinesthetic awareness" and a "sensitivity to the responses of other people and situations, whether they exist in dance or in everyday living" (p. 2) At the end of the curriculum, she added democracy to the mix:

> Education in general aims to establish principles of democratic living in each new generation. This book represents one method of achieving this aim.... [T]he creative approach to dance provides one solution to the problem of educating for democratic living. This approach is based on the principle of guiding individual development through problem solving.... Through such activity the student learns that no one has all the answers and that solutions to problems can evolve from many kinds of activity. (pp. 164–165)

These ideas certainly echo Dewey's emphasis, in education, on democracy as associated living focused on the need to solve social problems together (Dewey, 1944). They also reflect his concern for growth that is not random (guided individual development) in which the teacher has a significant role to play (Dewey, 1938) and is not merely a facilitator of the learner's agendas. Lastly, education, for Dewey, had to involve activities as a prime mode of problem solving and not remain fixed solely on mind work.

Prior to this explicit agenda that bookended the text, Turner wrote that the teacher must tailor the educational experience to "the needs and interest of the classes" (p. vii) to be taught. Hawkins wrote in just this way. Turner, however, had a somewhat different reason for such tailoring. She wrote:

> The student should come to know dance [as an art form] through her experiences with it—through experiences that are an essential and dynamic part of her life.... This may be most effectively achieved through intelligent stimulation to creative activity and continued guidance during the developmental stage.... Dance is for all students to experience, within the limits of their capacities.... Students have a greater capacity than they may be aware of. [No matter how limited the capacity] [s]he should be encouraged to continue her development ... for there are many other values which are by-products of dance experience. (pp. 1–2)

Hawkins did not argue that dance is a dynamic part of one's life but, rather, that life is enhanced by the dynamic of dance. Both Hawkins and Turner demarcated those who could dance from those who could not, and both argued that this is of no importance for the educational value of dance, which produces values beyond dancing. However, Turner's values did not focus on dance as a form of social adjustment of which problem solving is one species but, rather, on dance as a form of social change— problem solving for democratic living. For Turner, there was no focus on adjustment to the social status quo.

Hawkins emphasized the social values of dancing during the majority of her text. Turner, on the other hand, emphasized dancing itself. That is, Hawkins organized her text according to her notions of educational values and Turner organized her work according the order of events of a standard dance class, beginning with warming and stretching the body movements (chap. 2: "Body Conditioning"), moving to movement of the body in its various parts and as a whole (chap. 3: "Fundamental Movement Experiences"), and culminating in dancing through space (chap. 4: "Release Activities"). Turner concluded the text with two sections on creative movement (chap. 5: "Improvisation" and chap. 6: "Dance Composition") and a chapter (chap. 7: "Dance Clubs") on how to organize a dance club for purposes of promoting the creative experience on the school campus.

Turner's focus on dancing, per se, sets out the bridge between Hawkins and Penrod and Plastino, as the latter focused entirely on the profession of dance as opposed to its educational values. This point becomes even more evident as Turner noted: "It is an accepted fact that every student does not desire to dance and that some students will be satisfied by just an acquaintance with it. This acquaintance should at least open their viewpoints to such an extent that they are able to understand dance as spectators and, with each new experience, grow in their understanding" (p. 4).

Due to the relatively brief dance experience that most students will have, "it is very important to have high standards of performance both in the professional groups that may be brought to the school and in the student performing group" (p. 4). Penrod and Plastino emphasized their hope that if most students will not become professional dancers they will, at the very least, become appreciative and knowledgeable audience members. This is discussed at greater length later in this chapter when I examine their text, but at this point suffice it to say that Turner began with the educational value of dancing (with Hawkins) but included and, in many ways, emphasized the professional aspects of dance (good dance and dance audience development), which is contrary to Hawkins' intent but quite parallel with Penrod and Plastino. Turner's mixing of these two diametrically opposed agendas casts her text as a bridge.

Turner did two rather interesting things in this text. First, unlike the other two texts, she directly brought herself into the curriculum in the preface, writing of her own experience teaching dance. This appears anomalous, seeming out of synchrony with academic writing. Hawkins' book seems more the "norm" for academic writing. Second, Turner consistently used feminine pronouns and possessives. This is very strange (although totally reasonable, because her audience was almost exclusively women), because the norms of the day were to use *man* and its like as a stand-in for all people. This can alert us to the possibility of hidden dimensions of the curriculum.

This hidden dimension began in her strong valuing of work over play. By asserting that "Dance in education is very much in need of higher standards of work" (1957, p. 3) and that "It has passed the stage of being considered just another recreational activity at which one plays for a season," (1957, p. 3) Turner presented a classic Western dichotomy that favors work over play. For a clear exposition of this, see King and Apple, 1990. To that degree she was as sober as Hawkins. However, unlike Hawkins, she did not maintain this valuing consistently. In the chapter devoted to "Body Conditioning," she elaborately laid out the necessary body conditioning and fundamental movement experiences requisite to quality dancing and stressed the necessity of a work ethic, but in her "Release Activities" (leaps, jumps, hops, etc.) chapter she wrote, "Above and beyond all of these values remains a very important one—release activities are fun to do" (p. 84). This seems an unnecessary statement in light of her explicit agenda to underscore the serious, worklike, educational value of dance.

This opposition within her curriculum suggests that possibility that she was not as serious about her agenda as we might think; perhaps she was attempting to return to "play" through a devious route. A closer hermeneutic analysis of the concept of fun coupled with other aspects of her text reveals this possibility.

"Fun" and "play" are, conventionally, linked concepts. Work is serious and play is fun. Play involves pretending. When children play they often adopt a persona other than their own and live that persona (e.g., whether it be the persona of a baby or truck or train or animal). Such pretend play is a release from normal routines. Similarly, "release" may be understood as "release from the ordinary" or, in the case of dance, "release from the earth on which we ordinarily stand." "Release" also carries spiritual connotations. Some Western religions theorize the release from the present material life into a glorious afterlife. Meditation traditions teach to release, through spiritual techniques, from attachment to the here and now. We can assert that play and religious thinking share a common center: release from the ordinary. Whereas play is often associated with fun, transcendence is often characterized, conventionally, as a serious endeavor, which also brings, like play, great pleasure to the person experiencing the transcendent moment.

When Turner discussed creative activity and improvisation, she used language reminiscent of play/transcendence rather than play/fun: "[T]he individual must discipline her thinking and be able to concentrate so throughly on the stimulus that *she loses herself in the activity*" (p. 94, emphasis added). As in play, the player loses him- or herself, and as in certain kinds of religious experience, the purpose is to merge with a more universal self, so in improvisation there is the possibility of becoming lost in the activity. In Turner's case, the purpose of self-loss is to bypass inhibition so that the dancer can be more with the moment. Furthermore, Turner also wrote of the possibility of a "pleasurable experience in dance composition" (p. 118) that reintroduces the possibility of play as a valid aspect of dancing.

This analysis suggests that the "fun" and release activities are mediated, in other places, through the serious work of making art. This creates, on a very small level, a paradoxical tension within the text, which may be taken as either an aberration or as a sign of an unresolved difficulty. I prefer the latter, given my own horizon, in that there may be a striving for an as-yet unapparent possibility.

Applying this to our curriculum analysis, I would suggest that it seems as if two different curricula are being written here, one very consciously and the other implicitly. Consciously, Turner wrote for an audience of dance educators to provide them with the dispositions and arguments necessary to appeal to education policymakers. Implicitly, she wrote for her dance educator audience in a way that may have referenced their experience in dance, an experience that was much more about that "appetite for motion" than it was about problem solving. Her audience remained the same, but her appeals varied. My argument, however, is too strong. I don't believe we can locate a curriculum of play and transcendence beneath the curriculum of work. Rather, although the explicit agenda of the curriculum may be work, its opposite, forcefully absented at the beginning, has returned to the curriculum. In finding play submerged in the curriculum, the entire curriculum may be turned over and read quite differently from an initial reading, from the bottom up rather than the surface down. Turner asked us not to play, yet she could not wholly resist play, yet she refused to privilege play. Hers may have been a purely political move removed from her own dispositions, or her text may have been a Western modernist document characterized by the contradictions in Western modernist thought (Berman, 1982).

Unlike Hawkins, Turner did not seem as accomodationist to the status quo, although her lack of accommodation was veiled behind an accomodationist stance. That is, her resistance to what was demanded only appeared in marginalized ways, as in my discussion of "joy" and of the preface. The major portion of the curriculum was much more direct in the academicist way, forthright and commanding, no time for niceties: do this and do that, here are possible pitfalls for which to prepare, and here is why you should order dance class events in these ways.

PENROD AND PLASTINO, *THE DANCER PREPARES*

Curricularly, Hawkins presented dance education as a life-adjustment education. Turner explicitly argued, in Deweyan fashion, that dance contributes to problem solving and promotion of democracy. With Penrod's and Plastino's curriculum the curricular orientation is not, initially, so clear. They began by proposing that "We hope that you discover a new appreciation of the arts in general and to inspire in you a desire for self-discovery, self-discipline, and eventually self-expression in the art form of dance.... [The study of dance] is probably one of the most self-satisfying courses that you will take" (p. vii).

In other words, they apparently sought personal self-development, a form of the humanist curriculum promoted by Carl Rogers (Rogers & Freiberg, 1994). However, they also stated, "We hope these objective principles [of dance] will help you to form a subjective ideal that will inspire you to commit yourself more fully to the dance world" (p. vii), which removes attention from the self to an external world. What did they mean by "fully" in the preceding, and what was the nature of this commitment? They did *not* mean that students would become either artists or professional dancers: "No one can be taught how to be an artist, but you can be taught the craft of an art form.... We do not assume that you will become a professional dancer, although we have directed the ideas in this book toward that goal" (p. vii). Confusingly, they wanted the student to "experience the joy of movement well-executed, the exhilaration of creative endeavor, and the appreciation of dance—the most fleeting of the art forms" (p. vii) but for what purpose?

In the list of experiences, I would assert that the most important outcome is "appreciation." Penrod and Plastino stated that students would not be professional, could not be taught artistry, and yet would become fully committed to the dance world. Because being a professional dancer and artistry are denied them ("movement well-executed" and "the exhilaration of creative endeavor" being the attributes of these), only appreciation is left. As for their assertion of self-development, such a focus would logically require a commitment to oneself—dance would be only a vehicle. Additionally, there are no pictures of students in this book, only professionals. This is another way in which the beginning student is "left out" of the text. Therefore, the notion of self-development appears greatly weakened. Additionally, Penrod and Plastino never wrote of themselves, although they included themselves in the chapter opening's picture gallery. It is understandable, therefore, that the book's message is confusing: Even though hardly any of the students would become professionals, Penrod and Plastino "directed the ideas in this book toward that goal" (p. vii). They did this, I assert, because their real curricular interest was "appreciation."

We may ask: appreciation for what purpose? Later in the curriculum, they wrote of the need for dance companies to have audiences in order to economically survive. Appreciation leads to an increasing dance audience and improving the vocational life of dance performance. The agenda for developing audience was made especially clear on the very last page of the curriculum. They addressed the reader as follows: "Keep in mind that you as a member of the audience are a vital part of the process of the art.... Your sincere attempt to really see what is happening, to understand the artist's vision, and to critically analyze the work from your own experiences will strengthen your evaluative abilities" (p. 83). The reader is an audience member and not an artist, who is made to be other than the reader. This fulfills the early assertion that the reader would not become an artist. The notion of self-development is relegated to becoming an audience member, rather than personal development for personal reasons. To quote another film title, Penrod and Plastino were back to the future: They represented the very agenda against which Hawkins argued. Their interests were mediated through their position in a fairly successful, professionally oriented studio dance program in a major university. Their immediate connections with the professional world made it quite understandable why they had the focus they took. Indeed, were they to have written otherwise, they would have betrayed the agendas of the program within which they worked. Their institutional and social roles were consistent with the tone of the curriculum.

In the preceding discussion, I deliberately used the word *vocation*. In the educational climate under which Penrod and Plastino published this curriculum, connecting school experience to work experience was and continues to be the battle cry of both the conservative and liberal educationists and public in general. This is due to the economic fortunes of the United States being theorized to be tied to the rise and fall of school achievement. The school-to-work initiative, which appears to be steadily gaining momentum, is the present strongest instantiation of this thinking. The professional orientation of this curriculum appears to reflect this climate.

A focus on vocation was explicit when Penrod and Plastino listed the possible involvement one might have with dance:

In addition to careers in performance and choreography are: teaching at all levels and for all ages, dance notator, reconstructor of dances, dance therapist, historian, critic, journalist, accompanist, stage technician, stage manager, video artist, arts administrator, company manager, fund raiser, dance publicist, dance agent, dance producer, public relations specialist, movement analysis specialist, dance medicine/science specialist, dance trainer, expert in one of the aligned movement therapies such as Pilates, Alexander,

Feldenkrais, or Bartenieff techniques, dance orthopedist, performance-stress expert, and costume, set, and/or lighting designer. This short list gives you ideas to pursue in your love for the art, as all of these careers are necessary for modern dance to exist as a performing and developing art.

Modern dance can offer a diversion or a way of life—either a brief introduction to one of the most exciting of the art forms or total dedication to a life's work. The choice is yours. (p. 4)

This passage also presented a dichotomized vision of the place of dance in society. Turner had argued against the "play" (diversion) approach, and Hawkins wanted to undergird dance education with serious educational thinking. Penrod and Plastino, on the other hand, accepted the play/diversion position so endemic to the way the arts are viewed by many conventional school people in particular and society in general. This acquiescence only makes logical sense when vocation is privileged, because vocation necessarily contains its opposite, avocation.

Given Penrod's and Plastino's denials of the possibility of many people going on in dance, the "choice is yours" idea appears particularly disengenuous. Yes, a student can choose involvement in the field but, most likely, only in one of the peripheral support professions. The choice is sociocultural and not freely made (Bourdieu, 1994). The contrast can be made between these assertions and the Stinson, Blumenfeld-Jones, and Van Dyke (1990) study of seven adolescent dance students, several of whom were talented dancers, in great love with the art, who were opting out of dance because even the initial choice of entering had not been theirs. Their exits were brought on by a set of ideologies within the dance world that couldn't deal with difference, in this case difference in body types and in intellect. These girls were shunned and did not wish to be so. To say "the choice is yours" is to miss, entirely, Janet Wolff's arguments (1982) that art is socially produced, not the product of idiosyncratic individuals working on their own.

I wrote earlier of the break between dancing for oneself and public performance, and I pointed out the subtle turnabout in Turner's text. Penrod and Plastino made this difficulty simple by expunging the dancer's personhood: One only dances for and through others. They accomplished this by clearly distinguishing between choreographer and dancer, making the dancer the servant of the choreographer's desires and by giving the choreographer and teacher all the decision-making rights:

[T]he main concern of classroom technique is to align your body in a series of exercises that will strengthen and stretch it in order to make it responsive to the physical demands that will be made upon it. (p. 8)

The choreographer ... is forced to hire well-qualified, well-trained dancers who learn quickly and correctly. Dancers who can do any movement required of them by the choreographer are usually hired first. You cannot learn to dance on the job. (p. 13)

Developing a critical artistic eye is important to the dancer, but a word of caution is in order. Asserting that you know more than the teacher or other students (even when you do) is undesirable in the classroom unless your opinions are asked for. (pp. 15–16)

Additionally, they chided the dancer to imitate exactly:

[T]ry to copy the teacher's way. An important part of dance training is to develop your "artistic eye" to see all of the nuances of movement and then reproduce them as demonstrated. There are several reasons: Correct execution of exercise is imperative if injuries are to be avoided and physical control is to be established; mastery of the body is part of the satisfaction that comes from dancing; and those who want to be professional dancers must learn movement patterns quickly and correctly. (p. 22)

Finally, they asserted, "All teachers are working toward the same goal … the goal of developing a beautiful and artistically expressive body for you" (p. 13). Notice that the student has no role in these proceedings; rather, the teacher does it for the student. Penrod and Plastino consistently referred to the "training" of dancers, which, as has been pointed out by many people, ought to be distinguished from "educating." We train horses, but we ought to educate people. All in all, despite their initial assertion of the personal, their exclusive emphasis of professional, vocational concerns obliterated this dimension entirely.

SUMMATION

These four curricularists responded to their situations in differing ways. Hawkins stayed very true to her ostensive purpose to place dance on a firm educational ground. In so doing, I would argue that she desiccated the act of dancing as I understand it. Turner's curriculum revealed a moment when she remembered the joyful aspect of dancing, irrespective of its "work" aspect. I take this break to be an important sign of an underlying feeling that, perhaps for strategic reasons, she suppressed. I believe this is so based on my knowledge of her. When I began dancing, Margery Turner was head of the dance program in which I danced. I took only one class from her, later on. I did not know her at all when I took that first dance class, nor was she involved with the dance performances. She was centrally instrumental in the path I chose through the dance world, introducing me to the work of Alwin Nikolais with whom I subsequently studied and with whose protégé, Phyllis Lamhut, I subsequently danced for many years. I would say that Turner had a passion for dance tempered with a strong analytic intel-

lect. As for the Penrod and Plastino curriculum, here the curriculum pur-
ported to address the beginning, nonaspiring-to-be-professional student,
yet they couched everything in terms of the professional life. They asserted
that a beginning class ought to be for personal development, and yet consistently undermined this agenda by talking about the demands of the workplace. I believe they positioned the student as informed audience and failed
artist, hoping that they could develop the kind of backing that dancers need
if they are to survive as artists. Their problem, unlike Hawkins' and
Turner's, was to give professional dance a better financial future by creating
a better audience, rather than a better position in education. (This may be
because in the university in which they teach, the presence of dance is a
given. Their position also connects well with discipline-based arts education or DBAE.) This was not a problem, which they directly addressed as
central to their project, but it emerged through the ways in which they
spoke to the beginning dance student through the curriculum. In this
sense, like Hawkins, the phenomenological experience of which I have written appears to be entirely absent from the curriculum.

We can use these interpretations to do some curriculum thinking. Paul
Ricoeur has written that there are two sorts of hermeneutics: an hermeneutics of suspicion and an hermeneutics of the restoration of meaning
(Ricoeur, 1970). What I have practiced so far has been the former, as I sus-
pect the curricula of either not delivering what they ostensibly intended (especially Turner, Penrod, & Plastino) or delivering all too well (Hawkins).
The results of this hermeneutic may now be used to enact a restoration of
meaning, in this case by utilizing it to extend curriculum thinking.

In evaluating the quality of these curricula, if we use the practical
frame that the arts are in need of legitimating arguments to solidify their
presence in educational institutions, then a particular analysis emerges.
All three curricula are closely tied to conventional curriculum thinking.
In the case of Hawkins and Turner, the education thinking that they
were using was already under attack and at least partly discredited before
their work was even published. They were therefore already in difficulties if they wished to successfully persuade. In the case of Penrod and
Plastino, we have an old curriculum orientation (vocationalism connected with social meliorism in that they had already predestined most
student's positions vis-á-vis the social practice of the modern dance profession) reinstantiated in the school-to-work and DBAE movements.
Hawkins' work was a strong reaction to such thinking. Penrod and
Plastino could be characterized as insular in concern (how to improve
only the immediate situation that appears before their eyes) without new
ideas about dance *education*, thus without a way of convincing administrators of the importance of their work. Because it is almost a given that the
arts are still considered a frill by the educational establishment, Penrod
and Plastino, we might argue, ought to have taken on a legitimating project. To the degree that they did not, their approach was myopic. In sum,

all three curricula are weak in regard to forwarding persuasive arguments for the presence of dance in educational institutions.

Practical concerns, however, ought not be our only consideration in evaluating these curricula. A more fundamental concern pertains to why we ought
to dance at all. As I pointed out, my own reasons are strongly physical, emotional, and personal. I have also written (Blumenfeld-Jones, 1998) that re-
serving the arts for those who can skillfully practice them is educationally
unsound. Enabling others to encounter dance in the way that I did seems educationally sound (Blumenfeld-Jones, 1997). Thus, I have always found the
kinds of arguments forwarded by these texts unpersuasive. They have never
quite rung true for me. I am perplexed that they could have missed the physical pleasure and need to move. I do not believe that I am idiosyncratic in this
regard; one need not be or have been a professional dancer to feel this way.
This suggests that all three curricula are, generally, wanting, because they fail
to address dancers existentially. They fail to give the reader a more authentic
sense of what it means to dance. Generally, all three leave the person out.

Beyond this personal dimension, there is a parallel concern stemming
from aesthetics education. Greene (1978) argued that the arts belong in education because they provide aesthetic experiences, which are a fundamental aspect of human life. If such experiences can be construed as "good" or,
as Dewey might have it, "educative experiences" because they induce
"growth," then all students ought to have consistent and quality access to
them. Life-adjustment, problem-solving, and vocational/avocational foci
simply miss the point and, thus, are also found wanting.

One of the dilemmas faced by Hawkins, Turner, and Penrod and Plastino
is that ours is not a dance culture: Dance is not integral to our everyday life.
This does not mean, however, that ours is not a motional culture nor that we
lack in aesthetics. (Look at present-day popular culture, especially the aesthetic of skateboarding and trick bicycle riding.) Of all three examined curricula, Turner's is the only one that even hinted at this possibility. As I have
already pointed out, it might even be said that there are two curricula here:
the curriculum she had to write about work and so forth, and the curriculum
she implicitly wrote about joy. Although I have stated that this is probably far
too strong a statement, it still presents an intriguing possibility.

The question that surrounds these curricula, especially the Hawkins and
Turner curricula, is: How successful were they at getting the atmosphere to
change? And, if they were not successful, wherein did the problem lie? This is
an historical question, which might be answered most easily by simply noting
that, in the past several years, university dance programs have been disap-
pearing or, at least, have been demoted to program as opposed to depart-
mental status. Dance companies are continuing to struggle for existence
(thus, audience has not been developed). Many, many New York dancers are
seeking to leave the city for academic positions, which are becoming less and
less available. One of my students, who is head of the dance program in a local high school, reports that she uses many of the Hawkins and Turner argu-

ments to hopefully generate more administrative support, and that these arguments generally do not persuade. With all of this in mind, it seems to be time to seek a different curricular strategy, one that better matches the existential dance experience and can speak to the uniqueness of dancing, rather than how it is like other educational endeavors.

CONCLUSION

In contrasting the agendas of these three dance curricula with my own understanding of my own involvement in dance (which I consider to be nonidiosyncratic), I have tried to argue that what I would characterize as technical-rationalist ways of thinking (Macdonald, 1995) on the part of these three curricularists did not help forward the project of dance in education. Neither did these thinkers develop arguments that persuade administrators and the public of the importance of dance nor did they project an experience of dance, which reflects what many of us experience when we dance. They focused primarily on the technical aspects of dance as a set of useful outcomes, and they did not utilize theoretical understandings.

At the beginning of this chapter, I expressed the hope that through this analysis we might understand the curriculum design process itself as hermeneutic and, in turn, educational for the designers. I briefly address the implications, which this present study forwards. Given that curriculum writers work within ongoing traditions of which they must and do make sense as they propose changes to or departures from existing curricula, given that they proceed via interpretations of those traditions coupled with interpretations of present conditions, and given that all of this goes on within their own horizons, the curriculum design process is clearly hermeneutic. If it is not simultaneously educational, this is, at least in part, a function of a pure focus on practical solutions to perceived immediate problems.

A more robust image of curriculum as practical emerges when we link it with hermeneutics. Gallagher argued, as I wrote earlier, that hermeneutics can lead toward practical wisdom, toward a more ethical living of everyday life by enabling us to consider the grounds out of which our actions emerge and the possible futures toward which they might tend. I wonder what these four curriculum writers might have proposed if they had been hermeneutically aware in the complex ways I have used in this chapter to interpret their work. What might they have learned about themselves that might have brought about more self-aware work? For myself, I used to think like Turner and Penrod and Plastino. I have changed considerably, and this is due in no small measure to my hermeneutic practice. I am not averring that these curriculum writers would come to think as I do, but instead that whatever they produced would rely less on mere conventional and educational slogans (preparation for life, democracy, appreciation) and be more educative for those of us who read their work.

On another front of practical wisdom, they did not approach the practical wisdom that dancers can develop when they transcend technical thinking and utilize theoretical understanding (such as hermeneutical thinking) to do so. They did not recognize that we dance for reasons that go beyond the rational and are no less valuable for doing so. They did not argue for a different form of education that honors a more whole image of human beings. I am, in the end, arguing for such a wholeness that, I believe, may only be approachable through a hermeneutic practice such as I have enacted.

REFERENCES

Berman, M. (1982). *All that is solid melts into air: The experience of modernity*. New York: Penguin.

Blumenfeld-Jones, D. S. (1990). *Body, pleasure, language and world: A framework for the critical analysis of dance education*. Unpublished dissertation. University of North Carolina at Greensboro.

Blumenfeld-Jones, D. S. (1995). Curriculum, control and creativity: An examination of curricular language and educational values. *The Journal of Curriculum Theorizing, 11*(1), 73–96.

Blumenfeld-Jones, D. S. (1997). Aesthetic experience, hermeneutics, and curriculum: Conventional systems of classroom discipline. In S. Laird (Ed.), *Philosophy of education* (pp. 313–321).

Blumenfeld-Jones, D. S. (1998). What are the arts for? Maxine Greene, the studio and performing arts, and education. In W. Pinar (Ed.), *The passionate mind of Maxine Greene: "I am ... not yet"* (pp. 160–173). London: Falmer.

Bourdieu, P. (1994). *The field of cultural production*. New York: Columbia University Press.

Dewey, J. (1938). *Experience and education*. New York: Macmillan.

Dewey, J. (1944). *Democracy and education*. New York: Free Press.

Gallagher, S. (1992). *Hermeneutics and education*. Albany: State University of New York Press.

Greene, M. (1978). *Landscapes of learning*. New York: Teachers College Press.

Hawkins, A. (1954). *Modern dance in higher education*. New York: Teachers College Press.

Habermas, J. (1971). *Knowledge and human interests* (J. J. Shapiro, Trans.). Boston: Beacon Press.

King, N., & Apple, M. (1990). What are schools for? In M. Apple, *Ideology and Curriculum* (2nd ed., pp. 43–61). New York: Routledge.

Kliebard, H. (1995). *The struggle for the American curriculum: 1893–1958* (2nd ed.). New York: Routledge.

Macdonald, B. (Ed.). (1995). *Theory as a prayerful act: The collected essays of James B. Macdonald*. New York: Peter Lang.

Mann, J. (1975). Curriculum criticism. In W. Pinar (Ed.), *Curriculum theory: The reconceptualists* (pp. 133–149). Berkeley, CA: McCutchan.

Penrod, J., & Plastino, J. (1990). *The dancer prepares*. Mountain View, CA: Mayfield.

Reynolds, W. (1989). *Reading curriculum: The development of a new hermeneutic*. New York: Peter Lang.

Ricoeur, P. (1970). *Freud & philosophy: An essay on interpretation*. (Denis Savage, Trans.) New Haven, CT: Yale University Press.

Rogers, C., & Freiberg, H. J. (1994). *Freedom to learn* (3rd ed.). New York: Merrill.

Stinson, S., Blumenfeld-Jones, D. S., & Van Dyke, J. (1990). An interpretive study of meaning in dance: Voices of young women dance students. *Dance Research Journal, 22*(2), 13–22.

Turner, M. (1957). *Modern dance for high school and college*. Englewood Cliffs, NJ: Prentice-Hall.

Wolff, J. (1982). *The social production of art*. New York: St. Martin's Press.

Chapter 9

Education From All of Life
for All of Life: Getting
an Education at Home—
Precept on Precept, Line on Line

Audrey P. Watkins
Western Illinois University

Thinking Beyond

In this chapter, Audrey Watkins presents the reader with part of an ethnographic study of the formal and informal educational experiences of African American women. Watkins examines informal education in the home, and illuminates ways in which her study's participants' lived experiences function as sites of knowledge from which they theorize about the type of education Black girls need in American society. An issue Watkins investigates is how informal education in the home and community is valued on an equal basis with the formal curriculum of schooling. The chapter illustrates how Black women in particular seek to expand our notion of curriculum and develop their own lines of flight by finding spaces within the complex pathways of both the formal and informal curriculum to become not only consumers but also producers of curriculum theorizing.

Questions

1. How does this chapter demonstrate that a research concept like ethnography makes sense within curriculum theorizing that is dis/positioned?
2. Watkins' chapter also addresses a spiritual dimension. In what ways can the notions of spirituality expressed in this chapter be compared to the conceptualizations of Webber and McKnight? What are the differences and similarities?
3. How can the discussions of race, gender, and class be enriched through lines of flight research?

This is part of a larger study of the formal and informal education of Black women. Working-class Black women have been solely constructed as clients and consumers of education and schooling, as spectators at the spectacle of their education. We have not been perceived as knowers of valuable knowledge who can provide educational leadership. To address this issue, I designed a study and interviewed Ida, Gwen, Yvette, Colleen, and Trudy who were participants in a workplace speech and language training program. I was an instructor in this program, and because of our similarities, my educational experiences are also included in the study. In this chapter, I discuss participants' informal learning and their authoritative theorizing about the type of education that Black girls should receive.

Survival for most African American women has been such an all-consuming
activity that most have had few opportunities to do intellectual work as it has
been traditionally defined. (Collins, 1991, p. 6)

INTRODUCTION

In the foreword of Andrew Billingsley's book about African American families,
Paula Giddings welcomed Billingsley's "focus on the working-class family
which is virtually invisible in most studies" (Billingsley, 1992, p. 14). To enhance the visibility of these families, I designed the study to explore the educational experiences of Black working-class women. I examine the messages that
participants received from their families about education, how they interpret
these messages and the impact of these messages on their lives, and how they
theorize from their experiences. L. H. Whiteaker's definition of education—"acquisition of knowledge which can be obtained ... in a multitude of
settings, formal and informal" (1990, p. 3)—fits the purpose of this study.
Therefore, various types of learning that occur outside of school are discussed.

William Schubert (1986) found that "a paucity of writing exists on how
knowledge of nonschool curricula can be obtained in practical situations by
teachers and curriculum leaders" (p. 108). Some of the questions that Schubert (1986) suggested teachers ask about students' homes and families are:
"What messages do students get about the value of schooling? What do they
see it as good for? Do students come into contact with persons who are actively attempting to become educated in their homes and families? Is such
education of a formal or informal variety? What does the family teach? Is it
worthwhile to know and experience?" (p. 109). Schubert's questions were
helpful in conceptualizing the issues that this study addresses.

Home is where learning and preparation for life begins, but family life defies
simplification. Participants acknowledge the role of informal education in
equipping and orienting them for life and to formal education. Slavery and continuing inadequate and unequal formal education have meant that informal education has been indispensable in equipping African Americans for life under
conditions that require diverse skills. Learning from experience that occurs outside of school can prepare the individual to avoid or better negotiate future
problems. Cynthia Neverdon-Morton (1990) discussed the role of formal and
informal education in the lives of African American women in the South between
1895 and 1925, when Blacks considered education the solution to many of the
problems facing their community: "Education was seen as the first step toward
racial equality and racial equality was the essential precondition for the development of the individual's full potential" (Neverdon-Morton, 1990, p. 163).
Neverdon-Morton explained that during this period, 1895 to 1925:

The kind and quality of education appropriate for African Americans in the South
were subjects of continued debate. Black women participated in the debates,
but they also developed educational institutions, designed curricula, helped to

formulate educational policies, and taught in the classroom. But much teaching took place outside formal educational settings. The women used whatever forum was available, whether discussing such issues as proper dress, suffrage, or the treatment of black South Africans, or providing practical experiences in gardening, home nursing, sewing, or child care. The home was considered the major focal point of informal education, and every willing family member was included in some aspect of the educational process. (1990, p. 164)

Trudy, Ida, Gwen, Yvette, and Colleen were and are influenced by various sources of informal learning such as the media. Trudy got help with fractions from watching a television special starring James Earl Jones. A *Cosby Show* episode about dyslexia caused Yvette to wonder if she has this condition. Gwen remarks: "I find myself in these situations talking to people that I feel I don't have the education to talk to, but I always get out of it. And I'm amazed at what I know … from reading the newspaper from listening and from being at the right place at the right time. I know information!" Although Gwen alludes to the value of information she learns on her own, she expresses concern that despite being informed, she fears her knowledge will be inadequate. The latter reflects, in part, the denigration of informal learning in our society.

Formal learning can occur in the family because some parents use a structured curriculum to instruct their children at home. Informal learning occurs at school by means of interpersonal relationships with teachers, other students, and school personnel, as well as through other aspects of the context of school. Nonschool learning is any learning that occurs outside of school and encompasses the informal learning that occurs in the home. My goal in the following section is to focus on various educational experiences in the home, which become sites of knowledge from which the study's participants envision a curriculum for Black girls in the final section: the education of our lives: life education for Black girls. Therefore, *informal learning* here refers to education by parents and knowledge learned from the home environment. Ida's narrative reveals how highly she values out of school education. She explains disapprovingly, "When I was in college some people all they had was the book knowledge. They was lackin'!" Ida also believes that informal learning addresses innate potential that might be undeveloped were it not for education that addresses the whole person.

Education in participants' homes occurred through parents' conscious efforts as well as by parents' practice and the context of the family environment. Many life skills were learned informally through family communication. Orientation to formal education, work, self-reliance, and industriousness are some features of this family education.

COMMUNICATING LIFE'S LESSONS

Ida, Gwen, Yvette, Colleen, and Trudy perceive communication from and with parents as a way of acquiring critical knowledge that impacts personal and social development. Knowing what to expect in society and learning skills to deal confidently with the real world represent valuable information to participants. Trudy and her brothers wish their parents had better prepared them for the real world. Trudy used her mother's failure to adequately prepare her for her menstrual period to illustrate the latter, and she especially regrets that their father "didn't have time to just sit down and talk to us and let us know how it is out there and prepare us." Trudy's mention that an eighth-grade teacher, Mr. Compton, told the class "how the world really was" illumines the kind of information she and her brothers desired. The lack of insight from her parents' experiences acquires even more importance because of what Trudy omits from her accounts of family life. After her parents divorced, Trudy's mother struggled to support three children. Yet, lack of material comfort is never Trudy's main focus. Even after their father's death in 1993, Trudy and her brothers continued to lament the lack of information from their parents that would have prepared them for life. Trudy's dialogue reveals children's expectations of the parental role of teacher and initiator into the culture.

Yvette regrets the lack of open communication between her and her parents. She explains, "When I asked my parents questions they took them for accusations. They were always on the defense. 'Why do you wanna know?' 'Who have you been talking to?'" Yvette believes this style of communication with her parents resulted in her "not being able to get all of the knowledge—I don't want to say knowledge because that's not the word I'm looking for—but not able to be sincere, ah, a bonding. There wasn't a bonding there, you know." To Yvette, bonding that occurs through open communication is indispensable to any healthy relationship. Inability to demonstrate love to her children was a result of her family relations, as previously discussed. Yvette asks, "If you're not shown love, how do you expect to give love?" She worked to incorporate the missing elements in her family's life into her relations with her children. She longed for, prayed, and finally saw her own family of five children bond together.

Yvette believes that, in all relationships, communication that leads to bonding is essential for learning to occur. The interaction and exchanges resulting from open family communication affect the development of intelligence and confidence in the child. The quantity and quality of positive communication between parent and child determines the nature of their relationship. And the health of the parent/child relationship affects or determines the learning that occurs in the home. Yvette observes, "That's why the intelligence of a child of my generation was so mediocre [compared] to a child of my daughter Evelyn's caliber." Evelyn's knowledge and confidence based on open communication and family involvement in her education generates Yvette's belief that children of Evelyn's generation will "turn the country around because of their curiosity, their realism, their logic. They're making us aware of what they are being taught in school. They are more alert to what's being taught, and they're quicker to tell you, 'That's not what I was told. This is what I was told!'"

Yvette became curious about a commotion in her household, but received no explanation. Her parents believed that at 7 years old she was too young to be told that her mother had been raped. I cannot speculate on why Yvette's and Trudy's parents used the communication style they did. However, I do know that family and societal beliefs about communicating with children sometimes differ intergenerationally. The "children should be seen and not heard" approach was adhered to by my grandparents. The belief—which supported this approach for them—was that girls would become "womanish" and boys "mannish" if they acquired too much knowledge too soon about the world of adults. In this view, children should remain childlike and innocent as long as possible. In addition to the role of her own experiences, extensive influence by media images of families being demonstrative in expressing feelings and openly communicating with children probably contributed to Yvette's style of open communication.

Ida relishes the open communication that occurred in her family: "We would sit at the table everybody eat, we'll talk, and the kitchen be full. And we would just sit around and talk whatever on your mind. And that's another thing I like about them. You could talk about anything, sex or anything." Empowerment, intellectual stimulation, as well as family bonding are suggested by Ida's experiences of positive family communication.

Zora, one of the narrators in Etter-Lewis' study of older professional Black women, also prized the communication in her family: "We used to sit as a family and decide family issues around the table. We had consultations as kids, coming up. It seems big things which would affect us as children our parents communicated that to us and we talked about it around the table" (Etter-Lewis, 1993, pp. 21–22). Participants in my study work to develop open communication with their children, simultaneously preparing their children for life. Regarding sex, Gwen tells her preteen daughters, "Whatever you feel, talk to mommy before you do anything.... You talk to me first, cause mommy's not gonna lie to you." With open communication comes a concern Gwen refers to: "I don't wanna put things on their minds that maybe don't even have to be there right now, so all I say is talk to me first."

Colleen values encouragement. Her speech is laced with the word, almost drawing the hearer into a zone of encouragement. She notes, "Women are never encouraged.... We should encourage our daughters." Her "daughter was encouraged to do everything. She was encouraged...." Colleen also offers that her granddaughter "is very good and we encourage her...." Colleen reflects that her mother "encouraged me in ways that I don't even know how to formulate in words right now...." To Colleen, communication should embody encouragement. The act of encouraging demonstrates favorable expectations or hoped-for positive outcomes. Encouragement is not just a verbal act but also is expressed in providing material resources necessary to motivate or nurture. Her mother providing nice clothing and sending her to parochial schools were forms of encouragement to Colleen.

Gwen's communication with her daughters is reminiscent of her mother's communication with her. She admits that her daughters are 10 and 12, going on 21 and 40, meaning that the girls know as much about life as people twice their age: "And that's how I teach them cause they're right there and they see. Like I said my life's an open book, they see all my dumb mistakes, you know, and they see the good things too. And I tell them don't do this, don't be like mommy. Don't be one of those people that has to do it two times, three times, knowing that you should have learned the first time."

INTENTIONAL TEACHING IN THE HOME

One way of preparing participants for the real world is the intentional conscious teaching of parents. Colleen's narrative recounts how her father taught her to think critically by debating her about the credibility of information sources, such as the encyclopedia. Colleen's leadership role in struggles at work—such as getting management to make policy manuals available to workers and resisting the move to give her unit the workload of a defunct division—was motivated by her father's instructions:

> I was loud and outspoken. My father taught me from a child that you never accept anything anybody says to you without challenging it or until it's proven. My father was very, very critical in my education from the time I was about two or three years old. I remember he used to sit me on the table and we would talk. And he emphasized to me from the time, from as far back as I can remember to never, ever accept anything anybody says to me just because they say it to you. Do not accept anything that's written just because it's written.... When I was in grade school we'd have these big arguments because I'd say something about the encyclopedia, and he'd get an encyclopedia, and he'd open it and he'd show me a paragraph and he'd say, well, what makes you think this is true? And I would think he was insane. What do you mean why do I think this is true? It's in the book. He says well, do you know who wrote this book? Why do you think this is true? Have you verified this with anybody else? And I used to get angry with him. Then over the years you don't know how you retain things by osmosis, and that's how I've learned most of the things I've known.

Questioning and rejecting normative knowledge that supports oppression or that places more value on the elite than on ordinary people can be taught consciously, as Colleen's father did, or it can be learned from our contexts. I remember my mother recounting how she impatiently waded across police lines as crowds gathered to honor Queen Elizabeth during one of her visits to Jamaica. Mama had to get to work, and although she meant no disrespect, she did not regard the queen as being more important than her family's needs. My unwillingness to devalue my personal or my family's experiential knowledge in favor of the knowledge of others is part of a quest for equality, self-respect, and dignity. Wendy Luttrell's (1989) study suggests that White and Black working-class women favor forms of knowledge that "allow for subjectivity between the knower and the known, rest in women themselves (not in higher authorities), and are experienced directly in the world (not through abstractions)" (p. 400). I agree with Luttrell that we must "look more closely at the ethnic-class and race-specific nature of women's experiences, as well as the values that are promoted in each context in order to understand why certain forms of knowledge appear more amenable to women" (p. 400). Christians are told to give honor to whom honor is due. However, in the Bible, James (2:6) reproved some early Christians for valuing and honoring the rich more than the poor. He asked these Christians, "Do not rich men oppress you, and draw you before the judgment seats?"

In addition to sharpening her critical thinking skills, Colleen's father also taught her and her brother Standard English: "We grew up in the ghetto, but we were very well educated on how to speak correctly. We learned to speak incorrectly to survive in the neighborhood. And if he heard [us] say something incorrectly, he would correct everything we said. Even though we spoke the ghetto language outside the house, we could not speak it at home in his presence."

Ida has an almost reverential respect for her father's knowledge: "You could tell he's blessed with a gift of God knowledge. Because when my father says something, listen … !" She remembers his informal teaching and joyfully recounts his instructions:

> He was one of the first one to let us go to the bank and sign and put this money in the bank. He was showing us, and it never dawned on me he was teaching us this. He used to take us to the clinics to get our shots and stuff. He'd say put your name down there. Don't you know your name? Write your name. I did not know he was really training us. And he'll say go get me a paper. He'll sit up there and he'll read his paper and he'll say, here, give it to us to read. Look through that paper and find something you want to read in there…. You know it's a simple thing, but it was special. And it is so funny how it rubs off on each and every one of us.

When Ida explains to her daughter Lisa, "Everything you do will come back to you," she's using proverbial sayings learned from her parents. "They used to say, I'm thinking, stupid stuff. 'You reap what you sow'; 'You can't throw a rock and hide your hands'; 'Your problems go where you go.' I'm starting to understand now." My mother also used similar sayings to instruct us. One of her favorites is "Don't hang you basket higher than you can reach it." The latter means that in order to be successful, we should live within our means. "The higher the monkey climb the more him expose," and "If you dance at home you'll dance abroad" are other common sayings used by my mother and her parents before her to instruct their children. Many of these sayings are universal, but have particular meaning within family interaction.

Gwen's mother's schooling ended in the fifth grade, and she worked multiple jobs most of her life; thus, she taught her five daughters survival skills that she had proven herself. Gwen remembers her mother telling her and her four sisters, "'I know you girls, but I'm not raisin' any wimps, you know,' and she would whip you if you came home cryin' and let yourself get beat up, if you didn't fight back. She wanted you to fight back; she didn't want to raise any wimps cause she wasn't around...." Gwen comments that her mother was strong and proud and "she taught me values." She also taught "that bills must be paid ... and that you gotta have a roof over your head, food in the house, because even if you broke, you know, if you gotta stay in the house you gotta have a place to go...." These lessons have undoubtedly helped Gwen survive and maintain her independence through unemployment, divorce, and separation from two husbands.

LEARNING WORK ORIENTATION

An orientation to work that prepared them to be independent and self-reliant is part of the knowledge that participants learned in their homes. Through various life circumstances, parents taught self-reliance and industriousness verbally and by practice. Household responsibilities helped initiate participants into work early. Colleen explains why she refers to her mother as a "tough taskmaster":

> Every Monday of my life I had to go home. I was in the basement washing from the time I got out of school until 10:00, 11:00 at night cause we had one of those wringer washers, and my mother was a perfectionist. We washed the clothes, then we rinsed them in two different tubs of rinse water, then we hung them. Then on Wednesday we went an' took them out of the basement. They had to be folded and ironed and put away. I remember making starch, putting clothes in the refrigerator to iron them later.... I worked hard, very hard.

Colleen says the drive to work hard that she is herself imbued with seems to be missing from children of all races. She believes labor-saving devices contribute to this decrease in industriousness.

Until she became pregnant in her freshman year of high school, Yvette helped care for her eight younger siblings, and her schoolwork suffered as a result. Barbara Omolade mentioned Sara Lightfoot's observation "that in poor families, domestic chores such as childcare, food preparation, laundry, and errands often take precedence over school work" (Omolade, 1994, p. 141). Although her chores did not prevent Ida from attending school, her mother often relied on her to cook. "I was in grade school, about 8 years old. She'd call home and say, Ida, I left this out, would you cook this? That's probably why I don't like cooking now. I was more responsible and she'd say 'Here go the keys, make sure everybody in.' So she'd depend on me to do things around the house."

Expectations of work were nurtured within the family, but economic necessity also mandated work. Yvette's father was a seasonal construction worker and his salary barely met his large family's expenses. Because of this, Yvette worked as a waitress when she was 12 years old. Ten-year-old Colleen received a commission from each hot dog sold when she helped her father's friend sell hot dogs near local factories. From her early years, Colleen felt her parents would be unable to afford all the things she wanted, so she decided she would have to work. Gwen was 14 when she began working, and Trudy and Ida were juniors in high school when they began to work.

All participants attribute their work ethics to one or both of their parents. Even if the issue of work was not addressed verbally at home, the lives of hard-working parents taught eloquently. Mirza's (1992) study of African-Caribbean females in Britain found that "young black women were strongly influenced by their parents' orientation to work and education.... It was not the mothers' actual job that influenced the girls as much as their mothers' (and other black females') attitudes and rational strategies" (pp. 187, 188). Imogene, a former participant in the workplace-training program, discusses the influence of her mother's attitude to work: "My mom has always been a very strong Black woman. She raised seven children herself, for the most part.... My mom did a lot of work, she was a dedicated worker, and that's where I got my dedication to my job. I saw the way she struggled. I saw the way she put everything to what she was doing to make sure that her children got something out of it. So that's where I got that from."

Orientation to work takes many forms, but of major importance is the example of parents going to work every day and organizing their lives around work. "My mother worked from the time I was a child, that was where my work background came from," offers Colleen. Trudy attributes her work ethic to her family: "Both of my parents were working people. They wanted things out of life ... and it made me see that if you worked hard, you can get anything you want if you work for it." Ida exclaims repeatedly,

> I've always worked, so I don't depend on a man to give me some money, and I guess I got that from my parents. You know, they both got up and worked. They took care of their family; there was always food on the table, extra money if we wanted to do certain little things. So that was the subtle hint there, you know.... What they instilled in us, especially my father they wanted us to learn how to take care of yourself, bein' able to depend on yourself and not others.

Work orientation is linked to independence, and independence is related to schooling because getting an education prepares one for work.

ORIENTATION TO EDUCATION

Billingsley noted, "The value African Americans place on education has always been extraordinarily high. There is a deep historical and cultural belief in the efficacy of education. Blacks have sought education in every conceivable manner and at every level" (1992, p. 181). Not all the parents of this study's participants graduated from high school, whereas all participants are high school graduates. Billingsley's observation that "for more than a hundred years, each generation of blacks has been more educated than the one before" (1992, p. 172) is relevant to most participants. Gwen and Trudy have 6-month secretarial diplomas from Robert Morris College, and Ida has a 2-year college diploma. Although each family differs significantly, all value education, both formal and informal.

Our parents told us "get your education" just as we tell our children to get their education. "Getting an education" is the exhortation used by both generations, but what does this phrase mean in each case? Conceptions of getting an education differ for the women and their parents. To participants' parents, "getting an education" generally meant obtaining a high school diploma. Trudy remembers, "Our parents didn't even encourage us to go to college. They just wanted us to do good through high school, and then they wanted us to go out and get a job after high school. They didn't encourage us to further our education." Trudy believes her mother's Jehovah's Witness religious beliefs caused her mother to downplay post-high school education while encouraging Trudy and her brothers to enter some aspect of their religious organization's ministry.

Colleen's parents sacrificed to pay her tuition at Catholic grammar and high schools. Yet, they did not help her financially to attend Pepperdine University on a scholarship she had won in grammar school. Colleen believes her mother needed her as a source of strength in the midst of marital problems, and therefore failed to help her to attend Pepperdine. Ida remarks that her parents:

> Implanted ... you need your education, but it's up to you to continue it. I'm giving you the foundation; make sure you complete high school ok? They sayin' we want you to get the basics as long as you know how to read and write.... But they never went on to say I'm choosing you to go to college and make this and make that. She never did, but she say you have to finish high school. My mother would tell you, you need your education in order to write your name to fill out an application. She'd say be able to fill out an application, be able to read something.

Yvette completed high school at night after her second child was born. Although her parents rarely encouraged her to go to school, she believes they wanted her to complete high school. Gwen's mother rarely discussed education openly; she used her life as an illustration. She regularly asked her daughters, "Do you see how hard it is for me?.... Do you wanna be like me?" When some of Gwen's sisters joined a gang, stayed away from school, and one sister dropped out of high school in her senior year, their mother was sorely disappointed.

Participants had no family members in professional jobs or who were college educated to provide information and inspiration, as was the case with most of the older black professional women whom Etter-Lewis (1993) interviewed in her study. When I asked Gwen if there were any other family members who stressed education or who were role models, she replied emphatically, "There were none, there were none, there were none!" One of the women who provided background information for this study remarked that most of the participants' parents were from the South, where many African American children did not continue formal education beyond the eighth grade. Another woman corroborated the latter, relating that in the South, schooling was intermittent for many African Americans because some students had to work in the fields and often did not graduate from eighth grade until they were 17 years of age. To participants' parents, a high school diploma was a major credential. In 1950, when most of the participants' parents were young adults, only 13% of African Americans had graduated from high school (Amott & Matthaei, 1991). Factory and clerical jobs were increasing, and after World War II more Blacks got work in these jobs. It appears that participants' parents hoped that after their daughters received their high school diplomas they would find jobs that would allow them to live independently.

Despite these factors, I believe financial constraints played a major role in participants' parents not discussing college as an option with their daughters. Ida relates that her parents "never stipulated, 'I want you to go to college.' But I always felt that they want us to do better than they did, you know, take it a step farther." Ida's remark indicates that even though the finances and plans for college were not a part of their socialization, she, her brothers, and her sisters were expected to exceed their parents' levels of education. When Ida and her older brothers, and her sisters left the family home after high school, the only sibling remaining at home was able, with the help of the other children, to go away to college, where she received an engineering degree. Ida remarks:

> I can't remember when her birthday. All I know is that it's this gap between us … when she went to college she wanted money; we wired money. We put things into her account, y'know big care packages an stuff like that. Anything she wanted (snap) jump to it. So she was the one reaping all the [benefits]. Things were different when we were [younger] because it was so many of us that they didn't, you know, they couldn't do it, but after we all had moved on and graduated, they had this one that they could.

I infer from this quote that had funds been available, Ida's parents would have also helped their other children attend college.

Finances were one of the factors Gwen considered when faced with what to do after high school. Gwen knew college costs were above her mother's means, especially because her mother had just gone through a second foreclosure:

Right after high school, I didn't think about college because my mother had just lost her house. Ah, when the colleges came to our school, the tuition were just so high to me, I could not even dream of bringing this to my mother when I knew what she was already going through. So what I did was I just opted for the 6 months secretarial course because that was only like $3,000, and right, that was fully paid for … so I don't have any bills from that.

Participants' views of "getting an education" are different from those of their parents. For participants themselves, "getting an education" includes post-high school work such as college or vocational training, and they openly discuss the latter with their children. For their children, participants envision a higher level of education than they themselves were able to attain. Their children may not heed their advice, and the information, finances, and other resources may not be available for advanced training, but Yvette, Ida, Gwen, Trudy, and Colleen possess a greater awareness of the need for and possibilities of schooling than their parents had. Yvette says her children never spoke about their career goals when they were teenagers, and she did not discuss the issue with them. Yet, she expected her children to complete high school as well as college. None of her four adult children has completed college yet, but one is currently in college and another attends vocational school. Yvette is now aware of her children's goals and provides constant encouragement. She discussed vocational training with her 22-year-old daughter, who spoke of the difficulties of attending classes now that she herself has three children. "Well, what did I tell you?" Yvette questioned in an understanding voice.

Ida uses events such as college graduations to convey her expectations of college attendance to her daughter Lisa: "I think the first time I told her, I went to my baby sister[s] graduation. She graduated out of college with a engineering degree. Lisa was really young, and I whispered, 'This is what I want for you!'" Ida also used another family member's graduation to transmit this message of educational expectations. "We went to my nephew's [graduation] I keep on sayin' I want you to be able to go to a college (laugh)." Of her efforts to orient Lisa to becoming college educated, Ida says, "Yes, I'm pushing her, not really pushing her, but I'm suggesting, 'I would love to see you graduate from college.'" Family members who are college graduates provide role models or points of references that can motivate and inform the others.

Gwen contrasts the way her mother conveyed educational expectations to her and her sisters with the way she conveys her educational expectations to her two daughters: "My mother didn't stress education like I do with my kids. I stress to them that education is important. She never pushed … like I try to push my children. I don't try to push them beyond their limits, but I try, I do push. I must be honest." Gwen continues, "I let them know that it's your choice to go to college. I hope that you decide to go to college, and I hope that you become doctors or lawyers or whatever it is that you wanna be.

But I hope and pray that you aspire to something really up there. You could be a judge or something...."

My mother was unable to complete even elementary school, due to the poverty of her parents and gender stereotypes that operated against the education of women. After a divorce when she was in her 20s, she saw no other way to improve our lives except to leave us with her parents and join thousands of Jamaican immigrants seeking work in England. In England, she enrolled in a nurse's training program, which she was unable to complete. Her experience working in factories and performing domestic work convinced her of the importance, especially for women, of education, which leads to a good career. Mama explains that when a woman is educated she "don't have to take foolishness from no man." When my mother said "get your education"—"tek yu lesson," in Jamaican patois—although she did not specify a particular career, I realized it should be a professional field. As with Gwen's mother, I could see the struggle and the sacrifices she endured to support us.

My mother suggested I take secretarial training when I enrolled in junior college. She was not advising me on a career path, she wanted to ensure that I would have a way of paying for further education. When I asked her recently what kind of career she had in mind, she replied, "Whether teaching, nursing, get a skill." In the transmission of culture and values, many ideals are not spoken openly, but are still felt, shared, and understood. I believe such was the case with some parents who wanted their children to be college educated but did not openly state so because they could not offer their children financial support. Parents need to examine what educational options are available to them and their children so that they can determine and formulate what "getting an education" can mean for their family.

CONCEPTS OF EDUCATION AND FAMILY INVOLVEMENT IN SCHOOLING

The family as a resource is instrumental in the survival of individual members. Trudy and Yvette both lived at home after their pregnancies. Staying with their parents when they were young single mothers enabled participants to stretch meager resources. Yvette's four adult children and the children of her three daughters all live with her, and Colleen and her mother bought their first home together. This pooling of resources was undoubtedly mutually beneficial and provided help with Colleen's daughter while Colleen worked multiple jobs. Ida and her daughter have lived with her parents, and recently Ida and a sister bought a two-family building together.

Participants see a learning partnership with the school. They accept much responsibility for their children's education, and vigilantly exercise their knowledge and awareness to ensure that their children are educated as well as possible. Gwen sums up her perception of the role of parents and the role of the school: "I think that now it's 50/50. You used to be able to rely on the teachers to teach your child, and now you have to spend more time. I know I do! I spend more time making sure they know what's going on because a lot of the teachers will pass you anyway, even if you don't know."

Yvette's concern about her daughter Evelyn's education is demonstrated by her perpetual involvement in all aspects of Evelyn's education. When Evelyn was 7 years old, Yvette advised her to gain experience in her career choices. Yvette explains, "At first she wanted to be a teacher, you know. I told her … the only way that you'll be able to know what you want to do is to practice it. You said that you want to be a teacher, okay, then start doing it. You have nieces, so start trying to teach them."

Yvette and her adult children work closely with Evelyn to ensure her success. Yvette notes, "But as far as her body parts, I taught her that myself, or my other children with their help. And I told the kids the other day, I said well, Evelyn is being questioned on her tests about history, why don't you all start showing her or telling her about the different states—how this country was built?" Yvette demanded that Evelyn be moved to another classroom when the regular teacher was ill for a long time. Yvette was concerned about the quality of instruction and her daughter's ability to bond with various substitute teachers. Yvette pours all she has learned in raising her four adult children into educating Evelyn.

Ida consistently encourages and works with her daughter Lisa. Lisa gets frustrated when doing her homework because "she wants you to tell her the answer. She'll do it maybe one or two times and she doesn't grasp, she gets frustrated. So I have to stop and say let's go to something else, and then we'll come back later." Gwen does not hesitate to contact teachers when homework is confusing or when a teacher brought a bleeding dead rat to show the class, for example: "I left her a message on her voice mail. I said, 'My daughter told me that you brought a dead rat to school today, and I'd like to talk to you about it. Give me a call on one of my numbers.' She never did call me." Gwen recalls her conversation with a teacher about a confusing math concept that had Gwen and her daughters perplexed:

> I think I'm confused, you know, when I sit down an' I try to do their homework. I call it this new math but when I talked to the teacher, "Oh, well, some of the kids have problems, an' puttin' the zero just helps them find the answer, it really doesn't matter, does it?" I said, well, not really, I mean, what does a zero mean, nothing. But it doesn't go. You know, you teachin' a child somethin' different that when they get in the next grade or they try to teach the next person.…

Unfortunately, Gwen's subsequent conversations indicate that she never understood the math concept. She probably became frustrated and did not pursue further explanations from the teacher. Yvette was unsure if she was encouraging Evelyn's career aspirations appropriately. It would be beneficial for parents to have extra resources to help with such challenges. In many instances, these participants are already doing fine work, but validation or encouragement from other parents or educators would increase their confidence. When I interviewed Trudy, her son was only 4 years old. Yet, when he was enrolled in preschool programs at a YMCA, she attended swimming demonstrations and such and helped him with any work given by the teachers.

Although her mother was willing to help with her schoolwork, Ida could see that her mother was busy because she worked outside the home and cared for six children:

> My brothers and sisters were really right behind each other [in age]. So it was really me on my own, and when Ma came in from work, to ask her what's this, and she'll try. She's got a baby hollerin, she got my sister behind me want her attention, so she'll try, you know, to help me. And many times she'll stop and say read this, and you know, I always had this feeling that she was busy because I had the responsibility of cooking. Like when she did have time we'd sit down and we'd read a passage out the book and she would help me with a word here and there, but very seldom I would go to her. She was always busy. When I'd go to her, she would help me, but that would take her away from my baby sister or Mollie the one next to me, or she'd try to locate my brothers.

Ida saw older brothers and sisters and other family members who could help with homework as educational resources. Of children who were doing well in school she remarks, "They probably had someone helping them at home and probably just had a little edge up on me."

Gwen's mother was unable to help her children with homework, but Gwen's older sisters did. "My mother, no. My sisters had to check our homework, it was checked, you know, before I went to school," Gwen explains. Participants expect educational success for their children and are working to different degrees to ensure that their children succeed. Their understandings of their parental roles and responsibilities are demonstrated in their efforts to educate and to supervise the education of their children.

Participants who currently have children in school strive for the best formal public education within their means. Gwen did extensive research to find a better school than the neighborhood one designated for her children. She obtained a list of Chicago schools and their ratings from the board of education. I explored Gwen's persistence in researching schools for her daughters:

> People don't wanna tell you what you wanna know, and you have to sorta finally get somebody who's in their office by themselves who can talk to you. You have to keep talking 'til someone starts telling you what the real deal is. It's a school that they told me, an' it's South ... Bennett? Something starts with a "B," they say it's for more middle upper-class Blacks, you know, cause they have dues and different fees you have to pay for the school. I called and they had a 3-year waiting list for the school. Your child could be in college by the time you get in that school!

When Gwen moved to a new neighborhood, she researched the schools by talking to community residents: "I just talked. I talked to people outside of the church, comin' out of the store, and I would say, you know I'm new in the neighborhood, or, you know, they would say, 'Oh, did I just miss that bus?' Any little thing would start me a conversation, and I'd try to find out what I wanted to find out." Gwen obtained permission for her daughters to attend the school that community residents recommended. However, when I asked her what makes her think that school is a good one, she acknowledged, "It's not really good, it's just better than the one they were supposed to go to."

With rumors of schools closing, Gwen became concerned that her daughters' school may be among those closed: "I've always gotten involved with trying to get my girls in the best school possible because I can't afford private school, except for now, it's like I'm thinkin' about getting a second job if I had to send them to private school. So many schools they want to close, certain programs they want to shut down in the schools that will stay open in my area and that school might not open in September." Trudy's desire for quality education for her 4-year-old son led her to consider selling her car and using the proceeds to enroll him in a Montessori school. Before Colleen transferred her daughter from Catholic to public high school, she visited the Catholic school to observe conditions. She exclaims, "I was shocked, there was no discipline. Children were all over the place." Colleen did decide to transfer Rachel, but later wondered if she had made the right decision. Many single parents such as Ida prefer to do without a car or make other sacrifices to ensure that their children receive the best education possible. Ida has never sent her daughter to public school:

> That's another thing I like about the Catholic school she attends. They motivate! They bring it out in you. You may not get it through the books, but they have you up there saying a poem. It's not always grades. You have kids that are makin' the lowest grade, they have something for them to do. They bring out the potential in them. Lisa is into chess now and she loves that. They've started up a little chess tournament. Durin' the summer she was into that, little things like that. That's what I'm talking about; bring out their potential.

Ida notes that her parents wanted her and her sisters and brothers to complete high school in order to get a job, but Ida believes that now one needs an education "just to live." She explains:

> Everything is steady changing every day so you do need an education, and that's what I kinda like instill in Lisa. I'm tryin' to tell her, not just to support yourself, you need it for yourself, be able to read, you know, somebody lay a contract out before you, you are not able to read that before you put your name down there. It's not just to hold a job, it's for you, it's for your life, you know. And you know like my parents they wanted the education for a job, but the way things are now, you need an education just to live.

Ida consistently reaffirms that education is not just subject matter but information from all of life for all of life. One of the ways that participants prepare their children for life is by consciously providing motivation to achieve their goals and expectations and to realize fulfillment in every area of life. The belief that seems to underlie their actions is that children should be motivated both in and out of school.

MOTIVATION

My mother illustrates the link between her experiences of work and motivation to become educated in the following: "You have to motivate them to know that without a good skill in life they can't make a good headway…. I didn't get the education I wanted, and I see how you are pushed around without a good trade or education, and I didn't want that for my children." Motivation does not necessarily occur because experiences are immediately converted into actions. Experiences strike certain chords within individuals and the interplay of various internal and external factors stimulates reactions and responses within to advance, retreat, or possibly wait for future decisions to act or not act.

All participants are or were concerned that their children not become demotivated due to experiences that occur in or out of school. They see part of their parental responsibility as using various life situations to motivate their children and others in their families and communities to persevere and achieve. Protecting their children from various forms of discrimination that would decrease motivation is also important. For Yvette, receiving her high school diploma through the mail as she did represented the autograph of an alienating school system that devalued her. However, when I offered to bring her certificate for successfully completing our communication course, she refused. Instead, Yvette wanted her diploma to arrive in the mail, thus providing a forum for her family to note her achievement and be motivated themselves to set and attain their educational goals.

Ida lays a foundation to discuss an experience that has held far-reaching consequences for her:

> You have people that it seem like everything come easy to them or they stand out, and then you have the ordinary, and I'm considered a very ordinary person. And a long time ago I heard the reason there are so many ordinary people is because God loves ordinary people. He works through ordinary people. I used to sit up there and say, "Dag, why can't I do this!" I'm lookin' at someone else's gift like a singer or something like that. They right out there, or she was the cutest girl in the classroom so she gets all the attention, or she's a good cheerleader, good grades. They stand out. Then you have a person the more he tries, they [are] not recognized. They can get an "A" but it's not … the attention is on the straight "A" student—they're not recognized and they'll fall back. It happened to me in grade school.

Ida's analysis of the way those of us who are perceived as being without exceptional ability are treated goes to the core of how and for what humans are valued in society. She goes on to describe what occurred when the confidence resulting from her father's motivation collided with the actions of her second-grade teacher:

> My father, I used to sing to him. He would always say, "Oh, you'll be another Mahalia Jackson," something like that. And what stopped me, and this is why I talk about motivation a lot, is that I remember in first or second grade I had this teacher, and she had her little favorite and we used to read this book and at the end of it, instead of reading the part we would sing the part. And she would always have her get up and sing or you raise your hand and she would pick out who she want to sing the part. And I always wanted to sing that part. And what happened was this day the little girl had a sore throat or something so she couldn't sing right and I'm raisin' my hand, I wanted to sing. I get up, she said, "Go ahead Ida sing the part." And I'm puttin' ... just think a little young girl and you singin' to your heart['s] content because, you know, my father, you know you got a voice. I got through singing and the teacher just said, "Okay, out the door." Nothing like, "Ida, thank you." She would always compliment this little girl and that really hampered me.

Ida explains the effect of her second-grade experience: "I guess that's the reason I'm always sayin' I would love to sing but because of that in my mind it did something. And I said to myself, I would never let that happen to my child. Bring out her abilities, that's what I want. Do not—because this person may have a very beautiful voice, give others a chance." Ida gives strong emphasis to the importance of skills not directly addressed in school. Being confident and able to interact with others is critical. Ida is pleased that all areas of Lisa's life are being addressed in the Catholic school she attends. As she stated earlier, "Catholic school motivates." Ida's experience demonstrates the relationship of factors in the home and the school. She was encouraged at home and wanted to participate at school. However, her teacher's response created dissonance, which still affects her public participation. Ida added that because this teacher was White and the favored girl was light-skinned, she came to perceive the incident as a racial one.

Gwen explains her and her sisters' motivation to finish high school: "So it was mostly from inside of us, from I think watching. Yeah, I think from watching mom. The struggle is what activated something inside us or motivated us to wanna have something." Gwen refers to factors internal to the self that can respond to external situations to produce an impetus to act. Her experience also illustrates how negative as well as positive experiences motivate. An important aspect of motivation took the form of participants informally exposing their children to various positive motivating experiences. Gwen tries to keep her daughters "motivated, to keep them in atmospheres that will keep them motivated." One of Gwen's reasons for planning to attend college is to motivate her daughters. "I started thinking about school because ... I knew it would be a good motivation for my children," she says.

Gwen was especially motivated by a group of Black female teachers who encouraged her desire to remain in school and not get pregnant: "These are all Black teachers who motivated me." Motivation or its opposite—demotivation is affected by the social context. For some participants, the decision to enter college was affected by the status of Blacks who completed college degrees and were unable to find positions commensurate with their academic achievement. Gwen recounts how reflecting on the latter affected her thinking about getting a college education:

> For a few years I would work, um, side by side with Black people who just graduated from college and had their associate's, their master's, and here they are doing clerical work, frustrated, you know. We would get into problems because they don't want to be treated like a clerical person, but that's what you are.... So for years I thought, you know, good thing I didn't bother to go to college because I'd be just like them.... I'd have a degree, especially me being Black, you know I wouldn't have a job. I saw that some Blacks could get ahead with an education, but I also realize that some of the people, um, that have degrees don't get good jobs.

Ida also worked with educated Blacks who failed to secure jobs in the areas in which they had earned degrees:

> They had degrees a lot of 'em, now they are not working in what they went to school ... they got discouraged. One woman was sittin' up there with a bachelor at that time in accounting. She wasn't doin' accountin'. She was doin' clerk work, general office work. A lot of us went to school and because of that got discouraged. One guy, he got his degree over there at Loyola University in something. I'm sayin', "What are you doing here?" Got settled, couldn't move up, and that's what I was telling him at the time. It was very hard, especially for Blacks. You had to fight, and some of 'em they lost.... I just stopped. I left.

In addition to the negative effects of excluding degreed Blacks from positions for which they are qualified, Ida discusses the effects of inequitable education that results in segregated Black schools not offering subjects, such as precalculus, offered in White schools: "I wanted the same opportunity, even if they were giving it and I wasn't up to standard, at least it was there to motivate." In essence, the issue of motivation is a way to nurture dreams for fulfillment of goals, and mandates concern with social justice. How motivation for education achievement is affected by injustice is an important issue that needs attention.

THE EDUCATION OF OUR LIVES:
LIFE EDUCATION FOR BLACK GIRLS

As a result of their informal learning experiences, discussed previously, I wanted Ida, Gwen, Yvette, Trudy, and Colleen's perspectives on what knowledge should be included in Black girls' education. I asked them to delve into their experiences and perceptions, and suggest significant factors in Black girls' education that would improve their lives. Although the question required time for reflection, none of the women felt able to outline improvements. Colleen sighed, "I wish I could give you an answer, I just can't." Idamae answered, "You know what? I don't know how to answer." Gwen suggested that I ask the mother whose 8-year-old daughter helps to run her family's business confidently and proficiently. Trudy thought of the disparities in our lives and also could not immediately advance any ideas. Ida, Colleen, Gwen, Trudy, and Yvette had never been asked nor expected to produce this information, but throughout various conversations I returned to the subject, and their experiences and insights follow.

Colleen believes, "We should encourage our daughters to be educated. Black girls should be taught to be educated just like males, I mean, what is the difference?" All participants agree with Colleen's admonition that refers to schooling. However, it is clear that participants accord equal importance to education in the home and at school. Parents use their experiences to prepare their children for what they will encounter in society. Our discussions revealed the important role of informal education and the consistent overlapping of factors that should work across home, school, and work—all areas of life. Colleen maintains that children need to be "taught from many different sources and when they say, and this is as true as it can be, it takes a whole community to raise a child, that is true."

Valuing the Self: Unlocking Potential

Yvette believes an important part of education for Black girls is for them to "know who they are, where they can go, what is out there for them to be able to achieve.... They may not have a father in the house or they may have sisters who are having babies. That's not the way life really is, and they should be taught that at an early age." Yvette sums this up as what she refers to as a "sense of self" and of what Black girls can accomplish in life. I asked if this information should be taught at home or at school. Yvette emphasized that "this should be done both at home and at school. They should be taught that there are other goals a person can go for, there's other ways of getting these goals besides what you're looking at in the household. I tell that to Evelyn now. I was never told those things."

Yvette's words are centered in her personal experiences. She was a strict mother. Yvette counseled her daughters about the importance of avoiding the responsibility of children during their high school years, because she was pregnant as a freshman in high school. However, her three older daughters became single mothers when they were 18. Yvette therefore wants 9-year-old Evelyn to understand that what she sees at home does not have to be her reality. Yvette sees the need for Evelyn to learn from home and school the wide possibilities she can achieve, and to believe in herself to achieve her goals. Yvette's view is personally liberating, because the individual's future is not to be limited by past or present circumstances. Parents and teachers should develop and transmit expectations based on possibilities, not on limitations nor on what exists in the children's environment. Yvette believes in open communication with children at early ages. The openness empowers children by allowing them freedom of self-expression to express their being and what they are becoming. Consistent with the latter, Yvette and the other mothers provide motivation and opportunity for growth and development, and vigilantly work to provide safe spaces for development at home and at school for their children.

Empowerment Through Creativity

All participants feel that attention to discipline and personal guidance in the home is critical. Trudy and Colleen specifically refer to the need for parents to discipline and inculcate proper values in their children. Colleen defines a balance, however: "Black women, just based on my experience and from the neighborhood, you were really just turned loose so to speak on your own. Your mothers were very strict as far as discipline was concerned, but you were never taught to be creative." Although discipline is essential, forms of discipline that prevent development of creativity are not helpful to Colleen. Nonschool or informal education that prepares Black girls to face life's challenges creatively is the goal. In her dialogue that follows, and in the section on work, Colleen mentions the importance of Blacks learning survival skills to cope with the corporate environment. The problems Blacks face in society need to be openly addressed, and social contradictions need to be uncovered. We are required to maintain a sense of normalcy under unjust conditions, which only harms us. Our experiences need to be shared and multiplied as we help to prepare children for the environment they will face. Colleen explains:

> What I'm saying is that we have no formal training as Blacks, as women ... ah, our male children aren't taught how to survive in this world. What you are taught from family, from church, from association is how to be nonexistent, how to be, uhm, I don't even ... how do I say this? You're taught how to exist without being really heard or seen. It's like they tell children to be seen and not heard. You're taught how to get along so to speak out here. You're not taught how to cope or what to look for, or to know what the signals are. You learn them by rote and then in learning those signals by rote what happens is

you become very defensive. You learn how to defend yourself, and you get very, very self-contained. You realize how little power you have.

This statement intimates that knowledge in the areas mentioned would empower Black youths for the specifics of their daily lives. It would be helpful to understand how various people address this issue.

Encouraging Interests

Colleen believes in encouraging the interests and creativity of the child. She has implicit faith that parents will readily know what these interests are. She explains the importance of paying close attention to children: "Watch your children, find out what their interests are; you encourage what their interests are. Most children show you at a very early age what their interests are. They either like to dance, they either like to draw, they like to make things with their hands, some like to cook. You watch them, they will tell you what their interests are." Because of her daughter, Rachel, and granddaughter, Kim, Colleen is experienced in encouraging the interests of the child:

My daughter was encouraged to do everything she had an interest in. I pushed her, or I allowed her to do whatever her interest was at the time. When she wanted to skate she had skates, we took her over to the skating rink. When she wanted to ice skate she had ice skates, we took her to the rink, everything she wanted to do! When she wanted to be in art we gave her art classes, when she wanted to travel—we is me an' my mother that was her influence in life. Everything she's ever shown an interest in we've encouraged it. Even now, I still to this day encourage her to do whatever it is she feels she wants to do. She has no follow through. My granddaughter does and I do everything I can to see to it that she has the tools that are necessary for her to excel.

Colleen's 9-year-old granddaughter Kim is interested in computers, and the family makes sure that she has one. Kim is on her school's soccer team, and Colleen bought her a tape of Pele demonstrating soccer moves: "She sat there and watched that tape over an' over until she told me 'I can do that.' She went outside with the soccer ball an' started doin' it; she's in her second year on the soccer team. She's excellent, she's very good and we encourage her." Some of the tools Colleen provides to her granddaughter are those that Colleen's mother used to encourage and motivate Colleen: "I make sure that she can get to school, that she has nice clothes to go to school and I answer any questions she asks me, you know.... She's encouraged to really continue to read, she has a library card, she goes to the library." Colleen was obviously proud of samples of Kim's artwork displayed in her apartment: "I'll show you some of the things she's done when she was very little, and to show you her rationale at that time. I keep all of her artwork, she did this picture on my door. She's very artistic, I took her to art class when she was 3 years old. She was in a creative art class."

Motivation Through Entrepreneurship

Gwen believes a family business would be a source of motivation that could lead her daughters to accomplish significant goals in their lives: "I want my own business, some little tiny thing. I wanta work an' I want someone in my family to run this business, something that's ours, actually a legacy for my children." Gwen illustrates the benefits of working in a family business by pointing to the 8-year-old who assists her mother in a takeout restaurant on Ogden Avenue:

> She will take your order, ring it up, give you your change back, write the order down, take it back, she will answer the phone, take the orders over the phone, take it back to the back. She talks better than I do. She's on the calculator, and when she's done she sticks that pencil behind her ear and sits there and reads a book. I want my children to be that confident, you know. I want my children to have that now, to have a place that they run now, so that they really will want to do somethin' with their lives. Maybe even have the juices flowin' to own their own businesses. That little girl is amazin.' I look at her, I swear it's the look in her face, like she is no nonsense; she's like 8 years old. I see her sitting on a bench with the little gavel in her hand callin' everybody to order. It's beautiful, I mean, whatever her mom is teachin' her, ask that woman what it is that we need to do with our children.

Her account of the girl in the family business illustrates the value Gwen places on competence and confidence learned at an early age. The importance of informal education that is useful in the world is implicit. Colleen believes, "We should place more emphasis on business. We teach our children, I think this is all our children, we teach our children to find jobs, we don't teach them how to create jobs, we don't encourage them. My parents were both self-employed, they eventually went into the marketplace." Diminishing jobs for some and overwork for many who have jobs, as well as racial and gender discrimination, are contributing factors to Colleen's advocacy of entrepreneurship.

Removing "Dis" from Disadvantage: A Creative Approach to Work

For some time, Colleen has noticed increasing numbers of Black women babysitting White children in Loop parks. The numbers are reminiscent of when most Black women were engaged in domestic work: "The same stuff I saw when I was a child; my best friend's mother worked for the Jenkins[es], she cleaned their house, that's what's goin' on now, goin' back to cleaning.

They're hirin' you as professional nannies." Colleen believes the reentry into domestic service for some Black women should be made personally advantageous through entrepreneurship. She remarks:

> There is a business in that, but they don't want you to view it as a business. They wanna go back to the way it was before! You in my home, you gonna live here or whatever, you come and clean. I see it as a business, I think it's fantastic, but you have to have business skills to set that up as a business. I tried to talk my daughter into doin' the same thing, she had the opportunity to do it up there in Newport, but she didn't want to do that and I don't wanna do that. I can do it, but that's nothing I wanna do. I wasn't trained to do that. Unfortunately though, we're goin' to have to start doin' that, an' like I said, my subtle message, an' it wasn't so subtle, to all those who I would come in contact with is that we're goin' to have to learn, an' be willing to step out of corporate America. We're gonna have to suffer jus' like I'm doin' now....

Colleen's words are reminiscent of Black women immediately after slavery. Some Black women tried to escape the intolerable conditions in the homes of Whites by becoming laundresses or dressmakers, thus enjoying a measure of independence by working at home. Money management is an area that also concerns Colleen: "My granddaughter gets an allowance, I'm encouraging her to save her money, also to spend. I took her to the bank and Darcel Lewis opened her account. I'm teachin' her how to save her money."

Building Character

Some of participants' insights on education for Black girls are expressed in the form of religious messages. Ida and Yvette weave a God-centered focus into all areas of life, and Gwen believes the teaching of moral values is essential. She advocates teaching the girls "more strongly that their bodies are temples, and to be abstinent, you know, the old values." Yvette asserts her belief that a God-centered, two-parent family would be ideal. Trudy believes children who are taught religious values are better prepared for life.

Trudy stresses the importance of communication within the family and the influence of peer association. Her goal was to get married and have a family, but her association with girls who wanted to have babies in high school influenced her. Trudy was able to keep her focus until her father left the family: "I always wanted to get married first, but it was when my father left, it was like I clinged on to this guy...." She summarizes her views: "Who you associate with is very important because if you're around people that don't want anything out of life, you will tend to not want anything outta life. But if you're around people that are motivated and want to do things and want to be a better person, that's what you'll want."

Although the lives of all participants demonstrate resilience, Gwen believes racism is an obstacle to Black achievement, which—like all hindrances—must be met with resilience:

Everybody's responsible for how they live their lives, you know. There could be racism, um, an' it's a stumbling block, it's an obstacle, but do you let it get you down? Do you turn into a criminal, do you turn to drugs? I mean, you gotta be responsible for your actions. A lotta people get filled wit' hate. A lotta people have things happen to them and they lose their self-esteem, you know, an' then life doesn't go in a positive way. But I still feel like people should learn that whatever they do bounce back, whatever happens to you bounce back, believe in God, you know, just keep bouncing back because it's life, otherwise you gonna go down, you know, an you gotta be responsible, an' that's why I try to teach my girls.

CONCLUSION

Competence, confidence, encouragement, and interests are some of the recurring themes that overlap in participants' home, school, and work settings. The information presented in this chapter indicates the critical role of informal education in the lives of participants and their families. It is also evident that informal education is based on the curriculum of experience, which deals with material and spiritual concerns, emanates from life, and prepares the self to navigate and create.

Participants' experiences and association with others in the world stimulate desires and strategies for both formal and informal education. They are dedicated to helping their children learn formally and informally to realize their potential. Their conceptions of "getting an education" for their children surpass what their parents envisioned for them. This study's participants have higher expectations for their children than their parents had for them. Attention to motivation and nurturing relationships that allow learning through open communication are primary goals for these women. Participants desire to help their children avoid the effects of being unskilled in today's job market. However, the social, economic, and political effects of class, race, and gender discrimination present obstacles to quality education. It is impossible to generalize about all African American parents based on information collected from my study's participants. However, participants' experiences are comparable to those of many other African Americans. Jackson's call for a "major, large-scale, national research study of the relationship between family background, schooling, work, and income among specific subsets of black females over time" (1976, pp. 201–202) remains unanswered. Such a study is still needed, and more discussions of the effects of informal education on formal education also would certainly be helpful.

REFERENCES

Amott, T., & Matthaei, J. (1991). *Race gender and work: A multicultural economic history of women in the United States.* Boston, MA: South End Press.
Billingsley, A. (1992). *Climbing Jacob's ladder.* New York: Simon & Schuster.

Collins, P. H. (1991). *Black feminist thought: Knowledge, consciousness, and the politics of empowerment*. New York: Routledge.

Etter-Lewis, G. (1993). *My soul is my own*. New York: Routledge.

Jackson, J. (1976). *Career options for black women*. (ERIC Document Reproduction Service No. ED 138 812) Education and work section of the National Institute of Education, Washington, DC.

Lutrell, W. (1989). Working-class women's ways of knowing: Effects of gender, race, and class. *Sociology of Education, 62*, 33–46.

Mirza, H. S. (1992). *Young, female, and black*. New York: Routledge.

Neverdon-Morton, C. (1990). African American women and adult education in the South, 1985–1925. In H. Neufeldt & L. McGee (Eds.), *Education of the African American Adult* (pp. 163–177). New York: Greenwood.

Omolade, B. (1994). *The rising song of African American women*. New York: Routledge.

Schubert, W. H. (1986). *Curriculum, perspective, paradigm, and possibility*. New York: Macmillan.

Whiteaker, L. H. (1990). Adult education in the slave community. In H. Neufeldt. & L. McGee (Eds.), *Education of the African American adult* (pp. 1–10). New York: Greenwood.

Chapter 10

Gilles Deleuze and Jacques Daignault: Understanding Curriculum as Difference and Sense

Wen-Song Hwu
Brooklyn College

Thinking Beyond

In the final chapter in this volume, Hwu returns us to work that is unabashedly poststructural. The chapter centers on the work of Jacques Daignault and Gilles Deleuze. Hwu wants to move beyond the "death bound of deterministic and systematic curriculum planning." Hwu, like Daignault, wants to challenge us to rethink and do curriculum poststructurally. In this chapter, Hwu provides an excellent explication of the work of Deleuze and Daignault and the implications of their work for curriculum theory.

Questions

1. How is curriculum, as Daignault and Deleuze discussed it, a paradoxical and nomadic object? How is that notion of curriculum as paradoxical and nomadic related to the idea of multiplicity?
2. How does the concept of binary oppositions apply to much of our thinking in curriculum and education? How are the oppositions of theory and practice, teaching and learning, and thinking and action addressed by the work of Daignault and Deleuze?
3. How does Hwu's analysis of poststructural thinkers compare to the analysis of Reynolds, Webber, and Livingston?

Contemporary curriculum studies has been a turbulent and discontinuous field. Many scholars strive to reexamine the field through their own interpretive analyses; in so doing, they all bring "new" theoretical and practical frameworks into curriculum discourses and make us rethink curriculum and ourselves as educators (Apple, 1979, 1986; Cherryholmes, 1988; Doll, 1993; Eisner, 1979; Eisner & Vallance, 1974; Hlebowitsch, 1997, 1998; Hwu, 1998; Jackson, 1992; Pinar, 1988, 1998; Pinar, Reynolds, Slattery, & Taubman, 1995). In this chapter, one of my main concerns is the death bound of deterministic and systematic curriculum planning that prescribed to perish teachers' and students' social realities and their meaningful life experiences. I argue that prevailing structuralist-minded schooling has excluded the dynamics among students/teachers; that it offers false hope of certainty in achieving educational excellence; that it overlooks the social matrix embodied within itself; and that it diminishes the tensions of race, gender, class, and ethnicity by creating a homogeneous educational enterprise. I intend to ex-

181

plicate Gilles Deleuze and Jacques Daignault's works to problematize our understanding of curriculum theory and practice.

In reflecting on Deleuze and Daugnault's writing, I hope to lay out an interpretation of their "ideas" without losing the diagonal senses of their writing. These diagonal senses are "unsayable" (Foucault, 1972, 1977), akin to Derrida's "undecidable," or "trace," and Deleuze's "non-parallel" revolution—which is a "heterochronous becoming" (Deleuze, 1987; Derrida, 1978). Language has invented the dualism, said Deleuze (1987); therefore, we must pass through dualism because it is in language. In other words, to pass through dualisms is not to get rid of them, but rather to fight against language, to invent "stammering"—AND, AND, AND ... (1987). For instance, in Platonic dualism, we recognize that it is not at all the dualism of the intelligible and the sensible, of idea and matter. It is not the distinction between the model and the copy, but rather between good copies and simulacra—false copies (Deleuze, 1990). Deleuze and Guattari stated that "it is a subterranean dualism between that which receives the action of the Idea and that which eludes this action" (1987, p. 3). However, I hope that this chapter can be grasped in a conventional as well as poststructuralist way to cast light on the connection between Deleuze's thinking and curriculum studies.

IDENTITY, PARADOX, AND CURRICULUM

In Deleuze's (1990) comments on Mallarmé, dialogue from Zen master, he stated: "'If you have a cane', says the Zen master, 'I am giving you one; if you do not have one, I am taking it away.' (or, Chrysippus said, 'If you never lost something, you have it still; but you never lost horns, *ergo* you have horns')" (p. 136). The point is not to repudiate any identity, nor to embrace every possibility whatsoever. There is a paradoxical element implicitly being connected with the question of "What is curriculum?" raised by Jacques Daignault (1986). These curriculum questions and answers parallel the questions raised in poststructuralism. This paradoxical instance, therefore, has the property of always being displaced in relation to itself, of "being absent from its own place," its own identity, its own resemblance, and its own equilibrium. It is the question of "in between" or "boundary" that runs into all possible directions at one and the same time.

The curriculum field, Daignault argued, was a "stepchild" or "subdiscipline" to other disciplines. It was always associated with or derived from other disciplines and subject matters, such as psychology, political science, history, sociology, educational administration. Daignault contended that curriculum has been developed and became recognizable during the last 3 decades.

Daignault and Guathier (1982) did not define what curriculum is, rather, "how it functions—how to be" (pp. 182–183). We can understand their intention via Deleuze's (1986b) statement that "it is absolutely useless to look for a theme in a writer if one hasn't asked exactly what its importance is in the work—that is, how it functions (and not what its 'sense' is)" (p. 45). This also parallels the "technologies of self" in Foucault's dealing with self-formation (Martin et al., 1988). Daignault, then, approached this problematic of identity through the concept of paradox, adopted from Gregory Bateson (1972) and Deleuze's (1990) series of paradoxes. Daignault argued that identity is inherited from difference, and he remarked that the concept of identity presupposes the concept of "sameness." Two items have to be the same in order to be identical. Such a view was explained in Hegel's dialectical thinking; it is the identity, *both* between the identity of identity and identity *and* between the identity of difference and difference (Descombes, 1986), that constitutes the "difference" between identity and difference. However, Daignault went further to argue that the problematic of identity is focusing on the paradoxical instance of the "difference" itself, not yet differentiated. Paradox, said Deleuze, is at first what destroys good sense as the only direction, but paradox is also what destroys common sense as the assignation of fixed identities. Deleuze (1990) asserted that the function of the paradoxical instance is to "ensure the relative displacement of the two series, the excess of the one over the other, without being reducible to any of the terms of the series or to any relation between these terms" (p. 40). In other words, paradoxical instance functions to condition the possibilities of being related or divergent.

In this Deleuzean way, then, Daignault and Gauthier (1982) insisted that curriculum is a paradoxical and nomadic object, which is always transient (moving). In short, curriculum is "thought without image, object following an always moving empty space" (p. 182). Here we should not confuse the acts of thought with the image of thought; for Daignault, the curriculum does not exist, but it happens. As Deleuze (1990) pointed out, the idea of "a place without occupant" and "an occupant having no place" are not to be fixed or to be filled up in a place, which would simply stop the game (an "ideal game" in his mind); to the contrary, he insisted, the point is to keep on playing. The empty place and perpetual displacement of a piece in a game is a double sliding in a "perpetual disequilibrium vis-a-vis each other" (p. 40). However, Deleuze (1990) remarked that "the paradoxical entity is never where we look for it, and conversely that we never find it where it is. As Lacan says, 'it fails to observe its place' *(elle manque à sa place)*" (p. 41).

Daignault did not propose that we should stop defining but, on the contrary, to *multiply* the definitions, to invite a plural spelling. To define is to distort (Hwu, 1993). Daignault's intention here, with which Deleuze would agree, is that to define is not a question of probabilities, combining the heterogeneous elements, simply putting them together. Rather, to define is to portray that there are varied lines, in the Deleuzean (1990) term "*series*," made by people (or things) that do not know necessarily which line they are on or where they should make the line which they are tracing pass. The serial form is "realized in the simultaneity [of] at least two series" (p. 36). In short, there is a whole "geography" in people—with lines of flight, series of events.

DELEUZE'S THINKING AND PHILOSOPHY

For Deleuze, the truth is not merely the subject of enunciation nor the subject of statements, but the "event" itself—the boundary of two sides. In a Derridean fashion, Deleuze sees the concept of truth, as implied by harmonious agreement and what defines the "true" opinion of what something means, as itself a naïve notion.

The concept (or problem) of "difference" has been interpreted and reinterpreted by many scholars, poststructuralists in particular (Bell, 1998). In this chapter, I like to explicate Deleuze's notions of "sense" and the play of "difference"—as the only alternative to a deadlocked dialectical tradition (to reason itself) as reason tries in vain to overcome its oppositional nature—at the origin of values—that new light can be cast on a way of life. Pecora (1986), commenting on Deleuze, stated that "the history of reason in the West becomes, not the dialectic of pure conception, or pure representation, with an objective 'reality,' but instead the dialectic of reason *as* power" (p. 46).

Deleuze's (1983) philosophy of difference is interrelated to Nietzsche's notion of an "affirmation of affirmation" and can be briefly put as "only difference(s) can resemble each other." It is contrasted to "only that which resembles differs" (p. 74). There are two ways of making difference, said Deleuze: affirmative and negative. He insisted that it is not the reproduction of the same, but rather the repetition of the different that is important. Deleuze (1988) succinctly put it: "Resemblance then can only be thought as the product of this internal difference" (pp. 262–263). This internal irreducible difference is exactly where the world of simulacra is built. The simulacrum is regarded as the copy of a copy, in terms of Rousseau's model and copy (see Derrida, 1981a, 1981b).

Deleuze's philosophical thought adopts Nietzsche's notion of relation between knowledge and life. In *Nietzsche and Philosophy* (1983), Deleuze insisted that Nietzsche put knowledge into action, not as itself an end, but as a simple means of serving life. And he warned us that "the opposition between knowledge and life and the operation which knowledge makes itself judge of life are symptoms, only symptoms" (p. 96).

Furthermore, he averred that "knowledge *is* opposed to life, but because it expresses a life which contradicts life, a reactive life which finds in knowledge a means of preserving and glorifying its type" (p. 100). When thought is subjected to knowledge, with knowledge becoming the legislator, Deleuze remarked that "knowledge is thought itself, but thought subject to reason and to all that is expressed in reason" (p. 101).

In his interpretation of reason, Deleuze (1983) depicted "reason," following Kant's definition, as "the faculty of organizing indirect, oblique means," contrary to culture (p. 99); doubtless the original means react on the ends and transform them, but in the last analysis the ends are always those of nature. Reason, stated Deleuze, sometimes dissuades and sometimes forbids us to cross a certain limit or boundary. Because to do so is useless, would be evil, and is impossible—there is nothing to see or think behind the truth. He questioned the notion by asking, "Does not critique, understood as critique of knowledge itself, express new forces capable of giving thought another sense? A thought that would go to the limit of what life can do, a thought that would lead life to the limit of what it can do?" (Deleuze, 1983, p. 101). Deleuze agreed with the Stoic saying that reason is a body that enters, and spreads itself over, an animal body.

Although welcoming structuralists' dethroning the subject or attacking on the *cogito*, Deleuze questioned the status of impersonal structures that confine subjectivity. He thoroughly problematized the structural model—Saussurean analysis of linguistic structure—through a theory that emphasizes "singular points," "planes of consistence," "nomadic distributions," and his philosophy of difference. Deleuze (1990) argued that structuralist approaches may have no essential point in common other than "sense," regarded not at all as appearance but as "surface effect" and "position effect," and produced by the circulation of the "empty square" in the structural series (the place of the dummy, the place of the king, the blind spot, the floating signifier, the value degree zero, the absent cause, etc.). Deleuze (1990) remarked:

> Structure is in fact a machine for the production of incorporeal sense (*Skindapsos*). But when structuralism shows in this manner that sense is produced by nonsense and its perpetual displacement, and that it is born of the respective position of elements which are not themselves "signifying," we should not at all compare it with what was called the philosophy of the absurd, nonsense is what is opposed to sense in a simple relation with it, so that the absurd is always defined by a deficiency of sense and a lack [there is not enough of it]. (p. 71)

Following Deleuze, we can see not only that nonsense "makes" sense, this sense being precisely that it has none, but more importantly that the relation between sense and nonsense should not be based on a relation of exclusion. Rather, suggested Deleuze (1990), it should be considered "an original type of intrinsic relation, a mode of co-presence" (p. 68). It is an orientation that is not simply an alternative but also a possible complement, conjugation, or coexistent interaction.

Unlike many deconstructionists, Deleuze's notion of meaning (sense) can be expressed in a sentence, but that meaning can only be designated in a second sentence, whose meaning must be designated in a third, and so on. This paradox of indefinite regression attests to the weakness of the speaker, but "the impotence of the empirical consciousness is here like the 'nth' power of language, and its transcendental repetition, the infinite power of language to speaks of words themselves" (Bogue, 1989, p. 64). In Deleuze's views, meaning is a *simulacrum*, a paradoxical, contradictory entity that defines common sense. Roland Bogue (1989) elaborated on it as follows: "It is always expressed in language, but it can only be designated by initiating a process of infinite regression. It seems to inhere [subsist] in language, but to appear in things" (p. 73). The understanding of "sense," Deleuze emphasized, in *The Logic of Sense* (1990), is that words express things, but what is expressed is an attribute of things (i.e., an event). Meaning and events form a single surface with two sides, events only emerge within words, but what does emerge pertains to things. This surface of meaning/events forms the surface between words and things and functions as "the articulation of their difference" (p. 37).

In another book, *Kafka: Toward a Minor Literature* (1986b), Deleuze regarded Kafka as important because he invented a mode of writing—*minor literature*—that allows us to account for the different "machines" that condition our actual relation to the world, to the body, to desire, and to the economy of life and death. This can be portrayed through their understanding of art. Art, in modern sense, Deleuze and Guattari (1987) perceived, is no longer an art that proposes to "express" (a meaning), to "represent" (a thing, a being), or to "imitate" (a nature). Réda Bensmaïa (1987) noted, "It is rather a method (of writing)—of picking up, even of stealing: Of 'double stealing' as Deleuze sometimes says, which is both 'stealing' and 'stealing away'—that consists in propelling the most diverse contents on the basis of (nonsignifying) ruptures and intertwinings of the most heterogeneous orders of signs and powers" (p. xvii).

The notion of "becoming" is a pivotal point for Deleuze's (1987) philosophical thinking; for him, in becoming there is no past nor future, not even present; there is no history. This means that it is a matter of "involuting" (p. 29). It is neither progression nor regression; to become is to become more and more restrained, more and more simple, more and more deserted, and for that very reason populated. Deleuze (1987) explained, "This is what's difficult to explain: to what extent one should involute. It is obviously the opposite of evolution, but it is also the opposite of regression, returning to a childhood or to a primitive world. To involute is to have an increasingly simple, economical, restrained step" (p. 29). To become is to reach a process whose synthetic principle is "complication" that "designates both the presence of the multiple in the One and of the One in the multiple" (Deleuze, 1972, p. 44). To complicate the sign and the meaning is revealed in essence, not created by essence. Deleuze and Guattari (1987) remarked that multiplicities are made up of "becomings" without history, of "individuation without subject." Deleuze thus embraced Nietzschean perspectivism and aestheticism, arguing that all thought presupposes evaluation and interpretation, and that truth is created rather than discovered:

> I can talk of Foucault, tell you that he has said this or that to me, set it out as I see it. This is nothing as long as I have not been able really to encounter this

set of sounds *hammered* out, of decisive gestures, of *ideas* all made of tinder and fire, of deep *attention* and sudden closure, of *laughter* and smiles which one feels to be *"dangerous"* at the very moment when one feels *tenderness*—this set as a unique combination whose proper name would be Foucault. (Deleuze, 1987, p. 11)

Deleuze's fundamental problem is most certainly not to liberate the Multiple but to submit thinking to a renewed concept of the One. In Deleuze's view, it is through the play of "difference, a conceptual concept, and nonconcept" that the certainties of Western rationality are undetermined. Deleuze (1988) remarked that "the unthought is therefore not external to thought but lies at its very heart, as the impossibility of thinking which doubles and hollows out the outside" (p. 97). The theme is that of the "double," but the double is never a projection of the interior; on the contrary, it is an interiorization of the outside, a "fold" as Deleuze would say. It is not "a doubling of the One, but a redoubling of the Other. It is not a reproduction of the Same, but a repetition of the Different" (p. 98).

The multiplicity of forces, the multiple being of forces is an "act without activity." These forces are unfolded on the surface of internal depth and then folded under the surface; any given perspective can only be validated by reverting to still other perspectives. For example, Deleuze argued that

Time as subject, or rather subjectivation, is called Memory. Not that brief memory that comes afterwards and is the opposite of forgetting, but the "absolute memory" which doubles the present and the outside and is one with forgetting, since it is itself endlessly forgotten and reconstituted: its fold, in fact, merges with the unfolding, because the latter (the unfolding) remains present within the former (the fold) as the thing that is folded. (1988, p. 107)

Memory is contrasted not with forgetting but with the forgetting of forgetting, which dissolves us into the outside and constitutes death. Only forgetting (the unfolding) recovers what is folded in memory and in the fold itself. It is the question of "Are we capable of it?" instead "Is it still possible?" in which Deleuze was interested.

PEDAGOGICAL IMPLICATION: JACQUES DAIGNAULT

This section discusses some works of Jacques Daignault. It provides an interpretation of his thought and of its bearing on the current issues of contemporary curriculum studies. Because the influence of Gilles Deleuze on Daignault is enormous, a "reading" of Deleuze alongside a reading of Daignault will be presented as an intersecting "event."

The poststructuralist curriculum, Daignault (1983) conceived, is not simply the transmission of knowledge, or the transmission of values, nor the mastery of method—"know-how" or "know-how-to-be"—but rather is a "manner" to "stage" knowledge through a "passage-way." This passage-way is to think otherwise, as in Nietzsche's "will to" (as resentment), Heidegger's notion of "thinking" (thought-provoking) and Foucault's history of thought (as unthought), especially in the Deleuzean "sense" (French *sens*)—surface and event (as the fourth dimension of language or fourth person singular). Daignault suggested such a notion of thinking or sense in which to think oneself as self-educative, meaning "to experiment and to problematize"; to make sense, which by itself is a problematic and problematizing. Influenced by Kant and Deleuze, Daignault asserted that the separation of universality and particularity, subject and object, one's work and play, one's intellectual activities and everyday life, teaching and learning is all but unattainable. Binary oppositions are denied. Daignault thought of the "excluded middle" (in Deleuze's term "sense-event") being given ready-made unproblematically in curriculum studies. The excluded middle is the interest of determinations of signification. He argued that sense (event) is presented both as what happens to bodies and what insists in propositions. As Ulmer (1985) pointed out, classroom is a place for teacher and students' inventions, not simply reproduction; he insisted that "pedagogy is (a) theater that is not representation but 'life itself'" (p. 174). Lives become texts. Texts require interpretations and reinterpretations.

DAIGNAULT'S THINKING AND WRITING

Jacques Daignault has written on poststructuralism and curriculum theory in a "unique" (there is no organizing principle) yet consistent way. From a series of essays written by Jacques Daignault 2 decades ago, I have chosen a few of his works attempting to "stage" his thoughts on curriculum and pedagogy. For Deleuze and Daignault, thinking means to "problematize," to go beyond subject-identity toward "the thought of difference" and "the production of sense" (Daignault, 1991, p. 376). This leads to an aesthetics of problematization that neither excludes the subject nor centers it. Daignault insisted that this problematization does not exclude feeling or emotion without reducing everything to it either.

The problematic of theory and practice has been one of the major issues of curriculum. Daignault approached the problematic by using Deleuze's series of paradoxes to demonstrate the present dilemma within the curriculum field. For example, regarding the problematics of teaching and learning, Daignault claimed that there are many differences among theoretical practices, yet theoretical practices cannot be confused with the application of theories. Both Foucault and Deleuze recognized this point and reiterated that "theory does not express, translates, or serve to apply practice: it *is* practice" (Deleuze, 1988, p. 13).

Therefore, the problematic involves, observed Daignault, adopting Deleuze's third and eighth series of the proposition in *The Logic of Sense*

(1990)—that is, that the issue at stake is the distinction or gap between theory and practice. Daignault found that this can be understood as the "gap" between "signans"—as signifying—and "signatum," as the signified, which was called "Lévi-Strauss' paradox" by Deleuze (1990): "The Universe signified long before we began to know what it was signifying…. Man, since his origin, has had at his disposal a completeness of signifier which he is obstructed from allocating to a signified, given as such without being any better known. There is always an inadequacy between the two" (cited in Daignault & Gauthier, 1982, p. 187).

What is in excess in the signifying is a place without an occupant. What is lacking in the signified series is a "supernumerary"—an unknown, an occupant without a place. Daignault asserted that two conditions are present: "First, the elements of each series have to be determined by differential relations as in the case for phonemes and morphemes in the language and second, there must exist a paradoxical instance that pervades both series without belonging to neither a place without an occupant nor an occupant without a place" (p. 189). This instance has the function of articulating the two series to one another, of making them communicate, coexist, and ramify.

This Deleuzean "paradoxival instance," Daignault (1982) saw, is exactly the link between desire and promise, teaching and learning; in other words, "the promise of the other's desire" (p. 18). As Lacan (1977) would say, "the subject of a teaching is a learning" (p. 20). Along with these lines, Daignault ironically parodied Marxist approaches that are succinct (sufficient) but too dogmatic. He wrote wittily, "I would become sad as a Marxist should Don Quixote become a Roller Derby player!" (p. 3) In other words, Marxist approaches function to kidnap the readers to make them happy.

DESIRE AND THE OTHER

A notion of desire as seduction can be discovered in pedagogical situations. The notion of seduction means the interplay, dialogue, and encounters between teachers and students. The object of desire is to know and thus be seduced; it is unreachable or unattainable. We can never know absolutely, and yet our quest to know never stops. Once the object of desire has been appropriated, it loses its status as desirable; possession means death. Incidentally, in this regard Taubman (1990) pointed out that pedagogy is the question of achieving the "right" distance between teachers and students in complicity with the Lacanian notion of "desire."

Desire cannot be a question of "interior drives," or Girard's "lack of being," because to think of it in those ways is to reestablish the realm of interiority common to Man, even if one is Woman. Daignault (1982) insisted that "such is the romantic lie to which is opposed the 'romanesque' truth" (p. 5). According to Deleuze (1987) and Daignault (1982), the misconceptions of desire may be summarized as following three: "*First*, it can be put in relationship with lack or the law; *second*, with a natural or spontaneous reality;

third, with pleasure or, above all, the festival, celebration (i.e., reversal)" (Deleuze, 1987, p. 103).

We can see here desire represented as a lack, a function not of the presence of a desirable object but of its actual absence and thus of its sole imaginary and symbolic presence. On the contrary, Daignault (1982) asserted, desire is not "the inaccessibility of the object of Desire," but also the assumption that it comes from "an excessive appreciation of reality is rejected" (p. 6). Thus, he argued that it is rather from "a radical 'différance' coming from the pure fabrication of a double" (p. 7). This is an undifferentiated whole. This also can be interpreted in light of Deleuze's contention that desire is production, or "desiring-production," not acquisition or lack. Ronald Bogue (1989), commenting on Deleuze and Guattari, remarked, "Desire is essentially unconscious, and hence unrelated to negation (there is no 'no' in the unconscious), indifferent to personal identities or body images (central to Lacan's imaginary order) and independent of linguistic expression or interpretation (the core of Lacan's Symbolic order)" (p. 89). In other words, desire is "not internal to a subject, any more than it tends toward an object" (Deleuze & Guattari, 1987, p. 89).

The notion of Other is much related to desire. Deleuze & Guattari (1987) defined, "The Other, as structure, is the expression of a possible world" (p. 134). This means that it is the structure of the possible; that the expressed possible world exists, but it does not exist (actually) outside of what expresses it. Deleuze (1990) argued that "the error of philosophical theories is to reduce the Other sometimes to a particular object, and sometimes to another subject" (p. 307). The Other *is* the subject. Without the other there is no subject.

ANALOGY AND SENSES

Daignault explicated analogy in education through "common sense" and "good sense." He employed his understanding of Deleuzean "sense" to inquire into curriculum problematics, such as theory and practice, teaching and learning. Analogy, commonly understood, is a nonconclusive reasoning that proceeds through a fourth proportional term (A is to B as C is to D). For instance, a pen to a writer is as a gun to a soldier. Analogy, in Greek term "analogia or analogos," (from *ana*, "up," "upon," "throughout," and "continuous," and logos, "ratio," "reasoned") means the comparison of similarities in concepts or things. (Angeles, 1981) For Daignault (1983), analogy can be shown as proportional identity by the means of analog communication. He proposed four categories of analogy in education and further to fill a gap of "rigorous analogies" in education: "(1) The analogies of good sense and common sense; (2) the scientific analogies (or theoretical models); (3) the artistic analogies (or poetical metaphor); and (4) the pedagogical analogies" (p. 20). Here, Daignault (1983) again connected these analogies with Deleuze's notion of sense, repetition and difference, and paradoxical instance between signifiers and signifieds to deal with the problematics between teaching and learning. Teaching and learning represent two series that meet in pedagogy. There is necessarily a gap between these two. One knows and the other does not. Let us recall that the notion of sense, Deleuze (1990) wrote, is the fourth dimension of a proposition: It is "[N]either the designation (objective signification), nor the manifestation (subjective signification), nor signification (systematic signification). Sense does not ex-ist but sub-sists in the world and in-sists in language" (p. 38).

Daignault elaborated Deleuze's "sense" that it is expressed as an event of an entirely different nature. Deleuze (1990) asserted that "it emanates from nonsense as from the always displaced paradoxical instance and from the eternally decentered ex-centric center" (p. 176). In short, sense is produced by nonsense—"a donation of sense" (Deleuze, 1990, p. 69). Daignault (1983) also used Steve Reich's repetitive music to demonstrate that although "the shifting of the repetition [is being] accelerated at a constant speed," the differential value will be the same as the repetition itself to a certain extent; "repetition generates the difference"—interpreting the composition (p. 26). On the other hand, in the learning process, the difference needs to be annulled in order to repeat the same passage rigorously. This means "the repetition increases toward identity and the difference decreases to zero"; in other words, "difference gives birth to the repetition"—learning the composition (p. 27). We can see there is a paradoxical instance that circulates in the difference of teaching–learning process: "the 'non-sense' of the differential repetition of analogies analogous to themselves. And this *sui-reference* of the analogies is itself a function of the difference put forth for the joy of teaching" (p. 27). In this article, Daignault (1983) dealt with the notion of common sense and good sense again, but related directly to curriculum: "Common sense is a mechanism by which is conferred an identity to things—identity by virtue of which things may be known—and, good sense, a mechanism by which is imposed a direction, a good order in virtue of which a moral—which gives sense to life—may be founded" (p. 4).

Daignault (1983) used the analogy of common sense by reducing the teaching–learning processes as the transmission of informations—what he termed "the problematics of instruction." In the commonsensical processes of teaching and learning, there is an analogy of "going from the known to the unknown." The analogy of good sense as transmission of values is as "the problematics of education." It is a "mediation of relevance" (pp. 3–4). Here, as we can see, he protested these two notions of "intellectual" space—common sense and good sense. He warned us that we must not take the explanation of a fact for granted, but rather the birth or the suspicion of the existence of this fact—a preconceived opinion depending on good sense and common sense. Rather, he encouraged us to "wage a battle against the truisms and prejudices of [our] times" (p. 5). He was deconstructing the notion of common sense and the good sense of "complex prejudices."

Daignault (1983) proposed that curriculum is in a twofold paradoxical position, which is a "complex" prejudice. On the one hand, education transmits the cultural heritage of the past; on the other, it stimulates the youth to bring forth an improvement of present conditions—an example of an apparently contradictory prejudice as a paradoxical instance. We need not confuse contradiction with paradox, because the principle of contradiction points to the real and the possible, not to the impossible. The force of paradoxes is that they are not contradictory, but instead that they allow us be present at the genesis of contradictions. For instance, "writing has a double function: to translate everything into assemblages and to dismantle the assemblage. The two are the same thing" (Deleuze, 1986b, p. 47). The dismantling of the assemblages, observed Deleuze and Guattari (1987), makes the social representation take flight in a much more effective way than a critique would have done, and brings about a "deterritorization" of the world that is itself political and that has nothing to do with an activity of intimacy.

The problem again, Daignault saw, is that we confuse education with good sense and common sense. Paradox is opposed to *doxa*, in both aspects of *doxa*, namely, good sense and common sense. Deleuze (1990) explained as follows:

> Good sense is said of one direction only: it is the unique sense and expresses the demand of an order according to which is necessary to choose one direction and to hold onto it. Good sense therefore is given the condition under which it fulfills its function, which is essentially to foresee.... In common sense, "sense" is no longer said of a direction, but of an organ. It is called "common," because it is an organ, a function, a faculty of identification that brings diversity in general to bear upon the form of the Same. Common sense identifies and recognizes, no less than good sense foresees. (pp. 75–78)

Good sense and common sense are therefore undermined by the principle of their production, and are overthrown from within by paradox. This paradoxical instance is linked to Derrida's insistence that we must first try to conceive of the common ground, and the "différance" of this irreducible difference. For instance, Zen appears to be antimetaphysical, and yet Zen masters often make statements that are quite metaphysical. Zen masters seem to be fond of ordinary language, and yet their use of language is often extraordinary. This "paradoxical instance," for Zen masters, is the original teaching of Zen.

CURRICULUM, STYLE, AND DIFFERENCE

Daignault (1986) believed, "Education is the undying trace of the text of our day-to-day life, and such a text, which I call an expression, is nothing but the boundary itself. Writing about curriculum, in regards to the problematics of curriculum, is neither on the road or in the field but subsists in the no man's land" (p. 8). Daignault thought that the bridge between words and concepts is exactly the text of our day-to-day lives. Curriculum is the neverending trace of the text of everyday life. The trace, in disciplinary terms, is the boundary itself between literature and science. This trace is unnameable for it sub-sists in the world and in-sists in the language. What it "represents" cannot be represented. Or, as Derrida (1973) remarked, "The trace is not a presence but is rather the simulacrum of a presence that dislocates, displaces, and refers beyond itself. The trace has, properly speaking, no place, for effacement belongs to the very structure of the trace. Effacement must always be able to overtake the trace; otherwise it would not be a trace but an indestructible and monumental substance" (p. 156).

The boundary Daignault (1986) referred to is that "the no concept's locus in signifieds—expressible, no word's locus in signifiers—expressed" (p. 5). In Derrida's terms, this boundary itself is exactly a "différance"—a undifferentiated whole: a difference that makes the difference between identity and difference. The "différance" undermines the metaphysical hope of finding a "transcendental signified," a concept independent of language. The metaphysics of presence, which is self-presence, has been to find a stable place to stand outside, or above it. Derrida (1976) said "originary différance is supplementarity as structure" (p. 167). Here, structure means the irreducible complexity within which one can only shape or shift the play of presence or absence: that within which metaphysics can be produced but which metaphysics cannot think.

The "textual staging of knowledge," I believe, can be understood through Derrida's notion of silence. For Derrida (1978), silence played the irreducible role of what bears and haunts language, outside and *against* which alone language can emerge. Ulmer (1985) put the matter well:

> The risk in talking about silence (as many teachers must do, and for which the operations of the Mime are an analogy) is that a meaning might be given to that which does not have one (and this fall back into discourse is also a return to Hegelianism). To control this risk, sovereignty (a precursor of deconstruction) betrays meaning *within* meaning, betrays discourse *within* discourse, by choosing words, like "silence" itself, that "make us slide." (pp. 184–185)

Although silence can save one from conceptualization, one should not be attached to and be bound by it, according to Zen. Thus, the master Chap-chou was striking a flint for a light. He asked a monk, "I call this a light. What do you call it?" The monk did not say a word. Thereupon the master said, "If you do not grasp the meaning of Ch'an (Zen), it is useless to remain silent" (Chang, 1959, p. 156). The important point is not whether one should speak or should be silent, but nonattachment or Serres' notion of "detachment." It is an extreme to keep silent. Te-shan told his disciples, "If you say a word, you will get thirty blows. If you do not say a word, you will get the same thirty blows across the top of your head" (Chang, 1959, p. 133).

One should allow the mind to operate freely, naturally and spontaneously. Deleuze noted:

> The subject is this free, anonymous, and nomadic singularity which traverses men as well as plants and animals independently of the matter of their individuation and the forms of their personality. "Overman" means nothing other than this—the superior type of *everything that is*. This is a strange discourse, which ought to have renewed philosophy, and which finally deals with sense not as a *predicate* or a property but as an *event*. (Deleuze, 1990, p. 107)

Daignault (1988a) remarked that style is the most expensive form of writing. Style of teaching or writing is always autobiographic and self-educative. He could not imagine working on style—even in a very intellectual activity—without becoming someone else: myself different. In short, as Foucault insisted "one writes to become someone other than who one is" (Miller, 1993, p. 33) According to Deleuze (1987), a style is managing to "stammer" in one's own language but, he asserted, not "being a stammer in one's speech, but being stammer of language itself" (p. 4). Being like a foreigner in one's own language, it can be a gesture of the body that prompts an understanding contrary to what language indicate. In language, the equivalents of such gesture are called "sense" or "solecism," noted Deleuze, as Samuel Beckett (1976) did—to name the unnameable. However, I am "making" sense here.

So this neither means that speaking (mastery of a) different language is superior to those who only speak one language, nor simply to translate or to copy one into the other; but, in the sense of Deleuze's "becoming," it is not phenomenon of imitation or assimilation but of a "double capture, of a non-parallel evolution, of nuptials between two reigns" (1987, p. 10). To become is a matter of "involuting"; it is neither regression nor progression. Deleuze admitted that it is difficult to explain, yet he stated, "[T]o what extent one should involute. 'I' is obviously the opposite of evolution, but it is also the opposite of regression, returning to a childhood or to a primitive world. To involute is to have an increasingly simple, economical, restrained step" (1987, p. 29). Deleuze praised the following as to what the definition of "style" is, as Marcel Proust remarked, "Great literature is written in a sort of foreign language within our own language" (Deleuze, 1987, p. 54). In other words, we might be better to speak a kind of "foreign" language *within* our own language. In *A Theory of Semiotics* (1976), Umberto Eco insisted that "to re-write in another language means to re-think" (pp. vii–viii). We can clearly see that Daignault's endeavors present a rethinking of what curriculum means.

To think over something is to think oneself: that is, in this view, what thinking means. To know is not the same as to think. We can know many things, while not knowing ourselves: that is a matter of thinking. In regard to this matter, Michel Serres (1983) pointedly made a simple yet comprehensive comment. Serres stated, "For Plato and a tradition which lasted throughout the classical age, *knowledge is a hunt*. To know is to put to death—to kill the lamb, deep in the woods, in order to eat it" (1983, p. 28). In brief, to know is to kill, to rely on death. Rorty (1996) insisted that "academic disciplines are subject to being overtaken by attacks of 'knowingness'—a state of mind and soul that prevents shudders of awe and makes one immune to enthusiasm" (p. A48). This enthusiasm is what thinking strives for and what thinking is all about. Embracing a Deleuzean notion of thinking, Daignault asserted that to think is to experiment and to problematize. Deleuze (1988) put it, "Knowledge, power and the self are the triple root of a problematization of thought" (p. 116).

EVENT, PEDAGOGY, AND THE SUBJECT

The event, being itself impassive, involves the transformation of relationship between difference and opposition. The absolute difference allows both active and passive to be interchanged more easily, because it is neither the one nor the other, but rather the effect of their common result. The bridge or gap is paradoxical, for Serres; it connects the disconnected. Daignault emphasized that such a question "always implies an answer the destiny of which is to close space; that kind of space the opening of which is called problem" (1988b, p. 6). This cannot be confused with the relation of cause and effect; rather, said Deleuze (1990), "[Events] being always only effects, are better to form among themselves functions of quasi-causes or quasi-causality which are always reversible [the wound and the scar]" (p. 8). It is to think the possibility of thinking a relationship without thinking it.

Daignault strove to think of curriculum as a noncomplete relative difference—unilateral distinction. Curriculum is, said Daignault, an intransitive verb—to pass, only to pass, in terms of Joycean "riverrun." He also insisted that curriculum is regarded as an "event," which subsists in subject or inheres in language. Curriculum, like an event, simply happens.

Daignault (1988c) used a Frank O'Hara poem to explicate differences between theory and practice, which for him was analogous to painting and poetry. He cited from *The Selected Poems of Frank O'Hara* (1974), which is appropriate here:

I am not a painter. I am a poet. Why? I think I would rather
be a painter, but I am not. Well,
for instance, Mike Goldberg is starting a painting, I drop in.
"Sit down and have a drink" he says. I drink; we drink. I
look up. "You have SARDINES in it." "Yes, it is indeed
something there." "Oh." I go and the days go by and I drop
in again. The painting is going on, and I go, and the days
go by. I drop in. The painting is finished. "Where's

SARDINES?" All that's left is just letters, "It was too much,"
Mike says.
But me? One day I am thinking of a color: orange. I write a line
about orange. Pretty soon it is a whole page of words, not lines.
Then another page. There should be so much more, not of orange,
of words, of how terrible orange is and life. Days go by. It is even
in prose, I am a real poet. My poem is finished and I haven't
mentioned orange yet. It's twelve poems, I call it *ORANGES*. And
one day in a gallery I see Mike's painting, called *SARDINES*. (p. 47)

Daignault viewed this poem as an analogy to teachers and teaching. Daignault proposed that we can write something about teachers, entitled *Teacher*, while doing so without saying a word on teaching. This something he calls pedagogy.

Both research and practice languages "deserve" more than any reduction to what they have in common. According to the semiotics definition of language, anything could be seen as a sign to be exchanged against another sign. Within the limits of language, one could argue that there are similar structures between research and action, theory and practice. The one of knowledge is an example. However, the collaboration between researchers and practitioners at the language level must be encouraged, but not at the cost of reducing everything to fragmented knowledge or common language. For example, Foucault (1973) argued that there is no such thing—common language—any longer; he demonstrated the relationship between madness and reason: "The constitution of madness as a mental illness ... affords the evidence of a broken dialogue [between reason and madness], posits the separation as already affected, and thrusts into oblivion all those stammered, imperfect words without fixed syntax in which the exchange between madness and reason was made" (p. x). Daignault (1989a) argued that the irreducibility in discursive analysis is one of the major contributions of poststructuralist thought. He said, "It denotes 'today's unthinkable' in the midst of structuralism, in the possibly hegemonic situation of language, because language today has also become a problem: [T]here is no way out of it; but not everything can be reduced to it" (p. 8).

The concept of "flash" in the lightning of darkness, explained by Daignault, is exactly the sense of "différance" in relation to itself in which differentiation is realized; this also can suggest Derrida's "trace," which involves leaving a trace and erasing itself at the same time. Darkness has the same effect as Lyotard's (1987) concept of difference within identity, passion within reason, in light lies our darkness. Also in Deleuze's notion of "between," a passage from Virginia Woolf cited by Deleuze can be used to explain (which he recorded) that "I spread myself out like fog BETWEEN the people that I know the best" (1987, p. 27). Deleuze (1987) remarked, "The middle has nothing to do with an average, it is not a centrism or a form of moderation. On the contrary, it's a matter of absolute speed. Whatever grows from the middle is endowed with such a speed. We must distinguish not relative and absolute movement, but the relative and absolute speed of any movement" (p. 27).

In dealing with the notion of subject or subjectivity, many critical theorists, Marxists in particular, have been dissatisfied with and detested by the privileged "apparatus" of the notion of "general text"—textuality. Paul Smith (1988) argued that not only is such a notion as textuality questionable as that to which all conceptual phenomena must be submitted, but also problematic is the impotence to which the notion leads us, unless it leaves room for mediation by active subject/individuals. Daignault (1989b) emphasized that the subject is neither a person, nor any form of individual, collective or transcendental consciousness; rather, the subject is comprised of the "dynamics of an analyzer and of a synthesizer both dealing with expressions I call notes" (p. 1), or as impersonal plural agency. In part, this parallels the notion of "agency without agents" in Foucault's "subject-positions." Foucault (1972) said that a subject is not a "speaking consciousness," but rather "a position that may be filled in certain conditions by various individuals" (p. 115). Moreover, this echoes Deleuze and Guattari's (1987) "individuation with subject." Daignault (1989b) noted that the subject of education is the locus of the composition of a subjectivity in curriculum that makes sense. To describe a pedagogy qua the subject of education does not consist in analyzing the relations between the teacher and what he or she says, the students and what they say (or wanted to say), but rather in determining what position can be occupied by any individual if he or she is to be the subject of education.

Following Deleuze's "logic of sense," Daignault emphasized the composition of expressing that is "a process through which his/her self-consciousness offers less and less resistance to the reality of transcendental *expressibles* and to the emergence of new empirical *expresseds*" (1989b, p. 1). In Daignault's notion of "*composer*," we can clearly see that "expressing" is a present, ongoing process; the concept of "expressibles" is a transcendental, ideal concept of "what ought to be"; the concept of "expresseds" is simply the emergence of new empirical presence. He remarked that the composer is constituted in the "dynamics" of both "synthesizer" and "analyzer" in the work or play (pp. 3–4). This dynamic process produces the expressed as the doubling of the expressible, the doubling of a double, because the expressed has already incorporated the expressible as interiorized double.

The no concept's locus is called "expressible" and the no word's locus is called an "expressed." Both are not something. Both are not nothing. The expressible "sub-sists" between the world and the language. Difference is identical to negation in defining a concept by scientific usage. Deleuze (1990) noted that "they are not things or facts, but events. We can not say that they exist, but rather that they subsist or inhere" (p. 5). The subject can be reinterpreted, restored, and reinscribed. Daignault (1989b) asserted that "the subject of education [the frontier, once again, between an expressing and a composer] grows, through such a process of composition, towards a continuing problematization of the ego" (p. 15). Such an event, composition and de-composition, functioning against all personalism, psychological or ling-uistic, promotes a third person, and even a "fourth person singular," the non-person or "It" in which we recognize ourselves and our community better than in the exchanges between an I and a You.

It is not only the truth is what enables the mind to think; it is also the truth that enables us is to care for oneself and others. In Martin et al. (1998), Foucault insisted that to know oneself is to care for oneself. Daignault (1990) noted that "any pretention to reach the Absolute is a movement through which something is excluded; there is no absolute truth" (p. 3). The project of Foucault is to particularize the universal, not to deny it. The way of telling the truth is an endless interpretation, and to tell the truth is in-dependent of a political regime that tends to be indifferent to truth and while prescribing the truth. The challenge is to problematize prevailing practices and to interrogate power relations inherent in all social existence. It is to support local and minor forms of knowledge and a dis- location of commonly held conceptions about experiences, practices, and events. As Serres (1989b) warned, "Alexander [the concept] reigns over all, including his opponents. His power is so great that none remains who can object. To contradict the king is to belong to the king, to oppose power is to enter into the logic of the powerful" (p. 142).

Poststructuralism does not criticize the universal, but does criticize the juncture between the global and the universal. This juncture is what pro-duces dogmatism. Dogmatism is conceived as any local victory that tries to impose itself as a norm. However, this local victory is simply a universal ef-fect. Poststructuralism requires one to assume responsibility for truth. To champion localism without committing to truth is what produces nihilism. Daignault (1990) concluded, "Local emancipation is not nihilistic" (p. 36).

Structuralism is correct when it throws back into question the central position of the subject in humanism; it is by insisting on the fact that the subject is symbolically determined that it succeeds in decentering it, in-deed even dissolving it. But structuralism leaves intact the question of the sensible and not merely symbolic relationship of the subject to the body. From my view, one merit of Deleuze's work is that it has completely revived this question. It is important to note that the articulation of un-derstanding and speaking of the self are subjected to a different kind of reading. It is the novelty of shifting perspectives. The key concept, ex-plained by Deleuze (1990), is consequently that of individuation. He stated, "The essential process of intensive quantities is individuation. In-tensity is individualizing; intensive quantities are individualizing. Indi-viduals are signal-sign systems" (p. 47).

The question of signals is taken up again in *A Thousand Plateaus* (Deleuze & Guattari, 1987) in reference to the synthesizer, the synthesis of continuous variation; it is precisely at that point that the sensuality of sense is to be found. Not that sense is sensible, but its synthesis is. Furthermore, a synthesis implies a surface for recording differences in intensity, a sort of skin of differentiating sense; the condition without which the subject would never be anything more than a sign in a differentiating structure, or a differentiation subordinated to the identity of the plentitude of consciousness. Deleuze and Guattari (1987) remarked:

> The individual is in no way indivisible, but never stops dividing as he changes his nature. There is no me in what he expresses; because he expresses [I]deas as internal multiplicities made up of differential relations and points that stand out, of pre-individual singularities. And there is no I expresses there either; because there again he is forming a multiplicity of actualization, like a condensation of points that stand out, an open collection of intensities. (p. 143)

SUMMARY

In my view, Daignault's major contribution to the curriculum field was to challenge us to rethink curriculum and do curriculum *poststructurally*. These reviews hint at the minimum effect he has produced. Daignault provoked a notion of thinking or sense that to think oneself as self-educative means "to experiment and to problematize" (Deleuze, 1988; Foucault, 1989) and to think otherwise (Hwu, 1993, 1998); to make sense, which by itself is a problematic and problematizing. Fundamentally, Daignault's works can be grasped through the concept of paradox, the paradoxical instance, and nomadic movement. The notion of paradoxical instance is the movement of forces that circulates between two series of oppositions and moves in both directions at the same time. It is the moment of the simultaneity of coincidence when an occupant without a place is the same as a place without an occupant. As Deleuze (1990) remarked, "the younger becoming older than the older, the older becoming younger than the younger—but they can never finally become so; if they did they would no longer be becoming, but would be so" (p. 136).

In brief conclusion, problematics of binary oppositions (description and prescription, teaching and learning, thinking and action, method and manner, etc.) are presented as irreducible to either one. They are inseparable from the movement of paradoxical instances. In short, sense as nonsense produces meaning (*sens*). Daignault offered us a definition of curriculum as paradoxical. To define is to distort, but Daignault did not propose that we should stop the project of definition; on the contrary, one works "to multiply the definitions." To teach, for him, is to promise the other's desire: to seduce through knowledge. Through contrasting with analogy, *para-dox* is opposed to both aspects of *doxa*—paradox would provide us with pedagogical meaning. Regarding thinking, knowing, and feeling, Daignault insisted that thinking is different from knowing, but knowledge and feeling are not opposed to thinking (Hwu, 1993). As Serres (1983) remarked, "To know is to kill, to rely on death" (p. 28). In regard to the subject of curriculum studies, Daignault questioned and claimed that it does not exist, but subsists in things and insists in language; this questioning of curriculum as "event" gives us new understanding of curriculum and curriculum discourse.

REFERENCES

Angeles, P. A. (1981). *Dictionary of philosophy*. New York: Barnes & Noble.

Apple, M. W. (1979). *Ideology and curriculum*. Boston: Routledge.

Apple, M. W. (1986). *Teachers and texts*. New York: Routledge.

Bateson, G. (1972). *Steps to an ecology of mind*. New York: Ballantine.

Beckett, S. (1976). *All strange away*. New York: Gotham Book Mart.

Bell, J. A. (1998). *The problem of difference: Phenomenology and poststructuralism*. Toronto: University of Toronto Press.

Bensmaïa, Reda. (1987). *The Barthes effect: The essay as reflective text* (P. Fedfiew, Trans.). Minneapolis: University of Minnesota Press. (Original work published 1986)

Bogue, R. (1989). *Deleuze and Guattari*. New York: Routledge.

Chang, C. (1959). *The practice of zen*. New York: Harper & Brothers.

Cherryholmes, C. H. (1988). *Power and criticism*. New York: Teachers College Press.

Daignault, J. (1982, October). *To make someone know as we make someone laugh: A perverse analysis of promise and desire in curriculum*. Paper presented at the 4th Conference on Curriculum Theorizing, Dayton, OH.

Daignault, J. (1983, October). *Analogy in education: An archaeology without subsoil*. Paper presented at the 5th Conference on Curriculum Theorizing, Dayton, OH.

Daignault, J. (1986, October). *Semiotics of educational expression*. Paper presented at the 8th Conference on Curriculum Theorizing, Dayton, OH.

Daignault, J. (1988a, November). Autobiographie d'un style [Autobiography of a style]. *Urgences. Bagatelles et crases, 21,* 19–44.

Daignault, J. (1988b, October).... *Yn-X Cursus [...]TIA2 Arts aRe....* Paper presented at the 10th Conference on Curriculum Theorizing, Dayton, OH.

Daignault, J. (1988c, May). The language of research and the language of practice—neither one nor the other: Pedagogy. In T. Carson (Ed.), *Proceedings of the CACS' invitational symposium, Jaspers, Alberta* (pp. 46–59). Edmonton, Canada: University of Alberta Press.

Daignault, J. (1989a, April). *Where did the subject go?* Paper presented at the Conference of the Department of French, Louisiana State University, Baton Rouge.

Daignault, J. (1989b, October). *Curriculum as composition: Who is the composer?* Paper presented at the 11th Conference on Curriculum Theorizing, Dayton, OH.

Daignault, J. (1990, October). *Education, poststrusturalism and local emancipation*. Paper presented at the 12th Conference on Curriculum Theorizing, Dayton, OH.

Daignault, J. (1991). Curriculum as composition: Who is the composer? *Research Journal of Philosophy and Social Sciences, 16,* 1–34.

Daignault, J., & Gauthier, C. (1982). The indecent curriculum machine: Who's afraid of Sisyphe? *Journal of Curriculum Theorizing, 3*(1), 177–196.

Deleuze, G. (1972). *Proust and signs* (R. Howard, Trans.). New York: G. Braziller.

Deleuze, G. (1983). *Nietzsche and philosophy* (H. Tomlinson, Trans.). New York: Columbia University Press. (Original work published 1962)

Deleuze, G. (1986a). *Cinema 1: The movement-image* (H. Tomlinson & B. Habberjam, Trans.). Minneapolis: University of Minnesota. (Original work published 1983)

Deleuze, G. (1986b). *Kafka: Toward a minor literature* (D. Polan, Trans.). Minneapolis: University of Minnesota Press. (Original work published 1975)

Deleuze, G. (1987). *Dialogues* (H. Tomlinson & B. Habberjam, Trans.). London: Athlone. (Original work published 1977)

Deleuze, G. (1988). *Foucault* (S. Hand, Trans.). Minneapolis: University of Minnesota Press. (Original work published 1986)

Deleuze, G. (1989). *Cinema 2: The time-image* (H. Tomlinson & R. Galeta, Trans.). Minneapolis: University of Minnesota Press. (Original work published 1985)

Deleuze, G. (1990). *The logic of sense* (M. Lester, Trans.). New York: Columbia University Press. (Original work published 1969)

Deleuze, G., & Guattari, F. (1983). *Anti-Oedipus* (R. Hurley, M. Seem, & H. R. Lane, Trans.). Minneapolis: University of Minnesota Press. (Original work published 1972)

Deleuze, G., & Guattari, F. (1987). *A thousand plateaus* (B. Massumi, Trans.). Minneapolis: University of Minnesota Press. (Original work published 1980)

Derrida, J. (1973). *Speech and phenomena* (D. B. Allison, Trans.). Evanston, IL: Northwestern University Press. (Original work published 1967)

Derrida, J. (1976). *Of grammatology* (G. C. Spivak Trans.). Baltimore, MD: Johns Hopkins University Press. (Original work published 1967)

Derrida, J. (1978). *Writing and difference* (A. Bass, Trans.). Chicago: University of Chicago Press. (Original work published 1967)

Derrida, J. (1981a). *Positions* (A. Bass, Trans.). Chicago: University of Chicago Press. (Original work published 1972)

Derrida, J. (1981b). *Dissemination* (B. Johnson, Trans.). Chicago: University of Chicago Press. (Original work published 1972)

Descombes, V. (1986). *Modern French philosophy*. Cambridge, MA: Cambridge University Press.

Doll, W. E., Jr. (1993). *A post-modern perspective on curriculum*. New York: Teachers College Press.

Eco, Umberto. (1976). *A theory of semiotics*. Bloomington: Indiana University Press.

Eisner, E. W. (1979). *The educational imagination: On the design and evaluation of school programs*. New York: Macmillan.

Eisner, E., & Vallence, E. (Eds.). (1974). Conflicting conceptions of curriculum. Berkeley, CA: McCutchen.

Foucault, M. (1972). *The archaeology of knowledge* (A. Sheridan, Trans.). New York: Pantheon Books. (Original work published 1969)

Foucault, M. (1973). *Madness and civilization: A history of insanity in the age of reason* (R. Howard, Trans.). New York: Vintage. (Original work published 1961)

Foucault, M. (1977). *Language, counter-memory, practice* (D. F. Bouchard & S. Simon, Trans.). Ithaca, NY: Cornell University Press. (Original work published 1970)

Foucault, M. (1988). *Politics, philosophy, culture: Interviews and other writings of Michel Foucault* (A. Sheridan et al., Trans.). New York: Routledge.

Foucault, M. (1989). *Foucault live* (J. Johnson, Trans.). New York: Semiotext(e).

Hlebowitsh, P. S. (1998). *The burdens of the new curriculurist*. Paper presented at the annual meeting of the American Educational Research Association, San Diego, CA.

Hwu, Wen-Song. (1993). *Toward understanding post-structuralism and curriculum*. Unpublished doctoral dissertation, Louisiana State University, Baton Rouge.

Hwu, Wen-Song. (1998). Curriculum, transcendence, and Zen/Taoism: Critical ontology of the self. In W. F. Pinar (Ed.), *Curriculum: Toward new identities* (pp. 21–40). New York: Garland.

Jackson, P. W. (Ed.). (1992). *Handbook of research on curriculum: A project of the American Educational Research Association*. New York: Macmillan.

Lacan, J. (1977). *Ecrits: A selection* (A. Sheridan, Trans.). New York: Norton. (Original work published 1966)

Lyotard, J.-F. (1987). Re-writing modernity. *Sub-stance, 54,* 3–9.

Martin, L. H., Gutman, H., & Hutton, P. H. (Eds.). (1988). *Technologies of the self: A seminar with Michel Foucault*. Amherst: University of Massachusetts Press.

Miller, J. E. (1993). *The passion of Michel Foucault*. New York: Simon & Schuster.

O'Hara, F. (1974). *The selected poems of Frank O'Hara*. New York: Vintage.

Pecora, V. P. (1986). Deleuze's Nietzsche and post-structuralist thought. *Sub-stance, 48*, 34–50.

Pinar, W. F. (Ed.). (1988). *Contemporary curriculum discourses*. Scottsdale, AZ: Gorsuch Scarisbrick.

Pinar, W. F. (1998). *Autobiography, politics, sexuality: Essays in curriculum theory, 1972–1992*. New York: Peter Lang.

Pinar, W. F., Reynolds, W. M., Slattery, J. P., & Taubman, P. M. (1995). *Understanding curriculum: A comprehensive introduction to the study of curriculum*. New York: Peter Lang.

Rorty, R. (1996, February 9). The necessity of inspired reading. *The Chronicle of Higher Education*, p. A48.

Serres, M. (1983). *Hermes: Literature, science, philosophy* (J. V. Harasi & D. F. Bell, Eds.). Baltimore, MD: Johns Hopkins University Press.

Serres, M. (1989b). *Detachment* (G. James & R. Federman, Trans.). Athens: Ohio University Press. (Original work published 1986)

Smith, P. (1988). *Discerning the subject*. Minneapolis: University of Minnesota Press.

Taubman, P. M. (1990). Achieving the right distance. *Educational Theory, 40*(1), 121–133.

Ulmer, G. L. (1985). *Applied grammatology*. Baltimore, MD: Johns Hopkins University Press.

Afterword: Multiplicities and Curriculum Theory

Julie A. Webber
Illinois State University

William M. Reynolds
Georgia Southern University

> Who does not haunt the perverse territories, beyond the Kindergartens of Oedipus?
>
> (Deleuze & Guattari, 1983, p. 67)

The chapters in this volume have all been marked by the same interpretive style. At once an observer challenges an idea, concept, trend, movement, or act, and then immediately puts it under erasure, challenging his or her own presumptions to knowledge, power, and will in curriculum theorizing. This methodological focus does not come out of a tradition or learned paradigm of criticism, but instead out of a combination of training in the field of education, a will to debunk that training and use of one's own experience and affective inclinations to view curriculum as an invitation to *new* knowledge, not as an opportunity to have it defined once and for all. Students of curriculum are empowered by the opportunity to question, but the permission to question in a manner different from the traditionally accepted means is more important to them than worshipping the paradigms of questioning that even Bill's generation invented. As Bill and Julie began to work on this project, it became clear that members of a newer generation might have concerns about the progressive curriculum developments that were the outcome of the reconceptualization itself, and that as the dynamics of power that control and direct curriculum changed, so might the concept of "progress." Indeed, the theorists whose interpretive impulse best captured this situation were Gilles Deleuze, and his theoretical partner of many years, Felix Guattari.

By opening up "lines of flight," the authors entreated the reader to question not only their own presumptions but also those they have learned from their professors and teachers, in order to move curriculum theorizing forward into a more positive and enlightening future. Traditionally, the focus on critique, bounded by a tradition or methodology, has left the field of curriculum studies in an awkward position: Can we go further and see positive avenues for understanding curriculum by using these interpretive methodologies rather than

203

continuously relying on our own flawed and biased traditions? The answer has usually been no, and scholars who carefully read Deleuze and Guattari's work will find that "no" is simply a gap in thought that leaves the practitioner power-less to change the curriculum. For them, the answer is to "disinvest repressive structures" of their power over us as professionals and humans (Deleuze & Guattari, 1983, p. 61). Deleuze's concept of "lines of flight" has embedded in it several assumptions that are important if we are to see the next generation of curriculum scholars and practitioners opening up the field to new ideas. Guattari summed up the day when he figured out that he could no longer re-main faithful to psychoanalysis as a body of knowledge, when his patient said that he felt depressed and thought that playing golf might help him out of his funk. Guattari realized in that moment that the patient had the answer to his problem and that it was as good as any other answer, because he felt empow-ered by it. The lesson of this story is that although *methodologies based on lack* promise answers to scholars and professionals, they do not usually hit paydirt for the subjects and objects they are supposed to empower.

We have not argued that methods are unimportant because many of the scholars in this volume have used them, but what they have also done is used them to look at a problem or situation in a new light—they have been unor-thodox in their use of them, they have resisted using them the way that they are supposed to be used, and they have had the confidence to apply them heterodoxically. This is the world we live in, one that is chaotic and irrever-ent and does not respect disciplinary or methodological boundaries. So, the questions are these: Why do we have curriculum in schools that doesn't re-flect this heterodoxy? Why is the curriculum still so parochial? And what does it mean to have movements in schools to "restore" curriculum? Do we even know what it looked like before, and do we know that it was successful? Why go backward when we can go forward? Why shut down creativity and inventiveness when we can open up "lines of flight"? Against the trend to engage in the hopeless and philosophically conservative impulse to rein-state an idealized curriculum that never existed, we urge scholars and prac-titioners to dis/position themselves in the field. As this volume has demonstrated, this can be done, and it opens up discussion and debate about the future of curriculum research in a positive and confident fashion.

This is not easy. Certainly we are not saying *that* from our comfortable positions as professors in universities. We fight the same battles in our own disciplines and departments that teachers fight in schools, so we are not asking for practitioners to take risks that the authors would not themselves take or have not taken at some point in their careers. As Foucault argued in the preface to *Anti-Oedipus*, (p. xii) "Do not think that one has to be sad in or-der to be militant" Indeed, the struggle over the curriculum rages on, but if we say nothing the repressive forces win and new generations will emerge with this same negative disposition.

Several lines of flight have been opened by this collection. Whether the readers read alone, in a course, or combine these chapters and read them against others in the field, we are sure that they have seen just what the outcome of such a creative project can be. The editors of this volume did not anticipate the lines of flight opened up in this volume, and they were happy to applaud these outcomes. Reviewers for the book saw trends and ideas that we had not anticipated, such as the focus on religion in many of the chapters, as well as the role of technology in the curriculum. In what follows, we list a few of the lines of flight and give some background information on them. We have placed this discussion at the end of the book because we hope that the readers have seen new lines of flight in addition to those mentioned here. We did not want to frame the act of reading this book in such a way as to limit or impose closure on new lines of flight. We also wanted to open up the "in-between," which is the dialogue about those engaged readings.

We highlight five themes that emerged from the collection, because we believe that these issues are paramount to understanding curriculum in the present era. They emerged from a combination of theory, practice, and reflection on what is actually going on in schools today. These themes are virtuality, spirituality, the secular, the informal, and time. In a neoliberal era, where the only answer to "What knowledge?" is "How much can I get for it?" we must confront the foils of neoliberal repressive ideologies if we are to understand why they are so powerful over students' minds. We live in a virtual era, where meanings do not readily attach to material bodies but instead slide away from them as quickly as the media can come up with a new "spin" or interpretation for them. Thus, time is another factor that we must consider. As more and more laborers are asked to produce limited kinds of ideas and goods (we would include here the types of knowledges demanded on standardized tests as well), they are "comforted" by lax formal work requirements but inundated during their free time with informal requirements and lessons, disciplinary regimens that strike at the heart of personality, not merely their performance.

As more and more laborers become disaffected with work and life conditions and the two bleed together in an indistinguishable fashion, stress becomes a dull, thumping pain that coats the features of everyday existence with no point of respite or resistance. Spirituality becomes even more important to people who are subjectively destituted and routinely assaulted for desiring something positive in their daily routines. They want a "line out" of their daily grind in schools and universities. Faith in something else provides this for them when schools have become "perverse territories," beyond accountability, beyond Oedipus. This is a sign of the times. Secularism has come under fire because it is associated with the conditions of decline just outlined. The jury is still out on secularism, but it is clearly a point of inquiry that should not be dismissed lightly. The secular itself may be another foil for market-driven desires to the detriment of positive, caring relations of production. Next we outline several directions that these foils can take, and hope that they stimulate the reader to think of many more.

VIRTUALITY

Virtuality imputes an ideal element to thought as well as the temporal aspect that it is moving toward the future. In virtual states, we are moved by images and ideas, and our affective response to them drives knowledge and power forward. This can be positive or negative. Most critical media attention has focused on the virtual as having only negative dimensions, but new points of inquiry have found that the "virtual" can be used for any affective purpose because it seduces populations. It does not deductively explain the world to them. As Brian Massumi argued in a work that combines Deleuze, Guattari, Bergson, and James, "affect" is an important piece of the invention process. Knowledge does not proceed unaided; it is elicited through emotive states that arise when people look at an object of study or the world and have affective reactions to it (Massumi, 2000). It is in this process that virtuality itself is created. Ferneding, Blumenfeld-Jones, and Livingston have all opened up a path to understanding the role of the virtual in curriculum theorizing and in the technology that informs curriculum design and research. Virtuality is a condition of our present and future; we can no longer avoid asking questions about its role in the curriculum but must instead charge into analysis and inquiry lest the directors of the *Matrix* trilogy best us at our own game. By including the body in these interpretations, they have not made the usual mistake of worshipping technology to the detriment of the body that it is supposed to aid.

SPIRITUALITY

Spirituality has made a comeback in schools in the last decade or so, but in a new way. It no longer responds directly to political claims made by the New Right about interests and civil protections, but instead links itself to the pervasive traumas and wounds opened up by what Foucault called the "varieties of fascism" that range from "the enormous ones that surround and crush us to the petty ones that constitute the tyrannical bitterness of our everyday lives" (Deleuze & Guattari, 1983, p, xiv). In this way, we think a constructive line of flight can be opened up to spirituality as long as it is cautious to the interested parties lined up to dismantle the Constitution and Amendments in its name. Many of the chapters in this volume have critically evaluated the claims of religious movements in schools that play on students' and parents' real fears of the unknown to the benefit of an even more repressive curriculum. Spirituality that is open to progressive lines of flight, that comforts yet propels the subject forward into the future of positive production, is not to be feared. As Justin Watson (2002) pointed out, the major problem with spirituality in the schools is not whose spirituality but the uncertainty that has been generated by political leaders and interested parties who have taken their political battles to the schoolyard like children, instead of confronting each other as adults in the Capitol. Teachers, their unions, and administrators have capitulated to an unsophisticated concept of the "secular" because it protects them from these bullies, and they hold it up as a shield that merely deflects the rage at the very persons they are charged with teaching and protecting—the students. As we witnessed in West Paducah, the problem never goes away but is sometimes fatally resolved through bullets.

THE "SECULAR"

As the concept created in the 1600s to model the entire system of power and organization of world politics,[1] we have to question secularism, even though it's been a convenient means to protect the notion of civil society or the public sphere: owned by no one interest, but free to all. Recent interventions into the concept of secularism by scholars of world religions, coupled with real events like the attacks on September 11, 2001, make it clear that secularism has a checkered past in politics and may even be the belief system behind global capitalism, a crushing modernity, and yes, even U.S. hegemony. The outcome of this volume has been to secure a persistent doubt about secular claims in public schools and curriculum. Jakobsen and Pelligrini argued that, for secularism, "The relation between the secular and the religious that makes for secular equality and nonviolence creates another set of inequalities between those who are religious and those who are secular" (Jakobsen & Pelligrini, 2000, p. 5). Furthermore, the concept of secularism was established by European religious conflict and, therefore, what is secular is what is not Christian, which sets up an exclusionary basis by which what count as objective religious devotion and concern will be judged. Christian activists in the schools have argued, using secular ideas (e.g., the notion that schools are spaces where all religions get equal billing), that others should not view prayer as alienating and that everyone worships "God," but part of the power of religion in people's lives is that they believe they have found a separate answer, not a common one. Using the "informal" spaces of schools to reclaim public education for God, many have incurred the wrath of those excluded from belief. Indeed, the battle over curriculum may well be in the informal spaces of education that many specialists do not acknowledge as existing.

---

[1]The Treaty of Westphalia concluded the Thirty Years' War in northern Europe in 1648. The war was prolonged and unending, marking a change in the character of war in that period. Issues of religious control over territory made it impossible for parties to conclude the war. At the conference, the parties decided to make a rule that each leader (read despot) got to decide matters of religion within their own territories and no other state leader would interfere. It was also agreed that the state had its own reason, outside the boundaries of God or divine law, *raison d'etat*, establishing the basis for secular decision making with regard to the fate of nations. The nation-state (the only sovereign actor in world politics recognized by treaties, the UN system and states themselves) was born at the same time.

THE "INFORMAL"

The informal curriculum corresponds to all the informalisms that are power-fully generated to more effectively control individuals in schools and the world of work. The slackening of requirements in workplaces (dress, meeting style, performance, writing) have only set up workers to be more controlled by the idiosyncratic requirements of management and administration that are often the product of their own racial, sexual, and class-based anxieties. As Watkins warned in chapter 8, be aware of the lessons of informal education, but also be cautious because you are being tested by some criterion, especially some that are not enumerated or stated in policies. Often this category of "informal" is referred to as the "extracurricular" or the "hidden curriculum" that researchers have carefully noted is the site of disciplinary investments much stronger than those imposed by the formal curriculum.

TIME

All these "lines of flight" were opened because the contributors took time (out of work, teaching, personal lives, and especially the time they are still required to devote to thinking about curriculum from the perspective of the discipline and its history). Many critics have argued that the curriculum reconceptualization is "getting away with something" because it apparently does not have to pay attention to "real" schools or curriculum. This is far from any truth. Those involved in the reconceptualization have to teach standard approaches to curriculum before they can even show students how to take lines of flight or critique these methodologies. It takes more time to open up a line of flight then it does to administer a scantron exam written by a textbook manufacturer. There, we said it.

In an era of neoliberalism, powerbrokers are going to try to eat up people's time so that they can't protest the policies of a punitive curriculum. Globalization runs on time as it eats up whole spaces and remaps and territorializes people's minds and bodies. One of the most marked characteristics of this age is the way in which freedom of movement (a spatial orientation) is continuously shrinking as the number of activities and preoccupations required of schools hides the fact that they are becoming carceral institutions, with little movement assigned to practitioners and students.

As the field of curriculum studies moves forward, let it be rife with multiplicities and possibilities. Those, as Lyotard (1992) suggested, who would urge the closing down of experimentation, multiplicity, and possibility simply need to look for another field. Our hope for this volume is that it does, indeed, expand curriculum theory through dis/positioning and lines of flight.

REFERENCES

Deleuze, G., & Guattari, F. (1983). *Anti-Oedipus: Capitalism and schizophrenia*. Minneapolis: University of Minnesota Press.

Jakobsen, K., & Pelligrini, S. (2000). World secularisms at the millennium: Introduction. *Social Text, 18*(3), 1–27.

Lyotard, J.-F. (1992). *The postmodern explained: Correspondence 1982–1985*. Minneapolis: University of Minnesota Press.

Massumi, B. (2000). *Parables for the virtual: Movement, affect, sensation*. Durham, NC: Duke University Press.

Watson, J. (2002). *The martyrs of Columbine: Faith and the politics of tragedy*. New York: Palgrave Macmillan.

Author Index

Subject Index